THE
ROAD TO THE UNIFIED SOFTWARE DEVELOPMENT PROCESS

SIGS Reference Library

Additional Volumes in Preparation

THE

ROAD TO THE UNIFIED SOFTWARE DEVELOPMENT PROCESS

Ivar Jacobson
Revised and updated by Stefan Bylund

PUBLISHED BY THE PRESS SYNDICATE OF THE UNIVERSITY OF CAMBRIDGE
The Pitt Building, Trumpington Street, Cambridge, United Kingdom

CAMBRIDGE UNIVERSITY PRESS
The Edinburgh Building, Cambridge CB2 2RU, UK   http://www.cup.cam.ac.uk
40 West 20th Street, New York, NY 10011-4211, USA   http://www.cup.org
10 Stamford Road, Oakleigh, Melbourne 3166, Australia
Ruiz de Alarcón 13, 28014 Madrid, Spain

Published in association with SIGS Books

First published in 2000

Design by Kevin Callahan
Composition by David Van Ness
Cover design by Andrea Cammarata

Printed in the United States of America

A catalog record for this book is available from the British Library.

Library of Congress Cataloging in Publication data available.

ISBN 0 521 78774 2   paperback

*This book is dedicated
to you, the reader.*

CONTENTS

—

PREFACE

D URING THE CHRISTMAS SEASON last year I did what I had pushed
in front of me for so long. I went through old piles of papers to
clean up my office. I am quite good at throwing away old stuff, so
the oldest documents I had were from my work on my doctoral thesis, from
around 1985. Looking through the references in those papers, I found reports
I wrote in 1967–1970. That led me to think about how those documents got
into my hands in the first place.

In 1967, of course, we had no personal computers. It is hard to believe
now, but at that time we wrote documents on typewriters! Engineers themselves did not type; we wrote on paper with pencil. We revised what we had
written by cutting and pasting with scissors and glue. Then a secretary did
the typing, sometimes several days later. By the time we saw the typed copy,
we might be ready to revise it. Consequently, we did not write much.

Furthermore, since I am good at throwing away what I do not need, I did
not keep copies of my work. Thus, in 1978 when the success of Ericsson's
AXE telecommunications system had become a fact and its president, Björn
Svedberg, asked for historic evidence of the technology underlying the success, I had no documentation still in my office.

Since the work was more than five years old, the records were no longer
in the department in which the work had been done. I had to call around to
ask what happens to old documentation. The answer was that it might have
been stored down in the old archives in the basements—if I was lucky.

I went down there and found a huge archive with many long corridors
with shelves from floor to ceiling. It took me an hour to find the shelves that
held the documentation for my department from ten years earlier. To find
the documents of interest, I had to go through binder after binder. After hours
of searching, I found a handful of pertinent documents with my legible
signature. (My signature stood out, written in handwriting more readable
than it is today.) Now, with the Web, it is hard to believe that we once had
to work the way we did.

What was there to be found?

Component-based development!

However, very little about how we worked was documented at this earlier time. We focused on getting the software built; that is, developing its models—requirements, design, implementation, and testing—starting with the architecture and growing the architecture to the full-fledged system. And what was documented was in Swedish only.

Considering when the original idea of component-based development was born in my head, I have just refined it. That is essentially what I have been doing all these years; however, these years have been very exciting. It has been most exciting to work with all the brilliant people who have taught me what I know about software. In particular, Göran Hemdal, who implemented components all the way down from design to executable code (that is, through programming language, operating system, and computer architecture). It was Dines Bjorner who taught me how to formalize my modeling language; and Walker Royce who explained iterative and risk-driven development in the context of component-based development. Then there are all the fantastic people who have made the Unified Process and the Unified Modeling Language what they are today—the standard development platform.

Nevertheless, the future is even more exciting.

We now have the technology to successfully build the software that we need to make life easier. We are able to build systems we had not previously even dreamt of. With the Internet, some of the development practices that existed 30, 20, and even 5 years ago have changed. Essential words in this new world are e-business, customer-centric, creative design, business engineering, distribution, openness, standards, and worldwide availability.

Still, not all is new. We still need components; we still want use cases, architecture, and iterations. Since the Unified Process and the UML are both designed to be extended, we do not need to reinvent the wheel to support the new world. We can stand on top of what we already have, thus continuing to refine it.

I have very high expectations for the future of the Unified Process and the UML. They have the ability to grow and to serve us in new application areas and on new technological platforms.

The one thing we can be certain of is that the future is coming and everyone is welcome to join me in it!

Ivar Jacobson

Acknowledgments

First of all, all coauthors and special sources of inspiration regarding the articles collected in this book are especially appreciated: Jorma Mobrin, Patrik Jonsson, Doug Bennet, Sten Jacobson, Magnus Christerson, Staffan Ehnebom, Karin Palmkvist, Susanne Dyrhage, Dave Thomas, Grady Booch, and Jim Rumbaugh.

Then we want to thank Mick Spillane at SIGS Books and Lothlórien Homet at Cambridge University Press for helping us put this material together and finalizing the book; also a special thanks to the artist David Van Ness who had to re-create most of the figures.

Furthermore, we want to thank Adriano Comai, Jack Jackson, and the IEEE Computer Society from whom we got permission to reuse some of the article and interview material. We would like to extend a special thanks to Bob Hathaway, former editor of *Object Current*.

Finally, all friends, colleagues, and family members affected by this effort in one way or the other: Thank you for putting up with us!

INTRODUCTION

I T HAS BEEN A VERY exciting journey to edit this collection of articles by Dr. Ivar Jacobson. Not only because the articles span a wide range of subjects, issues, and problems related to the field of computer science; but also because the articles represent one man's perspective on it all. It is a viewpoint that has been adopted in one way or another by a very large number of people; a position that has yielded standards; a perspective that has yielded commercial success in many different areas; an outlook that has given its owner a guru status.

It all seems to have started back in the 1960s, where we find Dr. Jacobson as a young technician struggling with complex telecommunication systems that were becoming more and more software-intensive. Back in 1967–69 he helped introduce components and component-based development used to create the largest commercial success story in Sweden's history: the Ericsson AXE switch. As we will see, even today's component-based approaches, such as Microsoft COM+, are built on the same underlying principles as existed thirty years ago! The major contributions, including diagrams such as sequence diagrams and collaboration diagrams, state diagrams applied to components, subsystems, and many of the original ideas behind standard technology for developing with components, were created at that time.

Building on this work, Dr. Jacobson provided the major source of inspiration for the *Specification and Description Language* (SDL),[1] the very first blueprint standard language based on objects and components, which began to be developed in 1976. This is still a strong standard in the world of telecommunications.

Moreover, Dr. Jacobson was the "father" of use cases and use case–driven development as applied to both business modeling and software modeling. Use cases are now mainstream for capturing requirements on software systems, and they are suitable to provide each individual customer (of a business as well as of a software system) with the value chains that the customer desires. Therefore, use cases are important tools when designing customer-centric Websites.

Dr. Jacobson created Objectory, the first engineered business and software development process, which has now evolved into the industry-standard Unified Process (Rational Unified Process). This is a process for software development based on the Unified Modeling Language that is iterative, architecture-centric, use case–driven, and risk-driven.

Furthermore, he was one of the three original designers of the Unified Modeling Language, the new object-oriented blueprint language for component-based development. Many of his original ideas were standardized as they evolved into the UML. (The other original designers of the UML were Jim Rumbaugh and Grady Booch.)

Interestingly enough, all this work is reflected in the collection of articles as presented in this book, which thus serve as interesting complements to his other books.[2,3,4,5] These articles have been updated and refined according to new findings, terminology, and the UML (the book is "UML-compliant"). Moreover, each part opens with an introduction to the articles included, as well as a brief table of contents. Every part ends with an excerpt from an interview with Dr. Jacobson relevant to the subject. These sections entitled "In Ivar's Words" are compilations of interviews with Ivar Jacobson conducted by Jack Jackson, Adriano Comai, Bob Hathaway, and myself.

So, dear reader, welcome on-board. Let's hit the road to the unified software development process.

Stefan Bylund

REFERENCES

1. Specification and Description Language (SDL), ITU-T Recommendation Z.100, Mar. 1993.

2. Ivar Jacobson, Magnus Christerson, Patrik Jonsson, and Gunnar Övergaard. *Object-Oriented Software Engineering—A Use Case Driven Approach*, Addison–Wesley, Revised Fourth Printing, 1993.

3. M. Ericsson, A. Jacobson, and I. Jacobson. *The Object Advantage—Business Process Reengineering with Object Technology*, Addison–Wesley and ACM Press, Reading, MA, 1994.

4. Ivar Jacobson, Martin Griss, and Patrik Jonsson. *Software Reuse: Architecture, Process and Organization for Business Success*, Addison Wesley Longman, Reading, MA, p. 497, 1997.

5. I. Jacobson, G. Booch, and J. Rumbaugh. *The Unified Software Development Process*, Addison Wesley Longman, 1999.

PART 1:
PROLOGUE

———

THE MERGER OF THE Rational and Objectory corporations provided a major boost for the Unified Process and its "supporting technology" such as development tools and modeling languages. The evidence of this are the currently available products and standards based upon the process.

How did all this happen? Well, the right people with the right experiences got together. The people were the leading methodologists in the field: Jim Rumbaugh, Grady Booch, and Ivar Jacobson, amongst others. The experiences were the collected know-how of software development from corporations such as Rational and Objectory; experience collected over decades of involvement in thousands of customer projects.

In this part we can read more about this major boost of the Unified Process, and the circumstances that triggered it.

PART 1: PROLOGUE

Building a Complete Solution

Ivar Jacobson, March 1996

As many of you are aware, the merger of Rational Software Corporation and Objectory was announced in October 1995. Given the considerable interest generated by this merger, we are pleased to take this opportunity to summarize the purpose of the merger and present our vision for the direction of the new Rational Software Corporation.

This merger's purpose follows a pattern of many similar technology mergers and includes the following factors: market consolidation, strategic synergy, and financial synergy.

Market Consolidation

Object technology is a high-growth market that is still quite young. As any market matures, consolidation occurs as strong players combine to provide a more complete solution and increase market share, whereas weak players combine as a defensive strategy or disappear. In this case, both Objectory and Rational were strong players with high growth rates, combining to seize the market opportunity.

Strategic Synergy

Many technology mergers are justified on the basis of elusive, strategic synergy between technologies, sales channels, etc. In this case, the primary motivation for the merger is the strategic synergy.

FINANCIAL SYNERGY

The primary motivation for many mergers is the financial engineering that goes with combining two existing organizations. However, given the difficulties of successfully executing a technology merger, the financial synergy would not have been sufficient to justify the merger without the compelling strategic synergy. Although the standard arguments for consolidation apply here, there are some interesting aspects of this merger, that reflect on the maturity of our entire industry. These issues can best be understood by reviewing the basics.

The business basics involved here are evident to all professionals in the software engineering industry. Every sector of the modern economy is increasingly dependent on complex software, particularly high-growth sectors such as financial services and telecommunications. Software is becoming more pervasive, more complex, and more central to virtually every major corporation. After many years of neglect by senior management, companies in most industries have begun to recognize that information and software are key strategic assets that are vital in today's increasingly competitive business environment.

Meanwhile, the infamous software crisis persists and is, in many ways, worse than it was ten or twenty years ago, as the demands placed on software have outpaced people's ability to deliver software. Most companies have had some experience with the failure to achieve a significant business objective because the software was late, of insufficiently high quality, or of insufficient flexibility to meet the demands of a dynamic market. Companies have come to recognize that traditional software development practices are inadequate from both a technical perspective and a business perspective. This is causing companies to reengineer their software development (or acquisition) processes in the same way they are reengineering their other business processes. Most companies have discovered that simply acquiring lots of tools, processes, and technologies from numerous vendors does not necessarily result in fundamental improvement in the actual business results.

As with any other reengineering effort, achieving results often requires major cultural changes, insertion of new technology, and new business practices. Whereas some companies have tried to attack this problem on their own, many have recognized that their core competencies lie elsewhere (telecommunications systems, financial services, manufacturing, or whatever their primary business might be). These companies have selected a small number of software technology partners to both assist in the reengineering effort and to provide a complete and integrated solution. As the industry has matured, more companies are willing to turn to "off-the-shelf" solutions from reliable partners rather than feeling compelled to invent new solutions at every turn.

It is clear there is the opportunity for at least one major independent software company to be very successful in this arena—therein lies the opportunity for the new Rational Software Corporation. Rational and Objectory have, over the years, built their respective businesses around enabling customers to successfully reengineer their software processes in such a way as to produce fundamental business results. Both organizations have many years of experience applying object-oriented software engineering principles. Both organizations have focused on providing a complete solution combining process and tools. Rational has historically focused on software engineering from analysis and design through implementation, testing, debugging, documentation, and delivery. Objectory has historically focused on systems and business engineering, supporting tools based on use-case technology, and development of a powerful and configurable software process. The nature of the solution that we can now provide is a reflection of both the state of the market and the contributions of the two companies. This solution consists of three key interrelated elements:

1. The software engineering process.

2. The software engineering process support environment.

3. Training, mentoring, and consulting services.

SOFTWARE ENGINEERING PROCESS (SEP)

The first and most important element of the solution is the process. It is possible to build software systems using tools and a haphazard process, but it is not easy and, in the long run, is expensive. The complexity of today's software systems requires a more rigorous software process to reduce risk and improve quality. As part of the maturation of the industry, many companies have recognized the need for process with increasing focus on ISO 9001 and the SEI CMM model and other process initiatives. Objectory's contribution here has been well documented, allowing one to engineer a SEP framework that then can be reused and tailored as part of designing a specific SEP that is instantiated for a particular project.

In terms of the content of the process, the Objectory technology for use case engineering is one of the most critical elements. Use case technology is being used both as part of the object-oriented analysis and design process, and as an important project management tool for driving the overall development process. Rational's investment in process has historically been focused on object technology, controlled iterative development, and architecture-driven reuse. Combining these technologies provides a very powerful and complete process product offering.

SOFTWARE ENGINEERING PROCESS SUPPORT ENVIRONMENT (SEPSE)

Whereas process is critical, in practice it both shapes and is shaped by the tools used to implement and automate the process. Our experience has shown that without proper support it is difficult to implement a truly iterative process. Automation is essential to make iterations possible and manageable, and to supply the benefits of modern SEP to large-scale projects. The SEPSE and its SEP form an integral whole.

Rational can now provide a complete environment with tools that support use case requirements capture and analysis, object-oriented programming, configuration management and version control, change management and problem tracking, testing (test management, test generation, test execution, test coverage analysis, etc.), automated document generation, and other capabilities for development on multiple host platforms supporting multiple-target environments. The approach is based on an open systems concept where each component of the support environment operates as a part of the integrated whole, or as a standalone. In all cases, interoperability with tools from a variety of vendors is essential. The desired set of Rational and complementary third-party tools can support the specific SEP configured by a customer from the SEP framework.

TRAINING, MENTORING, AND CONSULTING SERVICES

Adopting new technology, particularly in the context of reengineering the software development process, requires more than high-quality products (process and tools) can deliver alone. High quality, focused professional services ranging from the basic in object technology education through to managing an object-oriented project help customers receive the maximum benefit from processes and tools. Frequently consultants act as agents of change within the customer organization, becoming part of the customer's development team to help make the project successful. Our services are driven by the SEP, which gives customers the benefit of real-world experience that our consultants have gained from participating in many diverse projects.

GOALS FOR INDUSTRY STANDARDS

As mentioned, the idea of a modern SEP is a driving force permeating our approach. A major part of a modern SEP software process is the extensive use of object technology, which consistently proves its technical and economic value in highly demanding projects. A major element of our efforts to accelerate the utilization of object technology is the efforts of Grady Booch and Jim Rumbaugh, whom I recently joined to produce a unified approach combining the major features of the Booch method, Object Modeling Technique, and Jacobson. There are great benefits in reducing fragmentation and making it easier for people to use object technology by collaborating to produce a single, unified notation and method.

The 0.8 version of the unified method was unveiled at OOPSLA in October 1995 and is available today. Developed before I joined Rational, the 0.8 draft already included basic use cases. With Grady, Jim, and myself together at Rational, use cases will be integrated even more completely into the unified notation; this work will be part of the 1.0 release. Our goal is to produce a unified model the industry can view as the basis for true standardization.

Change comes with any company merger; being a part of a bigger, new corporation is a change for the people at the old Rational and Objectory. This is clearly a change for the better. Objectory and Rational were successful companies with complementary products and processes. There is a genuine synergy within the combined company strategy, especially in our vision of a more seamless, automated support for software development throughout the lifecycle based on use cases and object technology.

EDITOR'S NOTE

There is evidence of the successful merger of Rational and Objectory. The SEP as mentioned here is manifested by the Rational Unified Process (RUP) product as provided by Rational. Similarly, the SEPSE is most obviously manifested by the Rational Suite of development tools, with all its variants and separate point products such as Rational Rose, Rational RequisitePro, Rational ClearCase, Rational TeamTest, etc. Please refer to www.rational.com for more information.

The "unified notation and method" is really the Unified Modeling Language (UML) that is continuously refined by Rational and many other companies and organizations; the UML is today a commonly adopted standard defined by the Object Management Group (OMG). Please refer to www.omg.org for more information.

An important message here is that the merger of the Rational and Objectory corporations provided a major boost of the SEP, the SEPSE, and the underlying standard modeling language (UML). Thus, this particular company merger provided a very significant "following wind" on the road to the Unified Software Development Process.

The notions of SEP and SEPSE are further elaborated upon in depth in Part 4 of this book.

REFERENCES

1. I. Jacobson and S. Jacobson. "Beyond Methods and CASE: The Software Engineering Process with Its Integral Support Environment," *Object Magazine*, 4(8): 24–30, 1995. (See chapter entitled "Beyond Methods and CASE: The Software Engineering Process with Its Integral Support Environment.")

2. I. Jacobson and S. Jacobson. "Reengineer Your Software Engineering Process," *Object Magazine*, 5(1): 12–16, 1995. (See chapter entitled "Reengineering Your Software Engineering Process.")

3. I. Jacobson and S. Jacobson. "Designing a Software Engineering Process," *Object Magazine*, 5(3): 79–81, 1995. (See chapter entitled "Designing a Software Engineering Process.")

4. I. Jacobson and S. Jacobson. "Designing an Integrated SEPSE," *Object Magazine*, 5(5): 96–93, 1995. (See chapter entitled "Designing an Integrated Software Engineering Process Support Environment.")

5. I. Jacobson and S. Jacobson. "Building Your Own Methodology by Specializing a Methodology Framework," *Object Magazine*, 5(7): 96–95, 1995. (See chapter entitled "Building Your Own Process by Specializing a Process Framework.")

In Ivar's Words

─────

Q: Could you discuss your move to Rational and Objectory's merger with Rational?

A: Before we talked with one another, Objectory had been able to grow on its own for eight years. We were about 100 people and we had significant interest in the United States. We believed we needed to grow much faster and to have a big channel throughout the whole world. We also felt strongly that we needed a different owner structure. Ericsson owned a majority of the company, which we had been very satisfied with. Ericsson is 120 years old, but focuses on telecommunications and not programming software development environments. So Ericsson and I agreed that we needed to find a new owner and we actually had been hoping to find a colleague of Ericsson's for a couple of years, and then Ericsson decided to take a close look at Rational. Both Rational and I received a proposal from Ericsson. At the same time Rational expressed an interest in collaboration with us. So we met in February, and for about three or four months we didn't do anything else besides talk to each other and try to get to know one another, and we met about once a month. Somewhere in the summertime, we thought to consider a merger, and we worked it through very carefully, because about 80 percent of high-tech mergers turn into disasters and don't work out very well, and we didn't want to be one of those. So we met and worked through all the important issues about what the new company would look like. We made agreements on all these important issues. At the beginning I didn't think that we needed to merge with another company, but having worked through all these issues, we felt very confident in one another. And the mode of inquiry had a very strong process content, after all our business is to tell a complete organization how to move into objects, that is to reengineer the way they are developing software to do it through object orientation.

At Objectory we made a very strong difference between a method and a process. A method is typically captured in a textbook like my own book on OOSE (Object-Oriented Software Engineering—A Use Case Driven Approach). However a book is not enough. A book presents some ideas, it can be read by single readers, it should have a wide market to be able to sell.

A process is something quite different. It is captured in a set of handbooks, it addresses the whole development organization not just single readers. Thus there are work-steps for every type of worker in a development project: analysts, designers, programmers, testers, project managers, etc. An author writes a method book, whereas process engineers develop a process. When I founded Objectory the main business idea was to engineer a generic software engineering process, what I call a SEP, and build tools to support that. Therefore we started by designing a generic SEP. We used our own approach for modeling a business to model SEP. This is described in my second book—The Object Advantage. Thus we modeled the SEP using objects. We had two stereotypes of objects. There were worker objects that represented work roles that people in the development organization played. And there were work products like a use case model, a design model, an object to be designed, the code of a subsystem. The SEP model described how workers interacted and developed work products. By using an object approach we designed a process framework that then could be specialized for every single organization, application, etc. So what we now can do is to shape an organization, not only the projects, but the organization, to move from, that is to say reengineering, in whatever way they are working, to working using an OO approach. And that was one of the things that Rational really wanted first of all. And another interest was our tool support, which was particularly strong in the front-end and in support of the process.

But anyway, we were strong in the front-end and Rational was very good in the back-end. I believe our work in the front-end with use cases and process is really complementary with what old Rational had. Rose is a very good design tool for C++, and Rational has developed a good programming environment for C++ and Ada, for configuration management, and of course testing and project management tools. All of these things are very complementary with what we had, so I think we had a perfect fit. And moreover our people were consultants on the whole life-cycle process. We were more generalists than experts in any particular field. Rational had people of that caliber as well working throughout the world, while we were at that time primarily in the United States, Germany, and the UK. So everything looked very well, I crossed my fingers, and it worked. But I can tell you now, there is always a vacuum after a merger. But now we are through that period and we are moving forward and we have a great deal of enthusiasm here, and I think it emerged in the best way.

The Objectory process has now been completely adopted by Rational; it is developed, marketed, and sold by Rational. We have also extended it so that it incorporates the experience from old Rational. It incorporates the work done by Grady and Jim, and our joint work on the Unified Modeling Language. It also incorporates work by other people at Rational, ideas on incremental development, process management, architecture. The result is called the Rational Unified Process.

An important specialization of the Objectory process product is the business engineering process. We called it Objectory BE. This is an implementation of my BPR book, The Object Advantage. This is a very important product. First of all, it's very important to be able to understand your business, and by using this approach you get a very good model of your business. You can use this model to communicate the changed business to the people that will work in the business. Furthermore, you can, based on your business model, generate requirements for the information systems for the business, the mechanics of it, if you will. Once you create an object model of your business, you can press a button and create a use case model of the information system to support the business, and that is a very, very strong concept. But also if you ignore the business model, I don t know of any other systematic approach to identify the necessary information system and the requirements of the software. Because if you don't know the business, you don t know the software for the business. Moreover, I don't know of any other systematic approach to find reusable assets for a family of systems, across the entire company, other than to use this approach. So we believe that these products will be a very big market for Rational.

This has been a very long answer, but it's extremely hard to merge two companies. We had different cultures, but they were very compatible, and so once we concluded that our ideas worked together, we were very glad, and since then our technology has been very well adopted.

PART 2:
A BRIEF HISTORY

Dr. Ivar Jacobson is probably most known as the father of "use cases." There may however be contributions of his that are even more important, such as when he participated during the introduction of component-based development at Ericsson, starting in 1967. This is because software components were already at that time starting to be designed as pluggable modules that provided well-defined services via interfaces.

With these fundamental and yet powerful ideas in place, there followed a wide range of methodological and architectural issues that called for attention, such as "How do we capture the requirements on these components?" and "How do we describe component interactions?" The solution was to introduce various methods and diagramming techniques to deal with this new kind of complexity. One of the most obvious results from this effort is the notion of "use cases." Other results include early versions of some diagram types such as sequence diagrams, collaboration diagrams, and activity diagrams, and how to use these diagrams in a pragmatic manner; and how to apply all this technology in an industrial software development process in general.

In this part we get a glimpse of those early days, the apparent problems of software development, and the proposed solutions that actually yielded a large commercial success to start with.

PART 2:
A BRIEF HISTORY

2

A LARGE COMMERCIAL SUCCESS STORY AT ERICSSON

———

Ivar Jacobson, MAY 1996

PARADISE TO MOST COMPANIES is developing a product that meets customer requirements and is superior to competitors. Few companies ever attain it; even fewer in mature businesses attain it. But thanks to objects and components, a Swedish company, Ericsson, achieved such a market position 18 years ago. The major telecom administrations around the world judged the Ericsson product—the AXE switch—superior to its competitors.[*] Ericsson has succeeded in using its competitive advantage to expand its business and become one of the largest players in the world of telecommunications. It has increased its market share in both traditional switching systems and new areas, such as mobile communication. At the same time, several of its competitors have suffered dramatically from not being able to provide a competitive product. Some of them, like ITT, have actually gone out of the telecommunication business. Others, such as GTE, Phillips, GEC, and Plessey have dramatically smaller market share.

Of course, technical superiority is not sufficient but an essential asset. It strengthens the self-confidence of everyone in the organization. Through objects and components, Ericsson developed a product that could easily be adapted to (at this point) 100+ different countries' individual needs, a product still being aggressively further enhanced and refined in a multinational

---

[*] The history of the AXE success story is in a book titled: *Teknisk Revolt* (Swedish for "Technical Revolt").

development organization. Ericsson developed a product that fulfills all reasonable requirements for a large-scale industrial product and succeeded in pleasing very demanding customers. Consequently, the AXE system gave Ericsson a significant long-term competitive advantage leading to an outstanding international success with the system.

BACKGROUND

Object orientation has been described as a fundamentally new technology used to build software systems, a technology that has grown in parallel with young companies like Apple and Microsoft—a technology that enthralls programmers, making them capable of creating elegant and reusable software.

In Scandinavia, object orientation has been applied as long as software has been developed. The ancestor to all OO programming languages is *Simula*, developed in Norway and currently celebrating its 28th anniversary. Everything essential to object orientation now offered by a language such as C++† existed in Simula in 1967!

THE PRODUCT

The AXE system is a *telecommunication switching system*. Switching systems are very complex and require thousands of programmers. The system must be very reliable and practically never out of service. It must be highly concurrent, able to manage thousands of ongoing telephone calls for hundreds of thousands of subscribers. Response times must be kept very short, at the level of milliseconds (or shorter). Every exchange is a large database that at installation time must be initiated with hundreds of thousands of personalization parameters for subscribers and trunks.

The database system supports atomic transaction handling, so either a transaction succeeds or it has no impact at all. The toughest requirement on a switching system is that it must be changeable during operation without disturbing ongoing traffic severely.

A successful switching system must be adaptable to the demands of various clients. The development is often geographically distributed in several different locations around the world. The system must be able to evolve over

---

† The principal designer of C++ was actually Danish—Bjarne Stroustrup.

several decades due to advances in technology—both hardware and software—impacting both development and implementation.

Therefore, it is no surprise that good switching systems are difficult to develop. The development environment for a switching system is extremely demanding, providing an excellent proving ground to learn and develop industrial-strength design methodologies.

The AXE Method: A Brief Overview

A major key to the success of the AXE system was the use of an OO design method supported by a similar OO implementation. The method was partitioned into four different workflows: requirements analysis, design, implementation, and testing.

Requirements analysis identifies the system's functional requirements and results in a set of textual specifications—one per use case.‡ In *design*, you model the whole system as a set of communicating objects (blocks).

The objects are assembled in subsystems to make the system manageable. You find the objects by working though all the use cases and, for each use case, identifying the objects that cooperated to offer the use case. You now know all the responsibilities for each object and can make a specification for every object. The design activities result in a set of static class diagrams with all the system objects, their interconnections, and their grouping into subsystems.

For each use case, a sequence diagram is developed showing how the objects communicate dynamically to carry out the use case. Furthermore, for each object, a specification is made that describes all the messages the object must take care of as well as the internal data of the object. For some objects, particularly objects interacting with the environment of the system, the specification includes a state diagram.

Those familiar with popular object-oriented methods have probably discovered that those methods have adopted techniques used 25 years ago!§ The *implementation* work is now straightforward. Every subsystem is assigned

---

‡ The term *use case* was not introduced until 1987.[1] Ericsson used two terms: (a) *traffic case*, for different types of telephone calls, i.e., local call, incoming call, or transit call; (b) *functions*, which today I would call *abstract use cases*.

§ We wanted support for subsystems, or rather their executables—that is what we today call components—all the way down to the computer architecture. We got this with AXE, which made a lot of difference.

to a responsible programmer who codes it in a language (PLEX) that supports subsystem and message management. The code for a subsystem is a source code component, which after compilation becomes an executable component.

Finally, every subsystem is unit tested until the programmer is satisfied with his/her own work. *Testing* is done by a special group of people and encompasses integration and system testing. *Integration testing* is essentially use case testing (ie, testing that each use case is correctly offered by the objects already being unit tested). *System testing* involves different concurrent use cases with high traffic load and interfacing an operational system environment.

The method as just outlined was developed into a Software Engineering Process (SEP) that made it possible for a whole project team to work together to develop a product. Every development project is planned as a sequence of workflows: requirements analysis, design, implementation, and testing.

But to support all the clients around the world, there may be a large number of such projects going in parallel. This means the four different workflows are subprocesses rather than phases. These subprocesses can be engaged concurrently in different projects. They exist as long as the system is in use, and require maintenance and support, allowing Ericsson to manage the AXE system during its entire life cycle.

SECRET BEHIND SUCCESS

Why did AXE 10 become such a superior product? The product was launched in the mid 1970s, when competing products were developed more conventionally. Software was structured in functions, and data was manipulated by these functions. The difficulty in maintaining such systems is well known.

Ericsson could now present a product with completely different maintenance characteristics and demonstrate a development process similar to one used for systems implemented in hardware. The process was understandable to decision makers at the telecom administrations. The whole software architecture was simple to understand, communicating subsystems where each subsystem corresponds to a recognized telephony service such as "wake-up" or "follow me."

Ericsson introduced the concept of *service modularity*, which meant the system consisted of pluggable subsystems and each subsystem offered a service. The system could be configured with different sets of subsystems for different customers. The implementation used interfaces that allowed Ericsson to exchange one subsystem with another without changing the surrounding subsystems, except in rare cases. These changes could also be carried out while the system was in operation mode.

Thus, understandability was extremely important. It made Ericsson's approach believable and it demystified the software technology, which was liberating to most decision makers. When Ericsson could demonstrate that the ideas held in practice, success was a fact.

Understandability was also necessary to allow Ericsson to manage the product internally and industrialize it. The product had to be adapted to hundreds of different customers. Obviously, the developers had to understand the product, as did the sales, production, and installation departments. And last but not least, the users! This was simply and naturally done thanks to the objectification of the system, which supported configuration and version management.

Today, the AXE system is over 18 years old. The computer architecture and its implementation have been changed several times and the capabilities of the system have undergone dramatic improvements. The software has been constantly refined and adapted to telecommunication requirements, some not even identified 15 years ago. This has been possible due to a consistent OO approach followed throughout the architecture.

HOW DID IT HAPPEN?

The events that resulted in the AXE 10 system took several years. Ericsson began to develop computerized switches in the early 1960s. Its main source of inspiration for this came from Bell Laboratories. Bell Labs was a pioneer for this technology and generously shared its knowledge. After a comprehensive field test completed in 1967, Ericsson was ready to begin developing a first true product.

Coincidentally, I began to work with computer-based switches at this time, having four years of experience from the development of electromechanical systems. This was invaluable, because I had learned how to think in terms of complete systems as well as a particular way of implementing them. After a couple of months, I realized we were not building a manageable system. We would have to take a novel approach to the whole development process—an OO approach.

The proposal was unanimously negatively received. It was only through my role as the technical project manager that I succeeded in convincing the project's steering group to listen to me and discuss the proposal. After six months of endless discussions (which had quite a negative impact on the project), we had to make a crucial decision: either do as we did in the early field trial or accept my proposal. We stood at a crossroads—a decision that would have an impact on Ericsson's future.

Emotions ran high. There was a lot at stake even for me personally. The manager with overall responsibility for the technical organization of computerized switching systems, Lars-Olof Noren, made the decision.

Apart from myself, Noren was the only person in the 13-person steering group who accepted the proposal. Noren made the decision and requested that everyone accept it. This was a historic decision within Ericsson. We developed a product that later turned out to be a precursor to AXE.

We did not have a good enough implementation environment. We programmed in an assembler language; our operating system and our computer architecture did not support our software architecture.‖ We had no support for managing objects and, therefore, could not get a pluggable system. Message communication was only supported by macro instructions. Even so, Ericsson was able to sell the product to about 10 countries. It was at least as good as the competitors' corresponding product. But internally, people understood that it would not be manageable for the anticipated sales volume. The maintenance costs would be astronomical; but it gave us critical expertise. We learned which development method and architecture we should implement.

Therefore, in the early 1970s it was decided to develop a new product, which became the AXE system. The same SEP and principal software architecture were used. They had been tried out and tested in a large-scale environment and the experience was positive. But now the product had to be manageable in an industrial environment. The implementation of the software architecture was consistently carried out in the programming language, the operating system, the computer architecture, and the micro program. We

---

‖ Actually, many of the constructs now in the Unified Modeling Language had their origins in the approach used at Ericsson. For instance, the following diagrams in UML have direct counterparts in the early modeling language used to design AXE: class, collaboration, sequence, state charts, and activity diagrams. State charts in UML are a much richer notation than ours, but our notation became later the major source of inspiration behind the CCITT standard SDL. Class diagrams correspond to subsystem diagrams statically showing subsystems and their interconnections.

got components all the way down! Some very innovative ideas were born and implemented. The key architect was Göran Hemdal, a genius with many patented ideas now used in a variety of companies.

THE IDEAS OUTLIVE THE PRODUCT

The AXE system is now 18 years old and will live far beyond the year 2000. I believe, however, that the basic ideas will outlive the product many times over. When the decision on development process and architecture was made in 1968, it was clear to me that Ericsson had made a historic decision. Not everyone agreed with me; many believed it was a dead end. It took 10 years before there was a general understanding of the importance of this decision. Not until 1978, when the sales force succeeded in winning strategically important contracts based on the technical superiority of the product, did it become apparent that the principles behind the system architecture and the development process were a key to success.

I was asked to "make science of the AXE method." I used seven years, one of them at MIT, to develop the ideas behind the AXE method. The result was a doctorate in computer science (1985) and a thesis formalizing these ideas into an OO modeling language. The software architecture of the AXE system was used as a basis for the work. Then I simplified and generalized it so it was also applicable to standard data processing. I further developed the technology so it could be unified with OO programming languages (e.g., Smalltalk or C++) and extended it with new language features.

Two years later, I left Ericsson to found a company specializing in object and component-based development processes. One lesson I had learned at Ericsson was that developing a method is very simple—I did it at Ericsson within a couple of weeks. But to develop a software engineering process is a major effort. A software engineering process must support an organization, not single users, in developing a product as a team.

The early ideas developed in 1967 and after have been the principal source of inspiration for SDL, a CCITT standard first taken in 1976 and extended every fourth year since. In 1976 SDL supported a kind of objects (called *processes*) and a kind of messages (called *signals*). Objects were packaged in subsystems and described in terms of a state diagram. Sequence diagrams were used to describe object interaction. Unfortunately, in the late 70s there were a number of language design decisions that CCITT took early on that have made it very difficult to make SDL a mainstream object-based# modeling technique.

Processes were a special kind of objects and signals a special kind of messages. Even the 1992 release of SDL (called OSDL) where one has tried to make SDL more object-oriented will not improve these early fatal decisions. OSDL supports an obscure kind of object-orientation. However, even given these flaws, it is fair to say that SDL was the first standard on object modeling. 10,000 developers today use SDL daily and several vendors provide tool support for SDL. Furthermore, the ideas have evolved into a mainstream object-oriented method OOSE.[2] An introduction to OOSE was presented at OOPSLA '87 and, to my knowledge, this is the first published object-oriented** design method. OOSE has inspired many other methods. Furthermore, we have only seen the beginning. The experience gathered from AXE has substantially influenced our work on architectural styles and reuse.[1] I believe these styles, developed on top of simple object-orientation, are fundamental to achieve systematic software reuse. Thus, object technology is a basic standard technology that will be further developed, and refined. But, most important, it will hold. Everyone who invested in this technology early on, like Ericsson, built up an infrastructure and experience base. These companies will not experience an expensive restructuring as technology changes. My guess is that Ericsson (if well managed) will harvest even large rewards in the future because of its early strategic decision on object technology.

CONCLUSION

The AXE product is the largest commercial success story in Sweden's history. I believe the AXE system is the largest product ever built using objects and components. Largest in whatever measure you want to use: lines of code, number of people, revenues of product sales, etc.

By selecting an object and component based approach for the software architecture of the AXE system; having it consistently supported by programming language, operating system, computer architecture, micro program;

SDL did not support inheritance—though it was object-based.
** OOSE supports inheritance.

and allowing it to impact all activities of the enterprise fully, Ericsson created a product technically superior to its competitors.

I also believe the success of the AXE system could be formulated in one single word: *reuse*. Thanks to a carefully designed architecture, Ericsson achieved substantial reuse of already designed software.

Furthermore, Ericsson also succeeded in reusing the AXE ideas and technologies in another system area, creating another great business success, the MD110 series of high-end business communication networks.

In summary, technology matters, and objects and components used consistently and systematically are a sustaining competitive advantage.

ACKNOWLEDGMENTS

I am grateful to Mobrin at Ericsson for reviewing this column and giving valuable feedback. Parts of this were originally published in *American Programmer*, 1992.[3]

REFERENCES

1. Ivar Jacobson, Martin Griss, Patrik Jonsson. *Software Reuse: Architecture, Process and Organization for Business Success,* Addison Wesley Longman, Reading, MA, 1997.

2. Ivar Jacobson, Magnus Christerson, Patrik Jonsson, Gunnar Övergaard. *Object-Oriented Software Engineering—A Use Case Driven Approach,* Addison–Wesley, Revised Fourth Printing, 1993.

3. Ivar Jacobson. "Object Orientation as a Competitive Advantage," *American Programmer*, 5(8), Oct. 1992.

3

AN AMBITIOUS GOAL: INDUSTRIAL DEVELOPMENT OF SOFTWARE WITH AN OBJECT-ORIENTED TECHNIQUE

Ivar Jacobson, MARCH-APRIL 1991

INTRODUCTION

COMPARED TO MOST OTHER BRANCHES of industry, the development and manufacturing of software systems is young. Moreover, it has hardly reached such maturity that it can be said to be industrial (or even rational); it is, in fact, rather more like a handicraft. Nevertheless, software is an important component in a great many industrial products, from simple control systems to domestic appliances to complex large-scale systems for telecommunication. To manufacture these products with the same quality requirements on the software as on the hardware, it will be necessary to manufacture the software components in an industrially acceptable way. In this article, we will argue that there is every reason to believe that this will be feasible within the next few years.

The term *system development* is used in a wider sense than software development. Thus, it is taken to cover the development of systems consisting of both hardware and software components. However, system development does not comprise the description of the surrounding activity, which is usually handled during the business modeling. On the other hand, it contains routine descriptions for those who are directly using the automated part of the system. Henceforth, we will use the term system development, thereby including also the special case that comprises only software development.

By way of introduction, we start from the need for a more industrial attitude to system development. Development is then viewed as part of a larger enterprise where, among other things, manufacturing, marketing, and sales are important components. With this perspective, we describe how the development process can be designed.

Then we focus on the system development process itself, bearing in mind that a product during its life cycle will have to be changed and redeveloped. System development must be designed as a process that can handle changes; this is particularly true about large systems. To be manageable, such a process must be divided into smaller parts. We summarize the traditional classification of system development phases and insert concepts such as incremental development and prototyping at their proper places within the development work.

Object orientation is, among other things, a basic technology for programming that soon will become increasingly important in all system development work. What we wish to achieve is an understanding of how this viewpoint can form a conceptual basis for all system development work.

In the following section, we expound on the concepts of architecture, method, process, and tools as viewed from a system development perspective. The architecture, i.e., the structure of the resulting system, is decisive for the life cycle properties of developed systems. The method shows how the system will be developed, systematically, to attain this architecture. Overlying the method is a uniting process that sees to it that the task descriptions are being followed and coordinated in a development project. Given this base, consisting of architecture, method, and process, it is possible to add tools to simplify the different tasks of the work. Finally, we concretize the discussion in a brief presentation of a development method, ObjectOry™, that has been developed along these principles.

INDUSTRIAL DEVELOPMENT OF SOFTWARE

Most complex products, such as cars, houses, and ships, are produced in some kind of industrial environment. Today, products are handmade only if the production is very small or if the handmade product has an added artistic dimension that makes it more valuable.

An increasing number of industrial products contain parts controlled by software. To make possible the maintenance and repair of products as a whole, the software must meet the same requirements as the other components of the system. It is particularly important that there be routines for continuous maintenance when the products are complex. Such routines form part of the product development and are well established in most branches of industry.

Unfortunately, this is still not customary in software production. There, the aim is seldom to develop a product that can be maintained and changed during its whole life cycle. There are several reasons for this. One is that software development is a young branch—only a few decades old—that is being integrated with more mature branches of industry, such as automobile manufacturing, which is more than a century old. There, considerable change has taken place over the years: even though cars have looked more or less the same for the last fifty years, it was quite a long time before there was a general consensus that cars should have four wheels, a steering wheel, and a gas pedal.

Moreover, a program is an abstract entity that makes great demands on man's intellectual capacity and tools. Most people find it easier to discuss concrete objects. It is, for instance, much more difficult to give the production criteria of a program than those of a machine part that is to be manufactured in a turning lathe.

Obviously, software must be developed on the same condition as other types of industrial products. There are instances of enterprises where this is already well established practice. In systems for potentially dangerous or sensitive enterprises, it is a requirement that it be possible to maintain and correct the systems for a long period of time, for instance, systems for telecommunications, population registration, and control systems for nuclear power stations or power distribution.

Another aspect of industrialization is that the ensuing activity is highly specialized and geared at making both the volume and quality of the production predictable. The activity then becomes a rational process with part tasks that can be clearly defined and delegated.

System Development—Part of a Larger Activity

System development is part of a larger activity. In many cases, this activity aims to develop a product where software is an integrated part. (This is usually the case in large industries.) In other cases, the activity comprises the data processing department within a large company (e.g., insurance companies and banks). The product can then consist of the administrative resources that the data processing department offers to the staff of that company. Figure 3-1 shows the system development as a partial activity of the company (or the department) whose assortment comprises products containing software. In this example, the company is called System Manufacturing, Inc.

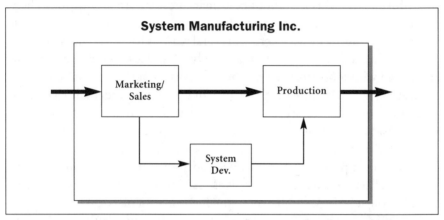

Figure 3-1. System development is an integrated part of a larger activity.

The entire activity of System Manufacturing, Inc. is a process that apart from system development contains at least two other processes: marketing/sales and production. The main flow typically passes directly from marketing/sales to production. The inflow consists of new orders from customers and the outflow of delivered customer systems. (We are using the term customer in a wide sense. Another department within the same company can thus be viewed as a customer.) The marketing/sales department orders product configurations for delivery to customers and formulates requirements for new products.

A product order goes from marketing/sales to production. The order is formulated in such a way that it is possible to identify the configuration of the final product immediately. The production department delivers a complete system to a customer. It should normally be possible to formulate an order in terms that are comprehensible to the customer without the aid of the system development department. Thus, no programmers or qualified technicians take part in the production process, but rather persons who are good at duplicating and assembling products into systems and who can test these before delivery.

New products are initiated as the marketing/sales department conveys new customer demands to the development department. Again, a customer-friendly terminology is usually employed that does not require the active presence of the development department. This is possible if products are described as sets of packages of functions—*services*—that can be ordered.

In the development department, new data for the production of the system are developed based on the new product requirements. Then the marketing/sales department is informed about the new service facilities.

Services perform a central role in the development phase. It is in the terms of services that the three part processes—marketing/sales, production, and development—communicate. Services must be designed so that they can be configured for a number of different products. Likewise, the software itself has to be reusable. In other words, the various parts of a system should, to a high degree, be reusable both within the system (general services) and between different types of systems (components). Even the system documentation should be made reusable between systems.

System Development

We will now concentrate on the part process of system development. Based on a number of changed requirements, it will develop an updated system (Fig. 3-2). This new system actually consists of revised data for the production process.

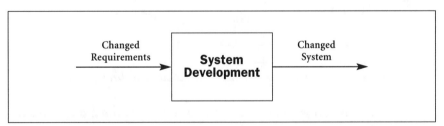

Figure 3-2. System development is a process for successive changes of a system.

For software, the production data are simply descriptions of the system to be produced. System development can thus be viewed as a process, manufacturing descriptions. This takes place at all levels—analysis, design, programming, and testing. In this context, source code is also a description that can be understood by programmers and by the production process (by a compiler). The descriptions present *models* of different detailing degrees.

The early models are very abstract, focusing on external qualities of the system, whereas the later models become more detailed and instrumental in the respect that they describe how the system is going to be built and meant to function.

To describe system development in a simplified (and "waterfallish") way, one might say that it consists of three different workflows that seamlessly follow each other (Fig. 3-3). In the first workflow, *analysis*, an application-oriented specification is developed, i.e., a specification of *what* the system is to offer the users. At this early stage of system development, when changes are still relatively inexpensive, the aim is to find a good structure of the system: a structure that is robust against changes and that gives the system a clear and comprehensible division into units that can be ordered (services). This specification, which we call the *analysis model*, outlines the functional behavior of the system under practically ideal circumstances and without regard to a particular implementation environment. In other words, in the analysis model we disregard any restrictions that might exist in the programming language, database management system, and other surrounding supporting system products. On the other hand, it is important to judge whether the analysis model can actually be realized under the given circumstances, e.g., as regards performance or development costs.

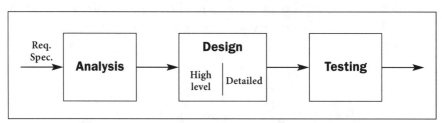

Figure 3-3. System development divided into three phases.

During the second workflow, *design and implementation*, the ideal conditions of the analysis will gradually be replaced with requirements from the chosen implementation environment. Here it is decided *how* the application-oriented analysis model will be realized with the aid of system software, database management systems, user interfaces, etc. The high-level design activities—the system design—could be seen as a formalization of the analysis model (now with regard to the implementation environment). The separate programs, identified in the high-level design, will then be coded in the detailed design.[1]

The final workflow, *testing*, checks that the system is really a functional realization of the analysis model, i.e., that all the functions comprised in the analysis model have been correctly implemented in the design, and that the performance of the system is acceptable. Testing takes place at several levels, from the testing of separate programs and various functions (i.e., unit testing) to the final testing of the system as a whole.

Each successive step in the development adds to the result of the previous step and furthers the development of the system. Thereby, both the formalism and degree of the specification of the system increase until the final detailing level is reached—the program code.

SYSTEM DEVELOPMENT— A PROCESS OF PROGRESSIVE CHANGE

All systems will change during their life cycles. This must be kept in mind when systems are developed that are expected to last longer than the first version, i.e., practically all systems. Most development methods of today focus on new development and treat revision work very briefly, although it is a known fact that changes constitute the main part of the total life cycle costs of a large number of systems. Therefore, an industrial process should focus on system changes.[2]

A system is normally developed through changes in a number of versions. New development is, from this point of view, only a special case, the first version, and it constitutes a change from nothing into something. Nonetheless, new development is an important activity, as it constitutes the base of the system and will last throughout the whole of the development work. If the base is faulty, it will have serious consequences during the whole life cycle of the system.

The analysis workflow begins when the marketing/sales department sends requirement specification to the system development department or, more correctly, when a specification of wanted changes of an earlier version is delivered; we call this a *delta* requirement specification.

As mentioned earlier, the development work is characterized by the development of a number of models and submodels, each of which has an increasing level of details. All of these models are really delta models; i.e., each is a changed version of an earlier model at the same level.

In analysis work, the changed (delta) requirement specification is the starting point from which delta analysis models developed. The delta analysis model is then delivered to the design team, which produces a delta implementation. Each new version of this system is thus a delta version. *System development is a process of progressive change.*

INCREMENTAL DEVELOPMENT

System development is usually regarded as a slow process, in which the turn-around time from concept to a finished system can take several years. At first, a requirement specification is worked out for the entire system. Then follow analysis, design, and testing of the system. The method can work if all requirements on the final system are known from the outset; however, this is rarely the case.

In most cases, it is therefore a better strategy to develop the system systematically, beginning with the architecture of the system and a few of the most important system functions (use cases). As it becomes clear that the chosen path is the right one, and a better understanding of how the system is to function is evolving, the next step is taken by adding a number of new functions. The system is incrementally enlarged in this way until the wanted level is reached, i.e., the finished product. By means of such an incremental strategy, there will also be faster feedback in the development process or, figuratively speaking, a more direct connection between the steering wheel rotation and the veering of the car.

PROTOTYPING

It is often difficult to determine how a system is supposed to work. The reasons may be technical, functional, efficiency, or user-oriented aspects. A prototype of the intended system is then often developed. The prototype is created to focus on the properties that require better insight. Moreover, it is important that the prototype be developed in an environment where an acceptable, functioning, and easily changeable system can be developed in a short time—so-called rapid prototyping. Experiments with prototyping will visualize a number of different design options. Another advantage is that the prototype can serve as a means of communication between the developer and the customer. It is easier to express viewpoints about something that can be demonstrated and used, if only partially, than to express an opinion about a specification that cannot capture the dynamics of the system in the same way as a "working" prototype.

Rapid prototyping is in relatively bad repute today; there are even those who criticize it as "quick and dirty." This reputation, however, has not been brought about by the method as such, but rather because of the way it has been used. In some cases, the prototype has actually been considered to be so good that it has been kept in use, and a full system development has been deemed unnecessary. This is, of course, quite in order, as long as those involved know what they are doing.

As a prototype is often meant to highlight certain properties of the intended system, other parts of the system can be disregarded, and are therefore only given schematic form. If, however, the prototype comes into regular use, this will presumably result in malfunctioning or lead to difficulties in changing those parts of the system.

Rapid prototyping is a useful technique for application comprehension. Furthermore, if the prototype is given a careful design, it may also prove useful in the final system.

Correctly used, rapid prototyping thus deserves a far better reputation than it has at the moment.

FROM ANALYSIS TO DESIGN

In every development methodology, it is possible to draw the boundaries between the successive work steps in a great many ways. What boundaries are chosen may even vary from project to project. In one project, a formal analysis model may be required; different contractors can then be asked to make design quotations. The formal analysis model will then guarantee that the final design corresponds to what was ordered. (By design is meant both traditional "design work" and implementation.)

In another project, it may be obvious how the implementation environment affects the system requirements. Then a less formal analysis model can be chosen, making it even more independent of the implementation.

At present, formalism during the analysis workflow should be restricted to the syntax and semantics of the static structure of the system. There is still no good, strictly formal technique to specify the system's dynamic behavior in the analysis workflow. A more practical, descriptive technique is preferable to a mathematical, formal method that has not yet reached full maturity. There are far better possibilities to use such a technique during the design work later, especially during the implementation.

Although the boundaries between analysis and design may seem vague, there are certain guidelines for what should be described in the analysis model and what should be dealt with in the design respectively.

- The analysis model is independent of the implementation environment, which means changes in the implementation requirements will not affect the analysis model. Even if an important part of the system is replaced in the realization, e.g., a database management system, the analysis model will not be affected.

- The analysis model is application-oriented. The work is carried out in an ideal world, and memory size, performance, and error tolerance requirements can be left aside.

- The analysis model describes the elements components of the application in application-related concepts (e.g., services). As it forms the basis of the design, the structure of the implementation will mirror the structure of the problem, rather than the other way around.

- The analysis model should not be too elaborate if what is done will still have to be adapted to the chosen implementation environment. This may happen, for instance, if the analysis model is too formal.

OBJECT ORIENTATION

In this section, we will give a summary of the basic ideas and concepts of object orientation. The aim is not to give a strict, theoretical definition of the object concept, but rather to introduce the point of view employed.

THE OBJECT CONCEPT

A system that is based on an object-oriented philosophy consists of a number of objects. By *object,* we mean a clearly delimited part of the modeled or designed system, usually corresponding to an entity in real life, e.g., an invoice, an automobile, or a mobile telephone. Each object has specific content and holds information meant for that particular object; thus, a car will know its registration number. Included in the content of the objects is their association to other objects, e.g., an invoice may know what customer to bill. All information in an object-oriented system is stored in the objects and can only be manipulated when the objects are ordered to perform *operations*. The behavior and representation of its information are *encapsulated* in the object—they are not visible from the outside of the object. The only way to affect an object is to perform operations on it.

CLASS

In a system, there are many objects that are described and that behave in the same way; all separate specimens of an invoice, for instance, behave in the same way. Such shared features are described in the various object *classes*. A class can be said to contain a definition—a pattern—of what objects belonging to that class should look like. Each separate object specimen of the system is an *instance* of a class, i.e., the general definition of an object will be found in its class. The class defines what operations the instances of the class can perform and what variables and associations the instances have. Information that is unique for one specimen/item is stored in one instance of the class.

INHERITANCE

It is possible to define a new class by describing how it differs from an existing class. We say that the new class *inherits* the existing one (Fig. 3-4). In other words, the inheriting class (Automobile in Fig. 3-4) can be built on established classes without changing these existing classes.

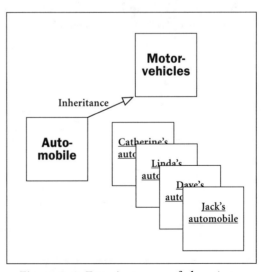

Figure 3-4. Four instances of class Automobile that inherit class Motor Vehicles.

COMPARISON BETWEEN FUNCTION/DATA ARCHITECTURE AND OBJECT-ORIENTED ARCHITECTURE

In this section, we will compare two different techniques for system development. The two chosen techniques are interesting, as they represent two extremes among system philosophies.

There is a decisive difference between the architecture of a system that has been developed with an object-oriented approach and the architecture of one that has been developed with a function/data-oriented approach.

To create a greater understanding of this, we will use as an example a system for spare-part handling. The customers buy the parts directly from the depot, and each requisition is registered in the data system.

FUNCTION/DATA DIVISION

In methods that are based on a function/data-oriented approach, a distinction is made between operations and data. Operations are described in the form of programs, "functions" (SADT[3]; RDD, which is based on SREM[4]), or " processes" (SA/SD[5,6]). Data are described as structures or variables in the programming language with abstract and application-related names as in Figure 3-5. Corresponding denotations in some other methods are "data" (SADT), "item" (RDD), or "store" (SA/SD). The relations between operations and data are at a read/write level (Fig. 3-5).

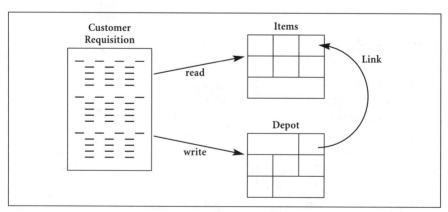

Figure 3-5. Schematic solution with a function/data approach.

Each function that performs an operation on data must know the internal structure of those data. A particular operation, e.g., a requisition of a spare part, often requires a number of references to several different data structures.

In our example, different spare-parts types might have different data formats. The operation must know about and pay attention to this. To handle such differences in data, we will need a number of conditional clauses (if-then-else). They have nothing to do with the requisition as such, but are only necessary because of the variation of data formats. Programs of this type are difficult to read.

A change of the underlying structure will immediately affect operations using these data. A change of a data structure may require changes of several functions and in a great many places. Every reference to data must therefore be checked and updated, an extremely meticulous task. The spare parts at the depot can, for instance, be kept in a list. If, however, it is decided later that they should be kept in a table, this will affect all the operations using the data stored as a list. By modularizing the operations so those working on the same data are combined within the same compilation unit, a step can be taken toward a greater coupling between functions and data; yet this does not solve the basic problem: Operations refer to data at too primitive a level.

OBJECT ORIENTATION

When the spare part example is developed with an object-oriented technique, the modeling is performed in term of objects only (Fig. 3-6). Obviously, the object types differ as far as properties go; nevertheless, they are all objects.

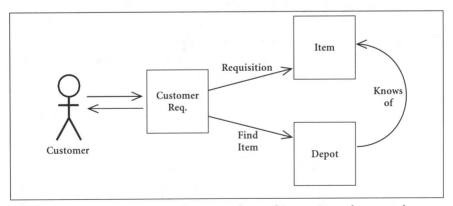

Figure 3-6. Schematic solution with an object-oriented approach.

Also in the object-oriented approach shown in Figure 3-6 are things such as Customer Requisition, Items, and Depot. There is, however, an essential difference between this model and the previously described function/data model. In an object-oriented model, all behavior connected with a particular Item is placed in the object containing all the data about Item. The object Customer Requisition does not know the internal structure of the data contained in Items or in Depot; it can only reach them via the operations of the objects. In Figure 3-6, for instance, the operation Requisition leads to a whole series of actions within the object Items. Yet, what happens within Items is of no interest to other objects; consequently, they need no information about it.

With the aid of inheritance it is possible to create several variants of item objects, e.g., for automobiles and uniforms, which have different internal data structures. All new object types have one thing in common however: They all know of the operation Requisition, a property they inherited from their shared parent, even though it is performed in different ways in the different objects. It is also obvious (as Fig. 3-6 shows) that the Customer Requisition object does not have to pay attention to what type of object is requisitioned, as Items all know of the operation Requisition.

The important difference between function/data-oriented and object-oriented approaches lies in the level at which relations can be modeled. In an object-oriented design the relations lie at a higher level of abstraction; they can therefore be made closer to life and thus become more comprehensible.

OBJECT ORIENTATION IS APPLICABLE IN ALL DEVELOPMENT WORKFLOWS

The function/data and object orientation approaches are examples of what in the next section will be called the architectural foundation of the method. They can therefore be applied in all development work, from analysis to design and programming.

It is understandable that a function/data division is used at a program-like level, as most computer architecture is built on such a technique. Moreover, most of today's programming languages, e.g., Cobol, Pascal, C, and Ada, are designed for compilation and execution on such computer architectures.

There are hybrid languages that combine object orientation and function/data programming, e.g., Object-Pascal, Objective-C, and C++. This is not news; the origin of object-oriented programming is Simula, which has been available for 20 years! There are also programming languages that are purely object oriented, e.g., Smalltalk-80 and Eiffel. Object-oriented programs tend to be more concise than corresponding conventional programs. The inheritance mechanisms encourage reuse of existing classes through specialization. A frequently cited example of this is the use of windows, where a new type of window can easily be designed by inheriting an existing one.

In certain cases, object-oriented programs, especially in Smalltalk, can lead to a performance lower than that of a non-object-oriented program. If the performance is of critical importance, the choice of a non-object-oriented programming language may therefore be justified. This does not hinder programming in an object-oriented style using a conventional language, however, nor does it hinder conventional programming in hybrid languages, particularly in performance-sensitive situations.

In other parts of the development, there is every reason to use object orientation as the underlying modeling technique. Its advantages show up clearly in analysis, for instance. With an object-oriented analysis technique, it is possible to avoid forcing people to think like machines in concepts similar to those of programs, which is a sheer waste of human creativity. In addition, we get not only a better system but also more efficient developers, who can communicate in a simple and comprehensible manner with their environment, which consists of persons with very different experiences in system development: customers, salespersons, production personnel, system installers, users, etc.

In methods such as SA/SD, SADT, and RDD, a function/data approach is used also in analysis and design. It is unnatural to keep this machine-like manner of description at high abstraction levels, where one is really trying to attain a better understanding of the problem. There are, however, clear signals that this is going to be changed and also that these methods will be given a more object-oriented approach.[7] The problem will then be that different structuring methods will be used during different phases of the development work. To make transformations between models of different structure is no trivial task, but will lead to extra complications.

To use an object-oriented technique in all work steps, as in ObjectOry,[8] will yield a homogeneous process where the real-life-like objects of the analysis workflow can be transformed into program-like models with a structure that closely follows that of the analysis model.

SYSTEM DEVELOPMENT FOR LARGE SYSTEMS

So far, we have been stressing the importance of the method used in system development. When developing large systems, it is equally important how the different steps of the method cooperate and how they fit into the development *process* as a whole. In this section, we will broaden the discussion to comprise both the development process and the basic ideas behind the method, in other words, what decides what *architecture* the final system will have. Finally, we will give a few viewpoints on how CASE tools should be designed, starting from the more fundamental properties of the architecture, method, and process (Fig. 3-7).

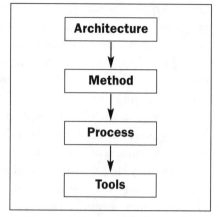

Figure 3-7. A method must be developed from an architecture. Starting out from the method, a process, as well as tool support for the process, can then be designed.

ARCHITECTURE

An important property of a software system is its internal structure—its architecture. A good structure makes the system easy to understand: it will be easy to change and to maintain. A comparison between computer systems and cars will illustrate what we mean. (However, all such comparisons are difficult to make and must not be taken too literally.) Most car owners are surprised to find that car manufacturers pay little attention to the fact that a car should be designed so that it can be repaired. Special tools are required for a number of simple jobs, or else it is practically impossible to get at a place that is to be repaired without dismantling other parts.

In more recent car models, a different kind of thinking is noticeable. Functional parts are assembled in large, exchangeable units. Repair work then means that a well-delimited unit can be removed and replaced in a few simple handgrips.

In the electronics industry, this idea has been developed even further. A television set is usually repaired through exchange of the circuit card with faulty component.

The architecture also decides in what way the system will have to be handled during its life cycle. Systems can be compared with houses. Stone houses and log houses have different properties, they are built differently, and they are maintained differently. Unlike card houses, these two types of houses represent good houses. The same differences are found in software systems. If a function/data-oriented method is used, the data of the system will be separated from the functions, and these will be structured top/down. Such systems have proven to have bad properties in the end; we will compare them with card houses. As was shown earlier, a small change of such a system, e.g., the change of a date format, can have very great consequences; that is why they can be compared with card houses. On the other hand, systems developed with an object-oriented technique are composed of a number of communicating and well-delimited objects. Such systems are much simpler to maintain, and have proven to have excellent properties in the long run. Furthermore, they are easy to develop and understand.

All aspects on internal system structure are found under the concept of architecture.

METHOD

A method can be defined as a planned procedure by which a specified goal is approached step by step (not to be confused with methodology, which is the science of methods). Most work descriptions for program development are method descriptions. They describe, often in a theoretical manner, how one should think and reason to develop a software system. Most methods also point out how the work steps of the method should follow each other in a particular sequence. The most common way to illustrate this is to line up the different steps after each other so that the information flow between them forms a "waterfall" (Fig. 3-8).

The different steps of the method can be divided into still more detailed elements. They all describe how the work is to be carried out assuming a certain underlying basic idea (or theory about the structure of the final system—its architecture). In other words, we see how a method is based on the preconceived

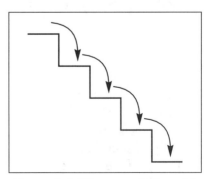

Figure 3-8. The waterfall model.

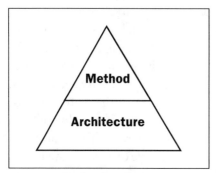

Figure 3-9. The base of a method is its architecture.

notion of the architecture of the final system (Fig. 3-9). This means that the descriptions of the method are formulated in terms of the architecture concepts in question.

A basic requirement of a good method is that it simplifies the development of systems that have the architecture it is meant for. Thus, a good method for object-oriented system development should help identify the right objects. This may seem obvious, but many methods for object-oriented development actually treat this aspect of development superficially, implying that there is no difficulty finding the objects directly in the activity that is to be modeled—an evasion of the problem. It is true that the objects of the system should have real-life counterparts, but they must also be motivated from the point of view of the system. What objects are needed and at what detailing level depends entirely on how the system is meant to be used. It is, for instance, hardly appropriate to include the whole spare-part depot in the system that supports the sales department, whereas it is most important that it be included in the support system of the service department.

It is usually not difficult to find suitable data-carrying objects in an enterprise. It is rather the dynamic objects describing how the system is used that are difficult to define correctly. Many people say that such objects need no modeling: They simply constitute operations on data-carrying objects and therefore can be included in those. However, behaviors cannot naturally be said to belong to a particular data-carrying object. For this reason, it is better to model separate dynamic objects.

PROCESS

A process is the natural continuation of a method. It comprises not only the work steps but also shows how these form a unity. The method defines how a development project should be carried out, whereas the process shows how the work is done in practice for many—possibly concurrent—projects.

There is, for example, a considerable difference between producing a new chemical substance on a laboratory scale and producing the same chemical on an industrial scale in a factory. In the laboratory, the goal is to find a method to produce the chemical. To make this method usable in practice, it must be developed into an industrial, large-scale process. This usually means that the working method needs to be changed. Nobody would dream of industrializing a laboratory method by simply building a large laboratory with gigantic test tubes and Bunsen burners. Yet this is often the way system development is carried out.

The solution lies in changing the working method so that it can be scaled up and carried out with great parallelism—as a process. If the method is developed for use on a large scale right from the beginning, the growing pains will not be so great when the work has to be scaled up. Therefore, it is an advantage if a development technique is adapted to designing large systems right from the start.

Just as a method can be split into a number of workflows with underlying work steps, a process will then consist of a number of small, communicating part-processes (Fig. 3-10). These must be defined in such a way that they are clearly delimited and can perform a task on their own. Each developer is responsible for the work carried out in one or several processes and is supposed to take care of the information that is sent to the process. Moreover, the developer should design the objects that other processes need as a basis of their process. The term "software factory" is coming into use for this division into processes and part processes.

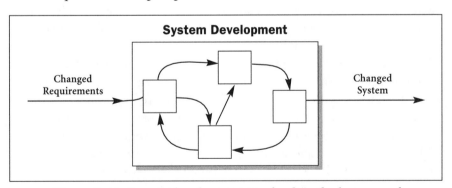

Figure 3-10. System development can be described as a set of communicating part-processes.

An interesting observation is that with this point of view both the developed system and the development mechanism itself can be regarded as a set of communicating objects. Processes are a type of object, a specialization of the general object concept. Each one of the part-processes needs to be described, including how they work and what input and output data they are working with. A good method description is about 100 pages long. To describe the corresponding process, ten times more text will be needed. The reason is that the method deals with a project only, whereas the process describes how a system will be managed during its entire lifetime.

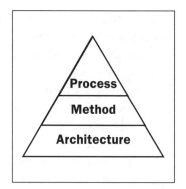

In other words, a process is an application or, if you like, the industrialization of a method. A process presupposes a method that, in turn, presupposes basic system architecture (Fig. 3-11).

Figure 3-11. A process is based on a method and its underlying architecture.

THE PROCESS MORE THAN THE METHOD

At the transition from principles to practice, there will be a number of new aspects that have to be taken care of. A process must therefore be able to express more than what is covered within the underlying method.

The process description defines how different part-processes are to cooperate and to what extent they should be carried in parallel, i.e., how the members of the project should cooperate. Each part process is independent as to the location of other part-processes. All development work can be split and carried out on several locations.

When program development is industrialized, the activity becomes less dependent on individuals. In an industrial process, there are fewer key persons. Most work tasks are well defined and can therefore be moved between different individuals. The whole process is more insensitive to disruptions due to the advancement of developers or other personnel changes.

If system development is viewed as a process, dynamics are introduced, as well as flow thinking. It becomes natural to see development as a change process. All development work is relative to the existing system. This is true both between different versions of a system and during the development of a particular version of the system. With a well-organized process, you will get a functioning version-handling into the bargain.

It is possible to replace a part-process with a new part-process performing an equivalent task. This is one way of adapting the development process to a completely new type of application or to a new development environment, e.g., a new programming language. Some part-processes may be of a type that cannot be designed in exactly the same way in all types of projects. They will have to be replaced by a process adapted to every specific project. Yet, this special part-process must have the same interfaces to other part-processes. This is especially the situation for the part-process responsible for coding the modeled objects of the design. It will be designed differently due to what data-base management system and programming language were chosen. To describe this specialization consistently, we allow processes to inherit each other. We say that a process can be a subclass of another process class (Fig. 3-12). We can start from a general process containing principal behavior, and make a number of specializations where separate properties are described.

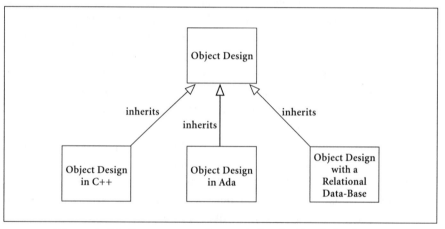

Figure 3-12. Processes can be specialized using inheritance.

COMPUTER-AIDED DESIGN

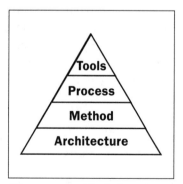

In the preceding sections, we have argued that the development of large systems requires that the development method be widened into an industrial process. To be fully efficient, the development work also needs computer-based tools (Fig. 3-13)—a computer-aided software engineering (CASE) environment. The introduction of tools need not change the actual form of the process, even though this is often the case.

Figure 3-13. Tools for system development form the top of the technique pyramid.

When large systems are developed, it is essential that all documentation of the system be consistent. This means, among other things, that an object must be given the same name everywhere in the documentation; often this is difficult to achieve. However, with a tool offering support for text links, this can be done very smoothly. When a developer wants to refer to an object in a document, he adds a reference to the desired object instead of "hard-coding" in the name. The presentation part of the tool then presents the reference as, for example, object names.

By means of a tool, a large number of the work tasks can be automated, especially trivial tasks that would otherwise become cumbersome due to their volume. If the work tasks in the underlying process are seamlessly interconnected, a great deal of the work can be automated, as the output result of a part-process can then easily be related to the input data of another part-process.

In the documentation of a complex system, it is desirable that the same information be presented in several ways. In that way, it will be easier for (different) developers to gain a better understanding of the system that is being modeled. Developers typically want to view association between objects as purely textual descriptions in a document, as arrows in diagrams, and as compilations in cross-reference editor (browsers). In a more sophisticated development environment, it may be more important to adapt the support to different categories of developers. Each developer can then receive exactly what information is needed. A project leader, for instance, is only interested in overall object descriptions, whereas a designer wants to see all the details.

A tool to be used on a large scale must support the process on which it is based. In an extension, the process can be integrated in the tool as part of it, for example, with decision support and the handling of change proposals.

Computer-aided tools can lead to massive production increases, but it must be remembered that they are parts of a greater whole. The choice of a development technique must start from the decided basic theory that governs the overall system architecture of the designed systems. To this architecture are then added a method, a process, and, finally, computer-aided tools.

BRIEFLY ABOUT OBJECTORY

We have described some important properties that can be expected of a modern development technique. We have stressed that system development should be carried out iteratively during the whole life cycle of the system, and that each iteration should be viewed as a change of an existing system. We have also placed system development in its proper context and spoken of system development as the whole chain from changed requirements to the functions system. Such a technique already exists. It is called ObjectOry, which stands for Object Factory for Software Development.

The framework of ObjectOry is a design technique, here called design with building blocks, that derives from Ericsson Telecom and is now spread throughout the whole field of telecommunications. The technique is the essential idea behind the CCITT recommendation specification and description language (SDL).[9] In SDL, a system is viewed as a number of connected building blocks, where each block represents a *system service*. With a complete specification of all required system services, building blocks are designed with a top-down technique, based on criteria for the development of systems that support functional changes and adaptation to new technology. It is this property that is particularly important if systems are to have long life cycle.

This technique has now been used for twenty years for the development of large commercial systems. It has been employed in projects involving hundreds of designers, and today more than 5000 designers worldwide are using it. The telecom technique has yielded very positive results when used in large centralized, as well as decentralized systems.

Combined with two other techniques, conceptual modeling[10] and object-oriented programming, the building block technique has been improved so that in ObjectOry, it now covers the whole development work.

This combination has been developed further in ObjectOry in a number of ways:

- The telecom technique has been generalized and can now be used in various systems such as information systems, real-time systems, process control systems, CASE tools, and graphic presentation systems. Furthermore, the technique has been adapted to different program languages (e.g., Ada, C++, and Cobol), database management systems, operating systems, etc. It has, moreover, been extended from having been object-based into being object-oriented,[11] i.e., it supports the concept of inheritance.

- The telecom technique has been simplified and scaled down for application also to small projects. The technique can, however, easily be scaled up again for large objects.

- The three techniques have been formalized and tied together as the concepts have been unambiguous and interrelated.

- The conceptual modeling has been extended with object-oriented concepts and the possibility of describing dynamic behavior.

The architectural concepts that form the theoretical base of ObjectOry were formulated as early as 1985. This base has, of course, been developed over the years, but the basic ideas are still the same. Thus, the service concept is still used when the marketing/sales department formulates customer requests to the production department. The service concept has, however, been given a wider meaning, making the analysis models more general.

At first method description, based on the existing architecture, could be formulated at the beginning of 1986. In the same way as the underlying architecture, the method component has been developed and later supplemented with, among other things, criteria for how objects should be designed.

On the architecture and method foundations, it was possible to develop ObjectOry's process descriptions. They appeared in a first edition in 1988. Experience gained since has led to extensive development. The present, third, edition is 1,000 pages. Since the publication of the first edition, process descriptions have been used in six projects. It is worth noting that ObjectOry itself can be viewed and described as a system that has made it possible to develop a new edition of ObjectOry itself. In other words, the technique can be used to advance system development techniques, as these are also a type of systems.

Even though it is possible to carry out projects without tool support, the need for such support has been clearly stated in all six projects. Above all, there has been an expressed demand for tools to keep document information consistent. Therefore, a first version of ObjectOry Support Environment (OrySE) was cleared for customer use in September 1989. This first version, with support for the analysis part of ObjectOry, has been extended in 1990 to support the design workflow of ObjectOry.

CONCLUSION

In this article, we have treated the development of complex systems with a large amount of software by drawing parallels with branches of industry that are better established than software development in an industrial framework.

We have presented a technique that yields object-oriented systems and that is itself object oriented. The development process has been viewed as a number of communicating processes that together produce a tested system. A new way of developing systems is necessary. This change has already begun. Important ingredients of this work are object orientation, a process aspect of development work, and a well-developed toolbox. In a few decades, the view of system development will have developed in a full analogy with the car industry example. There will be a large number of reusable components at different detailing levels, from small, very general components to large, application-oriented building blocks. Largely, the development work will correspond to the process model that we have described. The basic architecture and method foundations, e.g., object orientation, will, however, have been developed and enriched.

ACKNOWLEDGMENTS

The author is very grateful to Patrik Jonsson, employed at Objective Systems, for his contribution to this chapter.

REFERENCES AND SUGGESTED READING

1. I. Jacobson. "FDL: A Language for Designing Large Real Time Systems," *Information Processing 86 Proceedings.*

2. I. Jacobson and L. Wiktorin. "Modernisering av existerand system," *Proceedings of MILINF '89*, Konferns I Enköping, 06B1: 13-25, June 5-9, 1989.

3. D. T. Ross. "Applications and Extensions of SADT," *IEEE Computer*, April 1985.

4. M. Alfor. "SREM at the Age of Eight; The Distributed Computing Design System," *IEEE Computer*, April 1985.

5. E. Yourdon and L. Constatine. *Structured Design*, Prentice Hall, Englewood Cliffs, NJ, 1979.

6. E. Yourdon. *Modern Structured Analysis*, Yourdon Press/Prentice Hall, Englewood Cliffs, NJ, 1989.

7. Ward, P. T. "How to Integrate Object Orientation with Structured Analysis and Design," *IEEE Software*, March 1989.

8. I. Jacobson. "Object-Oriented Development in an Industrial Environment," *OOPSLA '87 Proceedings* and *SIGplan Notices*, 22(12), 183-191, 1987.

9. CCITT, Facsicle VI. 11, Functional Specification and Description Language (SDL), Rec. z.100-z.104, Geneva, 1984.

10. J. Bubenko Jr. and E. Lindencrona. Konceptuell Modellering Informationsanalys, Studentalitteratur, 1984.

11. P. Wegner. "Dimensions of Object-Based Language Design," *OOPSLA '87 Proceedings* and *SIGplan Notices*, 22(12), 168-181, 1987.

12. M. A. Jackson. "The General and the Particular," 1988 INTEC/Georgia STE University Symposium, *System Analysis and Design: A Research Strategy*, 1988.

In Ivar's Words

Q: *During all those years, what do you think is your most significant contribution to the field of software engineering?*

A: It may be the truth that I am most known as the inventor of use cases. But I also practiced component-based development back in 1967 when use cases still were not "there," so component-based development is something I've been working in my whole life.

Back then, when I was introducing a component-based approach at Ericsson, the main objection I had from developers was that the components that we developed were not easily related to the "functions" (read: use cases) of the system. If you take a use case, it can "cross" many components; that was a basic objection. The developers were thinking in terms of "one function, one component."

Whereas I was saying, well, that's not OK. Most of one function (read: one use case) will be implemented by one component; but then other components will also play a role in implementing that use case. Then I decided to turn this into something positive. And it turned out that this was exactly what we needed! We needed to have that complexity, because that's how reality is. So the outside world talks about use cases, whereas on the inside of the system we describe how use-case realizations cross its components.

Just having objects and components, and not caring about things (read: use case realizations) that cross them, is a smaller problem. One of the difficult things is to make use case realizations, and to manage dependencies between subsystems, and that's much harder. Thinking just upon objects is a much smaller problem, it's a subproblem.

So, this is how use cases helped me contribute to component-based development in general.

Another significant thing is architecture, I mean really to identify an architecture as one of the first important development tasks in the software life cycle. We talked about software architecture in 1968. We presented the software architecture when we went out to our customers, and I remember they had never heard about anything like that. They thought about architecture for hardware, but there was not an architecture for software at that time.

(Extracts of the answer above are reprinted with permission from Adriano Comai, an Italian IT consultant. It was first published at www.analisi-disegno.com and in the ZeroUno magazine (Italian translation).)

Q: How will components really help us to build quality software systems?

A: All these young people developing software for the Internet today think all the old laws are wrong—that we need to make it totally different than in the past. Then we have to start over again.

That has generally been the case with computer software programming for more than 30 years, the amount of time some companies have used software based on components. Component-based development—which uses the same principles at its core as the automobile, building, or electronics industries—has been pushed aside as developers have tried to reinvent the wheel. While those wheels have proven to be square with time, companies using component-based systems have flourished.

I never would have imagined 30 years ago that component-based development would still not be mainstream today. The percentage of companies using this approach is maybe only five to ten percent. In not many years we will all be using it. The reason it is so strong is because component-based software is built up in a logical way—it has an architecture.

You can understand the software's structure in a similar way that you can understand other types of drawings. If you build a house, for instance, your blueprint shows the toilet, bathtub, windows, doors—all separate components put together. On the contrary, the structure of other types of software cannot be illustrated and usually does not have an architecture that can be described. Anything made with components—from a car to a television to a software system—is built up with interconnecting parts, both ready-made and newly designed. Thus, component-based systems can be changed and improved over the years.

As soon as new components are introduced they can be added or exchanged within the system to accommodate a new function. An example: Your company, which does business with customers over the telephone, wants to launch a "shop" on the Internet. You use a component-based business system that interacts with employees, guiding them in taking orders over the telephone. For the net, you need something similar that interacts directly with customers, showing products available and helping customers shop. The cost and ease of installing such a new component is reasonable. But if you introduce a Web page and use other approaches than component-based technology, basically you have to introduce a whole new software. Component-based systems are designed with the help of "objects," such as customers and transactions. Objects offer developers a practical way to model how a component-based system works. By using a standard system of object symbols called the Unified Modeling Language (UML), developers can draw a blueprint of how different objects affect the system and data. You use the blueprint in the same way you use blueprints to build houses and bridges. We have now reached the point where programming is only one step in the development of software—and it's not even the most important. These blueprints are much more important to get right. As the software industry has gradually begun to shift to this type of development, it has now started to become an engineering discipline, instead of a very "techie" field, where you had to understand all these bits and bytes and programming languages nobody else knew. Consequently, it is "dumb" to invest major sums of money in software that uses old technology today. Component-based development is the future. There is no other alternative. Get to the future as quickly as possible. If you don't, your competitors will.

(Extracts of the answer above are reprinted with permission from Jack Jackson, a Danish journalist. It was first published as "Spinning the Wheel— Component-based developers have rolled along as others tried to reinvent the wheel," © 1999 by Jack Jackson; Freedom, Summer 1999, by Industrial & Financial Systems (IFS).)

Q: What do you think is the best method of bringing software development up to the level of an industrial process?

A: In the most general sense, bringing about a mature industrial process will only happen by companies desiring to be competitive. I don't think there is any simple way to make people understand that the way they do work is in-effective. I have worked in the telecommunications industry for many years with Ericsson. Ericsson developed objects back in the 1970s. Before then they had only say about three percent of the world market. Ericsson developed a product that their customers considered superior to their competition. Ericsson won basically every large customer and their market share has grown several times—and that in a mature business and within a very expansive business area. That forced Ericsson's competitors to also use object technology. Thus thanks to one company being successful other companies also moved into the same technology—Nortel and AT&T for example. Some companies like ITT are not in the telecom business anymore. And Ericsson has continued to be competitive among all of these very large public companies. I believe in the success of objects because of a number of very large success stories and many smaller ones. And of one thing I can assure you—it's not based on a programming language, it's not based on a fantastic tool, rather its based on having a complete software engineering process. Organizations with up to 500 people need a software process and that's the way you can beat the market.

PART 3:
THE SEEDS OF A VISION

———

MOST OF US ACKNOWLEDGE the importance of a commonly adopted language that can be used and understood, with no ambiguity, by all participants of a software development team. A language that forms the basis for communication among team members, but also with external parties; a language whose various statements and sentences are intuitive, can be visualized if necessary, and suit their fundamental purpose: to describe a software system.

Such a language is the Unified Modeling Language, which currently is an adopted standard by the Object Management Group (OMG). However, to reach this standard was not trivial, and involved many individuals and organizations, including Dr. Jacobson as one of the three original designers. In this part we will get his view on this standardization work: how it was initiated, how important it was, and what we will gain from it in the long run.

In this part we also see some articles about the basics of object-oriented technology, and how it can be applied to components, reuse issues, and even to businesses themselves. Moreover, we present some articles about the fundamental importance of having a well-defined software development process in place, and how it differs from just using a textbook method. This is a good preparation for reading the subsequent parts of this book.

PART 3:
THE SEEDS OF A VISION

———

4

Time for a Cease-Fire in the Methods War

Ivar Jacobson, 1993

Is There a Methods War?

THERE ARE PRESENTLY 27 different object-oriented methods described by OMG's special interest group on analysis and design (SIGAD). There are probably hundreds of others not published but used in system development organizations. The number has grown explosively during the past few years alone. And it is still growing by leaps and bounds.

So, of course, you may say that there is a methods war. The immediate effect has been the confusion created in the system development community. Most end users prefer to sit on the sidelines rather than betting on the wrong horse. In most cases, developers buy our books and try to cook their own method. It's expensive and rarely successful.

Do We Need a Methods War?

No, it is time for collaboration. While it is a sound strategy to suggest and evaluate different approaches during an initial period to facilitate understanding a new technology, object technology has now matured. It is our duty to begin to converge and unify our achievements.

DO YOU MEAN STANDARDIZE?

No, I don't believe in standardization here in its conventional sense. I am against enforced standards. I worked for eight years with CCITT developing a design modeling technique: SDL. I learned how it should not be done. Standardization for object technology should be done in a modern way. When it comes to methodology, those of us who are the leading practitioners with the most practical industrial experience must meet to agree on the basics and let that become a de facto standard.

WHAT WOULD WE BE ABLE TO AGREE ON?

All good methods support object modeling. The differences between the leading object modeling languages are minor. You can model objects and classes, as well as instances, and their relationships such as inheritance and associations, etc. Objects have attributes and they offer operations so that they can communicate with one another. We could use a technique being used to formally specify programming languages. I have used it myself to clean up my own modeling languages and to specify an object-oriented programming language for real-time systems. You ignore notational differences by specifying an abstract syntax. Static and dynamic semantics can be specified using a kernel specified by techniques like VDM (an extended version) or pi-calculus. Since our modeling languages must be extendable, we must leave "holes" of not yet interpretable constructs.

In this way, we can agree on a basic object modeling language. Every methodologist would then be able to specify his own modeling language using this basic technique. In my case, I would have to extend these basics with use cases, robust objects (in addition to domain objects), and support for layered architecture. Others would also make their specific extensions.

Furthermore, we should be able to agree on a formal technique to describe different activities used in creating a model, using a common meta-method to describe our different methods. This would remove unnecessary differences in the way we describe methods. Terminology would be cleaned up. We would agree on what we mean by the terms *methods, methodology, activity, step, phase, process, subprocess, incremental, iterative, project,* etc. We may even go so far that we could agree on terms like *analysis, design, implementation*, and *testing*. Further down the road, we would be able to agree on a language to describe our individual development process.

Notation? Unfortunately, people, including most methodologists, spend too much time and attention on syntax or notation. It is, of course, very important to have a powerful syntax, but there are so many good alternatives. Personally, I would be able to accept several other alternatives than my own. I don't care as long as the notation is expressive, concise, intuitive, and simple. Not every syntactic construct must be given a special symbol; text is still very useful. To expedite the process, we should first concentrate on an abstract syntax.

How Should It Be Done?

A standardization body as a first step should not do the work. There is no reason to encourage the political and tactical games that formal standardization activities often entail. It would be far better to form an ad hoc group of knowledgeable and motivated people who believe that sound agreements are necessary.

Why Should We Do It?

All consumers of object technology would welcome agreements on method issues. The transition to object technology is tough enough. Complicating the transition by overlaying yet another decision—the selection of one of myriad proprietary methods—delays and hampers the whole introduction process. Being able to move an object model from one environment to another would make a lot of difference. The decision to invest in one method would not be cataclysmic. The whole market for object technology would flourish. End users would dare to invest in methods and CASE products.

The methods war may not disappear, but differentiation would move to a higher level, focusing on process-oriented issues such as flexibility, productivity, scalability, traceability, and quality assurance. Users would feel confident that methodologists have left provincial issues behind them and are working for the common best. Because, after all, there is one thing that we can all agree on already. Methods are not an end but a means. And the goal is to improve the engineering of complex systems.

EDITOR'S NOTE

The UML is today a commonly adopted standard that lies under the responsibility of the Object Management Group (OMG). However, it is important to note that the UML version 1.1 emerged from a task force involving no less than 17 corporations, including Rational Software, Microsoft, Hewlett-Packard, Oracle, Unisys, and IBM amongst others.

The abstract UML syntax is specified using the UML itself, primarily by the use of so-called "meta classes" and "meta associations." This abstract syntax is then extended by Object Constraint Language (OCL) expressions that constrain the syntax. Given the abstract syntax, a graphical syntax is separately specified, commonly called the "graphical notation." The semantics of the UML is primarily specified in natural language.

Please refer to www.omg.org for more information on the UML. To read more about the syntax and semantics of the UML, please refer to the *Unified Modeling Language Reference Manual*[1] and *User's Guide*.[2]

However, standardization of the modeling language is not all. The Unified Process is an effort towards unifying the development process itself, using the UML as its underlying modeling language.[3] The Unified Process is a "process extension" of the UML.

This is a pretty good realization of the vision outlined in this article.

REFERENCES

1. Jim Rumbaugh, Ivar Jacobson, and Grady Booch. *Unified Modeling Language Reference Manual*, Addison–Wesley, Menlo Park, CA, 1998.

2. Grady Booch, Jim Rumbaugh, and Ivar Jacobson. *The Unified Modeling Language User's Guide*, Addison–Wesley, Menlo Park, CA, 1998.

3. I. Jacobson, G. Booch, J. Rumbaugh. *The Unified Software Development Process*, Addison Wesley Longman, 1999.

5

YES, THERE IS
LIFE AFTER METHODS:
THE SOFTWARE DEVELOPMENT
PROCESS

Ivar Jacobson & Doug Bennett, NOVEMBER-DECEMBER 1993

IN THE FACE OF THE "SOFTWARE CRISIS," solutions are being sought in the techniques and approaches used to develop software products. New technologies are being introduced, books on new methods are being published, and development environments and CASE tools are being released. Companies are buying the technologies in the hopes of improving the quality of their products and the economics of development. Unfortunately, all this activity in tools and methods is not addressing the factor that has the biggest influence on product quality: the process used to develop the product. The relationship between tools, methods, and process in software product development, and how tools and methods can support process improvements, is key to improving software product quality and productivity.

After World War II, first in the United States and then in Japan, W. Edwards Deming said that the main determinant of product quality is the process used to develop the product. He also observed that the process was more important than the individuals or the tools used developing the product. In the software industry, interest in the development process is relatively new compared to interest in programming languages, CASE tools, and design methods. The most visible indication of this new interest is the reception given to the Process

Maturity Index and the process-assessment techniques published by the Software Engineering Institute (SEI) at Carnegie Mellon University.

SEI has defined five levels of process maturity: (1) ad hoc, (2) repeatable, (3) documented, (4) measured, and (5) optimized. There is also a method for determining at what level an organization is currently functioning. There has been some debate as to the effectiveness of the assessment process, but it remains a significant advance over previous practices that offered no way to measure the maturity of the development process. In 1988, the SEI found that 85 percent of the organizations in the US had a process maturity of Level 1! This finding indicates that there can be little improvement in the economics of the development process without corresponding improvements in the process maturity of the organization.

We can track the progress of an organization as its development process matures by following the design materials. Organizations working at a Level 1 maturity typically produce almost no design materials. While creating design materials does not by itself improve the development process, the presence of these materials and how they are used are indicators of process maturity. To function at Level 3 or above, multiple design and analysis models with appropriate documentation are required.

Maturity begins with the introduction of development materials for each stage of the development process. Evaluating those materials, measuring the time and effort required to produce them, and, finally making changes in the process to reduce the time required to deliver each of these documents is also necessary. We can say, then, that the role of CASE tools and design methods is to support the growth and optimization of the development process. Design methods simply become tools used by people in a mature development process.

The role played by process in an organization and the distinctions between process, method, and project are important. The organization is concerned with delivering products; the process is the way the organization goes about delivering those products. A development process for an organization should have a product focus and should live at least as long as any individual product. In fact, it may be more productive to think of the process as existing for as long as the organization exists.

The life beyond methods is a rich development process that can carry a product through its complete life cycle, from early, risk-reducing prototype projects through projects that deliver new functional increments to the product. The process should offer several different types of more finely grained projects, e.g., a feasibility study project, analysis project, prototype project, etc. Each project that is carried out advances the product along its life cycle. The output of some projects, like design studies and early prototypes, might consist only of design materials or an answer to a question. Others, such as projects, are different from what we typically recognize as a development project. Typically, a single project consists of analysis, design, code, testing, and possibly a feasibility study and/or prototype. The small discrete projects we propose have shorter time spans and demand a definable deliverable. This contributes to management and control of time and money and is one element that enhances the quality and productivity of the software product.

In an effective process, many different kinds of projects are available and each consists of a sequenced series of steps or tasks. Different kinds of projects use different steps. The kind of project and its related tasks can be matched to the needs being addressed. The description of most design methods consists of a set of steps of tasks that correspond precisely to a design project. For example, a prototyping project requires fewer design steps and reviews than a project that is to deliver a fly-by-wire system for a commercial airliner. Organizations that attempt to adopt a single method for all their projects are limiting the potential effectiveness of their process.

In organizations of Level 1 maturity, the process is embedded in the heads of the individual developers. There is little the organization can do to measure or improve the process, so there is little they can do to improve the product quality. Merely introducing a method, with no other changes, effects only marginal improvement in product quality. It is vital that some process steps be visible to the organization. Defining different project types and the materials required for each is an excellent way to get a handle on the development process. It is also a much easier to manage and control these smaller-grained projects.

Viewing a product's life cycle in terms of parallel projects is somewhat different than the more commonly held view. Traditionally, software development is broken down into two phases: a development project that takes the product from nothing to its first release; and maintenance, which includes the rest of the product life cycle. Most published methods address development only. In this traditional view, the "method" is the process while maintenance is somehow different. The problem here is that most projects begin with a product in some state and move it to another state. Very few projects begin with nothing and deliver the first version of a product, particularly with object technology. A single sequence of steps for initial development only is not a complete development process.

We recognize that this emphasis on process is rather unusual in the software industry in the US, but it is less unusual in Europe. On the contrary, it is quiet natural to most European software organizations to clearly understand the appropriate development process first and then to develop the supporting tools. This approach results in great frustration to US developers. It is difficult for people here to understand why CASE tools cannot be sold simply as a box with software inside. However, the results of a process-centered approach are consistently excellent. Organizations that aspire to SEI Levels 3 and 4 should look to examples offered by the application of process in Europe.

Where, then, do our beloved tools fit in a process-centered organization? Compilers and development environments, the lower CASE tools, are the hammers, saws, and lumber of the development project. They are used to fabricate the executable, deliverable product. The upper CASE tools provide help in carrying out the product design. In particular, they support and encourage the development of the various design models. Design materials in software, as in every other engineering discipline, make the end product tangible and visible before the product actually exists. Tools help developers to deliver the tangible milestones for each project.

Having argued that CASE tools and methods should be subservient to the process, we can ask what a CASE tool that supports a mature process would look like. From the process point of view, flexibility is a very important attribute of a method and supporting tools. The need for flexibility comes from at least two sources. The first is that multiple kinds of projects are required to support a mature process. The second is the process itself is continuously maturing and changing. This means that the steps, the sequence of the steps, and the documents and models produced at each step can change for every project. Many organizations will be moving upward in the process maturity index. But even when they reach Level 5, the process will not remain static; rather, it will be continuously improved as the process is optimized.

We have described why we believe the process used in a development organization is more important than individual tools or methods. We have also described some aspects of a CASE tool that support a flexible and mature process. We believe, however, that an emphasis on process has a much larger impact than simply specifying which tools get used. Most organizations have the same kinds of goals for their products: robustness, flexibility, ease of growth, shorter development cycles, and higher quality. Having common goals, it is likely that the process they use will be similar. An emphasis on process yields the same results in the software industry as in other industries: Good practice becomes standard throughout the industry. The suitability of individual programming languages, CASE tools, or design methods will quickly become evident when measured against the product and documents required by the process.

This could result in a reduction in the emotional debates over languages, methods, and CASE tools. With a rich process in place and a means of measuring and evaluating the performance of each step, organizations can try new tools and measure their contribution to the process and product quality. Tools that result in improvements will be kept; those that do not will be changed or discarded.

6

BUSINESS PROCESS REENGINEERING WITH OBJECT TECHNOLOGY

Ivar Jacobson, MAY 1994

IN A VERY SHORT TIME, business process reengineering (BPR) has become one of the most popular subjects at conferences on business management and information-systems design. It may become the number one buzzword of the 1990s. BPR, as defined by Hammer is "the fundamental rethinking and radical redesign of business processes to achieve dramatic improvements in critical, contemporary measures of performance, such as cost, quality, service and speed."[1] BPR implies that you take a comprehensive view of the entire existing operation and think through why you do what you do, why you do what you do the way you do it, and why…

In short, BPR requires that you question the entire existing operation and try to redesign it in a way that uses new technology to serve your customers better.

ROLE OF INFORMATION TECHNOLOGY

The most important enabler of BPR is information technology (IT). IT integrates the activities that make up a company's process.

A *process* is a set of linked activities that produce a specific product or service for a customer or for some other individual in the surroundings of the business (Fig. 6-1). When you perform BPR, processes come into focus, are named, and are assigned a slot in the organizational chart.

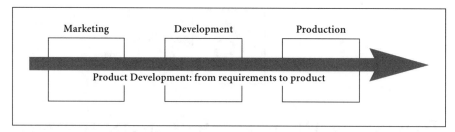

Figure 6-1. Processes are cross-functional.

Each process has an owner, someone who has a budget and drives the process across a company's functional divisions. Functions become resource centers as an organization's hierarchy is flattened. Each resource center also has an owner, someone who has people but no budget. The resource owner must have the right people with the right skills to be able to sell those skills to process owners.

BPR and modern IT can radically change the way you run your company. Businesses become more effective, customers more satisfied, time-to-market shortened, resource needs reduced, product quality raised, and employees more competent and responsible. It sounds like a dream. Why don't we all do it at once? Because we don't know how, and because the risk of doing it wrong is extraordinarily great.

WHAT ARE THE RISKS AND HOW DO WE REDUCE THEM?

There are many opportunities for failure in pursuing BPR—Hammer estimates that 50–70 percent of the companies that try it fail. I think the risk of failure is even higher. BPR risks fall roughly into two categories: (1) risks associated with the change process, and (2) risks associated with the technology used.

It has been estimated that 80% of the failures are caused by "soft" factors, such as motivation, management commitment, leadership, the need for expert guidance, etc. Most books and methods on BPR tackle these soft factors. I am convinced that BPR's success rate could be dramatically improved if its methods offered guidance that is more concrete. I don't underestimate the need to address the change process. But, I believe you can almost guarantee successful BPR if you have a formal reengineering process.

At my company, we have extensive experience in reengineering software-development organizations to adopt object-oriented processes. Our experience is unambiguous: A formal reengineering process and less hand waving is a must for success.

FORMAL REENGINEERING PROCESS

A formal reengineering process includes:

- **A description that specifies every activity and deliverable involved.** This process description must be adaptable to the reengineering project. For instance, the size and maturity of the organization and the type of process you are reengineering will influence the process description.

- **Deliverables, in the form of business models, that focus on the company's architecture and dynamics.** These are different from traditional business models, which fail because they model the company as a computer with a database and a program that manipulates the database. The business models should be presented in an engaging language so that everyone involved—the CEO, executives, process owners, process managers, process operators, resource owners, and customers—can understand them, not just the reengineering team.

- **A process for the development of an information system truly integral to the reengineering company.** An integral information system is one developed in parallel with new business processes that both influences the design of those processes and is influenced by them. This is often the most overlooked element of BPR. IT organizations are generally not as competent as other engineering disciplines in fashioning their product (information systems). The Software Engineering Institute (SEI) at Carnegie Mellon University estimates that 85 percent of all software development done in 1989 was done without any real method. A good word for this type of work is "hacking." This is a rich source of failure.

A tight, seamless relation between the process to develop the business model and the process to develop the information system is imperative. These processes primarily involve concepts, models, tools, and documentation. Only if this is done do you increase your chances for success. Establishing this relationship enables business people to communicate with IT people and IT people with end users. It also eliminates the separation between the business models and the information system's requirements models and tears down language barriers.

Object-Oriented Business Engineering?

Objectory's approach to BPR, Object-Oriented Business Engineering, is closely related to our object-oriented software engineering (OOSE) method. We use OO Business Engineering to develop the business model and OOSE to develop the information system plan.

With OO Business Engineering we describe a BPR project intuitively— and even a little naively—by the formula:

Business reengineering = reverse business engineering
+ forward business engineering

As Figure 6-2 shows, top management issues a *reengineering directive*, which triggers *envisioning.* Envisioning is the process of visualizing the new business or its processes, and requires both an understanding of the business and a known business strategy.

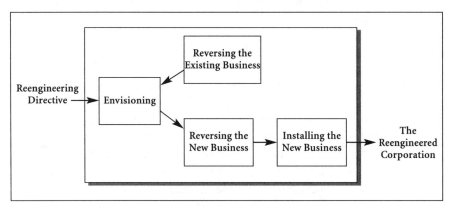

Figure 6-2. The BPR process.

Envisioning triggers an activity called *reversing the existing business*, in which you produce a model of the current business. Why, as Lenzi asked, should you reengineer something that never was engineered in the first place? Because you must know what you have and what you want to change. However, we warn against digging too deeply for some obscure truth that you cannot—and do not—need to unearth.

Envisioning produces an *objective specification*—a vision of the business as it will manifest itself in the future. This is the input to the next activity, *engineering the new business.*

The success of the entire BPR project rests on this activity. In engineering the new business, you seek to clearly understand what the new business should look like and how it should be implemented, e.g., what types of resources it requires and what kind of IT support must be developed. This requires the design of one or more new processes, development of an information system integral to them, and perhaps the simulation and prototyping of the information system. These activities must be prioritized in terms of lead-time, so that everyone can get down to brass tacks and avail themselves of the new possibilities. The output of this activity is a model of the redesigned business.

As a rule, BPR includes another activity, *installing the new business,* that is, implementing the redesigned business incisively in the real organization.

Models

Both reverse and forward engineering require models. OO Business Engineering recommends two models of the company, an outside view and an inside view. Of course, they should be consistent: *What* a company does should correspond to *how* it does it.

The outside view (Fig. 6-3) describes a company's process and customers from the perspective of the outside world—the "what." To do this, OO Business Engineering employs use cases. A use case model views a business

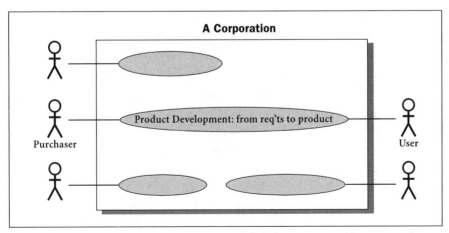

Figure 6-3. A company's processes modeled from an outside perspective.

as a system, and its processes as different use cases customers can make of the system.

The inside view describes a company's structure so that its processes can be used by its customers—the "how." It is an object model. A company is a complex system, and an object model is an excellent way to describe complex systems because it is easy to understand, change, specialize, and reuse. You design this object in a use-case model, which represents either a set of activities to be carried out by one person, or a thing such as a part, deliverable, or report. Each object's role is akin to its responsibility,[2] although this is a simplification of that concept. A company's structure is modeled by integrating the design of all the use cases. One object can participate in several use cases, and you may need several object models of the company (to model, e.g., an ideal versus a real structure). Again, the new business and its information system must be developed in harmony and tightly integrated. Therefore, these activities must be concurrent, with a great deal of alternation and interaction, as Figure 6-4 indicates.

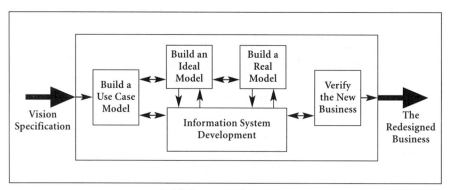

Figure 6-4. Concurrent development of the new business and its integral information system.

Our approach to developing the information system, OOSE, is described in *Object-Oriented System Engineering*.[3] OO Business Engineering and OOSE are closely related: Objects in the business model that represent work activities are directly related to information-system users. To begin, create a user for each such object in the business model, then design a use case for each responsibility that object has. Next, for each object that represents a thing in the business model, create an entity object in the information system's object model. You almost certainly will have to refine this first attempt. Some objects and some of their responsibilities may not require IT support. Some responsibilities may be so fragmented internally that you must develop more than one use case for them. But, in principle, this is how you relate the business model to the information-system model.

SUMMARY

Our OO Business Engineering approach is built on six key ideas[4]:

1. A business has several customers, and it wishes to treat each one according to the customer's individual needs. It offers these customers services and products by means of business processes. Internally, a company should be organized according to these processes, which cut across functional divisions.

2. Use cases are a simple, natural way to identify business processes. A customer is a user of a company, and uses the company through a business process. Each way of using the company is a use case.

3. A company is a very complex system around which many interested parties orbit. To clarify its workings for these parties, the company must be described in the form of models. Usually, different parties will need different models.

4. Object orientation is an excellent way to clarify the inner workings of a company—its processes, products, services, resources—and how those things depend on each other.

5. Reengineering a business and developing an integral information system are separate, parallel, tightly linked activities. The design of a business process is greatly influenced by creative IT solutions—it is essential that the two be developed in harmony.

6. The business model of the redesigned company and the requirements model for the information system must be seamless. This is achieved by a harmonious pairing of OO Business Engineering and OOSE.

EDITOR'S NOTE

A variant of OO Business Engineering as discussed here is included as a separate development workflow in the Rational Unified Process (RUP) product as provided by Rational. Please refer to www.rational.com for more information. A variant of OO Business Engineering is also incorporated in the Unified Process.[5]

REFERENCES

1. M. Hammer and J. Champy. *Reengineering the Corporation: A Manifesto for Business Revolution*, Harper Collins, New York, 1993.

2. R. Wirfs-Brock et al. *Designing Object-Oriented Software*, Prentice–Hall, Englewood Cliffs, NJ, 1990.

3. I. Jacobson et al. *Object-Oriented System Engineering—A Use Case Driven Approach*, Addison–Wesley and ACM Press, Reading, MA, 1992.

4. I. Jacobson, M. Ericsson, and A. Jacobson. *The Object Advantage—Business Process Reengineering with Object Technology*, Addison–Wesley and ACM Press, Reading, MA, 1994.

5. I. Jacobson, G. Booch, J. Rumbaugh, *The Unified Software Development Process*, Addison Wesley Longman, 1999.

7

Building with Components: Toward Mature Object Technology

Ivar Jacobson, May-June 1994

O BJECT TECHNOLOGY IS WINNING increasing acceptance as a way to develop every type of software, from commercial to defense, process control to robotics, telecommunications to presentation graphics. It is being used to develop systems that are technical as well as purely administrative, systems with severe real-time or security requirements, and systems that handle huge volumes of data. These development trends are reflected in computer-science research, which is focusing on object orientation. The only programming languages that will survive will have object-oriented features, which is why old languages such as Ada and C are being renovated. New database technology is object oriented, as is every user interface built today. Tomorrow's operating systems and computer architectures will have object-oriented features all the way down to the system core. In short, modern system development is object-oriented and it is no exaggeration to say that object technology will be the platform most developers will choose by the end of this decade (see Fig. 7-1).

More areas of computer technology are converging on object orientation as the preferred platform on which to build computer-based systems.

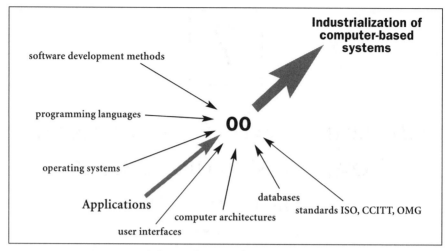

Figure 7-1. The evolution of systems development.

THE OBJECT-ORIENTED ADVANTAGE

Object technology's strength is that it lets you build systems with components. The advantage of this approach to construction has long been self-evident in other disciplines—mankind has been building with objects for many thousands of years. In the context of manufacturing, objects are tangible things that can be combined to form a larger, more complex object. Compound objects that have enough function to be of definite use to people can be seen as systems. Object orientation for software development brings similar advantages. With it, you can build systems using both simple and compound objects, much as you can build a community from:

- Simple components, such as bricks, cement, and lumber.

- More complex components, such as stoves, refrigerators, and bathtubs.

- Still more complex compound objects, such as kitchens and bathrooms.

- Entire systems, such as detached houses or apartment buildings.

So an object-oriented system can be viewed either as a collection of components or in toto. Its modular construction makes it easier to modify and adapt to meet new demands, and it can be constructed with reusable parts. Another important advantage to the object-oriented approach is that customers find they can more readily understand it. This lets them get more involved in development, so object-oriented systems can be made easy to use.

WHAT MORE DO WE NEED?

However, a software system is not a house or even a community. Today's large software systems are much more complex than that, and developing them differs form manufacturing in several important ways. Neither simple design methods nor the simple objects supported by today's object-oriented languages are sufficient. To develop a system that contains thousands—indeed, tens of thousands—of classes, all related in a vast number of ways, you must supply a more sophisticated architecture and employ more sophisticated objects than object-oriented languages now support. A successful project needs other things, too—I usually talk about the three Ps of management: project, product, and process—but here I want to focus on the importance of a sound architecture and the use of different object types to support this architecture.

ARCHITECTURE FOR WHOM? THE WORKERS

A system's architecture is its most prominent structure. However, different groups of people working with a system perceive different architectures; they have different models of it. The greatest insight we have gained is that a system's success depends to a great degree on whether the developer has identified which models are needed and we have originated the concept of a worker. Workers are all those people who will affect the system during its life. To ensure a system's success, you must account for every type of worker correctly when you develop a system (see Fig. 7-2).

The models you need are largely dependent on the type of system you build. Among programmers, there is a general misconception that the source code and, at the very most, the design model are sufficient to describe a system. This is because the source code is all you really need to have the system work. Source code is a model that both the compiler and (hopefully!) the programmer can interpret. Mature development organizations

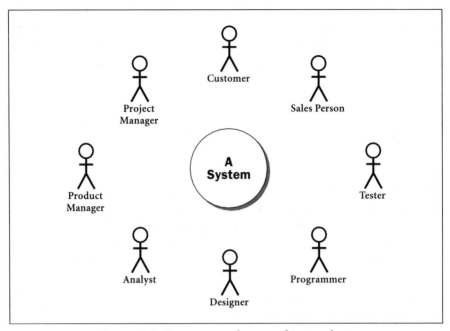

Figure 7-2. A system and some of its workers.

have their designers usually also build a design model, which is an abstraction of the source code. Some also build an analysis model, which describes the system's ideal design. For organizations that have adopted object technology, these models are object-oriented. All these models, although they are more or less abstract, describe a system's inner workings. A system's outer workings—what it should do—are usually captured as a natural-language-requirement specification. Unfortunately, a requirements specification is not a good tool for understanding the required properties of a commercial product: It is difficult to structure, wordy, and ambiguous. You need a considerably better modeling technique to ensure that you build the product that your customers want. Here the use-case concept, which I introduced in 1987,[1] plays a very important role. You develop a model that describes every user—the actors—and every way each actor might use the system—the use cases.

A use-case model is an important instrument with which you can capture and clarify the customer's needs and wants to make sure that the right system will be developed. It is also very easy to understand, considerably easier than an object model.

Among other things, a use-case model can complement the contract between the buyer and the developer. Thus, it is a model for customers, product managers, project managers, and analysts. I have already identified the use case (code) models. In addition, you may need a test model that describes the various test cases and their results. And you may also need separate models for sales people, production personnel, installers, end users, and so forth. Each model serves one or more workers. Workers differ from actors, because workers work with the models, whereas actors are modeled. To put it simply, one worker creates a model and several other workers use this model to create other models or to physically use the system. Thus, a model captures either what its workers must do with the system or what they must understand about the system.

Therefore, to decide which models should be produced and updated during the system's lifetime, I recommend that you identify the workers and proceed from there, making sure that each of them has access to exactly the model he or she needs. Then be clear about what each model is meant to capture, because this will tell you what architecture to include in each model. (When building more formal models, like use-case or analysis and design models, you must also decide which modeling language to use.)

Finally, when you have identified the models and determined what kind of architecture to include in them, you must relate them to each other so that the complete picture is consistent. The consistency relation between two models can be loose or tight, and can take many forms. One of the simpler and more common consistency relations is traceability between an analysis and a design model. I have also noted that the idea that models must be handled throughout a system's life has not been completely accepted. Most object-oriented methods depict the analysis model as something that evolves into the design model and thereafter loses all value. These methods disregard how you will continue to develop the product. It is fairly obvious to us that (1) the analysis model should be allowed to live its own life and should be linked only loosely to the design model, and (2) the work of analysis and design should be carried out in parallel for completely different releases of the system.

MANAGING COMPLEXITY WITH SPECIALIZED OBJECT CATEGORIES

Programming languages treat all objects as equals, as if they belonged to one superclass. Smalltalk does this literally; other languages do it through a formal definition of classes and instances. This may be reasonable, considering the level we have reached with these languages at present, but it is a poor system of classification.

You can substantially reduce the problems associated with building complex systems if you use more than just one category of objects. In our Object-Oriented Software Engineering (OOSE) approach,[2] there are several object categories: ordinary objects, use cases and actors, megaobjects,* application objects, and component objects. They are similar in that they all belong to classes, they all have instances, and their classes can inherit properties from each other.

Yet, their primary object properties, that is, the meaning of their classes, instances, and inheritance, are fundamentally different, as are the ways they are related to one another. Thus, OOSE defines a kind of generic object whose characteristics are "inherited" by all these object categories, while they are all different.

- Ordinary objects are abstractions of those you find in object-oriented programming languages. Most object-oriented methods deal primarily with these objects, which can be easily identified from real-world counterparts (why I call them "naïve" objects).

- Use cases and actors are the two object categories found in the use-case model. Use cases can send and receive messages from actors in their environment, but they cannot send messages to one another.
  This is an intentional restriction of what an ordinary object can do. Use cases in the use-case model are mapped onto objects in an object model of the system.
  Thus, you can find—for every use case—all the objects that participate in the use case. And for every object, you can find its responsibilities by identifying the use cases in which it participates.

- Megaobjects are instantiated as the software is produced. An instance of a megaobject in it simplest form is a composite object that consists only of its constituent parts, whether that part is another megaobject or an ordinary object class.
  One megaobject can inherit properties from another, but the implications of the inheritance are fundamentally different. Inheritance in

---

* In this chapter, the term megaobject instead of subsystem is used to indicate that megaobjects have semantics. Most object-oriented methods have subsystems that are semantically empty.

this case implies that every class in the super megaobject is passed in its entirety to the inheriting megaobject, which can add, specialize, or remove classes it has inherited.

What is usually called a *framework* in the context of object orientation is nothing more than an abstract megaobject whose properties are meant to be reused and extended. A *pattern*[3] is also a megaobject that resembles a framework, but with a pattern you can benefit only the existence of corresponding classes and communication patterns.

In OOSE, megaobjects have semantics. In an article in 1986,[4] I showed formally, using the Vienna Development Method (VDM), how megaobject semantics could support changing classes during operation and could also support handling atomic transactions, thus lending sound formal support to work that today must be done manually.

- There are three types of application objects: boundary, control, and entity. Each has, in part, different semantics. In practice, these categories, which Wirfs-Brock calls *stereotypes*,[5] are different in how they are found by developers.

  An object model that includes these three categories and is correctly prepared will be considerably more robust with regard to future changes than will a traditional object model.

- Component objects are utility objects, such as Set, Array, Dictionary; graphical user interface objects; and objects that hide and implementation techniques, such as distributed architecture, a specific database-management system, or an operating system.[2]

  Component objects are managed very differently from application objects: They are documented extensively to simplify reuse and are subject to extensive testing before release. They may not be exchanged with other components until every application has also been changed over to new components.

All these new object categories share the characteristics common to objects: All of them "inherit" a generic object type—which has still not been formally identified. However, objects that belong to one object category are handled in their own special way, quite apart from objects that belong to other categories.

The distinction between application objects and component objects as described here is only a special case of a more generic approach, namely, managing complexity with layered architecture. This will be the subject of the next section.

MANAGING COMPLEXITY WITH LAYERED ARCHITECTURE

Dealing with complexity by layering the system's architecture is a technique that was first applied to communications protocols. In a layered architecture, the underlying layers are close to implementation, and the upper layers are close to the applications.

Figure 7-3 shows a sample layered architecture. A large system can have more layers than those shown in Figure 7-3, and a system can also have layers in several dimensions, so that one layer can itself be layered. As a rule, changes at the lowest layer only affect the component object layer, whereas changes at the upper layers affect the applications that will be offered to, and built for, users.

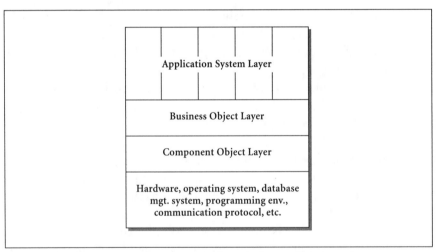

Figure 7-3. Schematic of a sample layered architecture.

Nowadays, the layered technique is used to structure complex systems in general, systems that can be developed in software, in hardware, or in a combination of the two. Layers are used, for example, to structure management-information systems, defense and telecommunications systems, and financial and CASE systems.

For example, a banking system might include a layer containing the business objects: customer, account, loan, and bank-office. All these business objects can be affected by, for example, a borrowing system, a loan system, or a transferral system. These systems are application-specific—they provide the business processes the bank needs to function. Competing banks offer different IT support to their customers, so the application-system layer is really a tool that one bank uses to compete with other banks.

The application-system layer can also be divided vertically. Thus, a single application system could have three vertical layers: boundary, control, and entity, which would contain the boundary, control, and, entity objects, respectively.[1]

The objects in the business-objects layer are usually of type entity objects. They might be used by many application systems. Business-level objects can be expected to become relatively stable after several releases.

The lower component-object layer is not specific to banking or to any other application. An insurance company, for example, should be able to use the same component-object layer as a bank, with different specialized services layered on top.

How higher level layers use lower level layers is an important architectural decision, and there are several kinds of relationships to choose from. Higher layers view component objects as primitives because such objects are used only when they are encapsulated in objects in higher layers. They should not be seen in the design of the higher layers, only in the implementation part of its objects.

In essence, this approach conceals the communication with component objects. Because a large object-oriented system may have thousands of classes that communicate very intensively, concealing communication with component objects makes it vastly easier to get a comprehensive view of the system. Business objects are not primitives, because to understand the design of an application system you must "see" how these objects participate. You must show these objects, but you may not change them. You may only change objects that belong solely to the application system you are designing.

If you want to change an object in the business-object layer, you must take into account all the other applications and make the change at the same time in all of them. Layered architectures also require well-defined interfaces among layers. In OOSE, each layer is a megaobject. The interface to a megaobject consists of the interfaces to its public objects. Object-oriented technology provides an elegant way of doing this and should be an essential part of any object-oriented method. New business ideal will develop around providing business-object layers—or business frameworks, as they are called—to entire branches of commerce. The difficulty here is not technical, it is cultural.

Summary

Object orientation is an important basic technology for building software. However, basic technology is not sufficient to build complex commercial systems. We need an array of architectural constructs. The ones I have discussed in this chapter have proven to be helpful in developing real systems:

- Models developed for each worker, not just for programmers, also help guarantee that the customers get the system they need. To develop more formal models such as use case, analysis, and design, you should use semiformal modeling languages. And you should make sure your models can be updated throughout the system's entire life.

- Use cases are essential in order to specify the correct system and direct the development so that the correct system is built.

- Object categorization must become far broader in scope than today's programming languages permit. We must distinguish, for example, between objects and megaobjects; between boundary, control, and entity objects; and between application and component objects. Every category has its own semantics, but each category belongs to the same generic family of objects.

- Layered architecture is a powerful technique for building robust systems that are extremely tolerant of changes in implementation technique, and this technique offers high potential for reuse of both business and component objects.

REFERENCES AND SUGGESTED READING

1. I. Jacobson. "Object-Oriented Development in an Industrial Environment," *Proceedings of OOPSLA 387, Special Issue of SIGPLAN Notices,* 22 (12): 183–191, 1987.

2. I. Jacobson, M. Christersson, P. Jonsson, and G. Overgaard. *Object-Oriented Software Engineering—A Use Case Driven Approach,* Addison–Wesley Publishers Ltd., Reading, MA, & ACM Press, New York, 1992.

3. E. Gamma, R. Helm, R. Johnson, and J. Vlissides. "Design Patterns: Abstraction and Reuse of Object-Oriented Design," at *European Conference on Object-Oriented Programming,* Kaiserlauten, Germany, July, 1993. Published as Lecture Notes in *Computer Science* #707:431, Springer–Verlag.

4. I. Jacobson. "FDL: A Language for Designing Large Real-Time Systems," *Proceedings of IFIP,* Sept. 1986.

5. R. Wirfs-Brock. "Stereotyping: A Technique for Characterizing Objects and Their Interactions," *Object Magazine,* 5(4): 50, 1993.

6. J. Davis and T. Morgan. "Object-Oriented Development at Brooklyn Union Gas: A Case Study," *IEEE Software,* Jan. 1993

7. I. Jacobson and F. Lindstrom. "Re-engineering of Old Systems to an Object-Oriented Architecture," OOPSLA 291, ACM Press, pp. 340–350, 1991.

8

SUCCEEDING WITH OBJECTS: REUSE IN REALITY

Ivar Jacobson, JULY 1996

LL THE TALK ABOUT REUSE THESE DAYS is a bad sign, because it probably means we have not yet achieved it in reality! At Ericsson, way back in the 1960s, we did not talk about reuse. We didn't need to, because we actually did it!*

Ericsson has built telecom switches for almost 100 years. Because its domestic market is very small, Ericsson has always sold its switches globally. That meant it had to tailor its switching systems to the needs of customers around the world. Reusing system assets to the greatest possible extent was the only way this small Swedish company could compete in the world market. At Ericsson, reuse went without saying!

THE MARKET DEMANDS REUSE

Over the years, Ericsson had achieved reuse by separating the core of its system architecture from the parts that could be adapted to specific customers.

In the late '60s Ericsson wanted to develop a new generation of software-based switching systems. Having worked on the previous generations of electromechanical switching systems, I became a project manager of this new endeavor. My task was to make sure that these new switches were cus-

---

* The term we use here is different from the term we actually used within Ericsson but the semantics, at this level of abstraction, are the same.

tomizable, which now was to be done primarily with software. Implicitly, my management asked for a system design that had a reusable core.

In building these new systems, we had numerous important goals, including adaptability. But we also had to be able to manage our software-based systems the way Ericsson had traditionally managed its hardware-based switches:

- We had to be able to describe the entire system architecture (not just the hardware), so salespeople could explain it to our customers.

- We had to be able to produce thousands of installations that could be operated independently of the others

Recall that this was in 1967! Back then we had to develop a new way to design software systems. I've described our method in a previous column[1]; I will summarize it here: We used use cases (or their equivalent), subsystems, and objects. We used sequence diagrams to describe every use case in terms of subsystems or objects. And, we used state diagrams to describe every object. In other words, nearly 30 years ago we were using many of the key techniques the object community has now adopted. This occurred years before the term object-oriented, or languages like Smalltalk were created. It was also long before there were any "OO methodologists" or "OO gurus" around, and that includes those who are well-known in the object community today!

REUSE LESSONS LEARNED
FROM ERICSSON'S SUCCESS

At Ericsson, the result was astonishing! We not only developed a system concept that fulfilled the requirements for adaptability and manageability, but— or maybe because of that—we also achieved a very high degree of reuse.

The key was that we designed the system architecture, the development process, and the organization in harmony. All three supported reuse as the natural way of working. This was extremely successful then and has proven to be successful ever since!

In other words, objects are not enough to achieve reuse. You must design your own organization so that it is one in which architecture, process, and organization work together in harmony!

Using current nomenclature, this is nothing more and nothing less than a reengineering task, in which you reengineer your development organization into an organization designed for reuse. (But that's another story—read more about it in "Reengineering Your Software Engineering Process."[2])

ARCHITECTURE WAS KEY TO SUCCESS

One of the important architectural constructs we identified early was the Service Package.[3] Service Package grouped frameworks and classes into a "service." Each Service Package was a unit for configuration management and version control. And they were the atomic work or responsibility-unit given to a single programmer. We considered Service Packages to be indivisible: a customer needed either all or none of a service.

For the purpose of reusability we also categorized Service Packages. As Figure 8-1 shows, a Service Package was either Mandatory or Optional; Standard or Customer Specific. We identified every Service Package so that it fell into only one of the four quadrants.

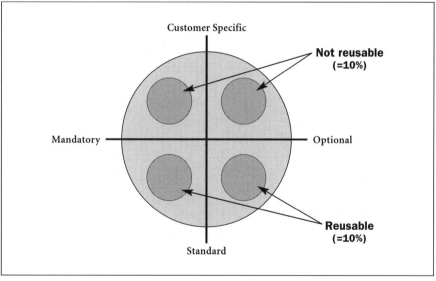

Figure 8-1. Classification of Service Packages.

Furthermore, Service Packages were reusable. We tried to identify a core set of Standard Packages that every customer needed (Mandatory-Standard). We also made sure that Optional packages were either Standard or Customer Specific. Naturally, we wanted as few Packages as possible to belong to the upper two quadrants as they largely could not be reused. We worked hard to make Standard Packages very good, so our customers would prefer to use them rather than funding the development of a specific package.

Even if we did not use the word reuse, we were still thinking of reuse as a way to save as much work as possible and to also keep quality assurance and testing costs as low as possible. This may sound obvious today, but it was not at all obvious that we could do this at the time. However, we did achieve a very high level of reuse. In most cases we had a reuse level of more than 90% between customers and systems!

We also identified an equally important architectural construct, the message. One of the key lessons I learned working on hardware-based switching systems was that interfaces between the building blocks were the backbone of the system. This was one of the key ideas behind the new method we developed back in 1967, and that defined a way to "design-by-interfaces" to achieve interchangeability and exchangeability.

We knew we had to be able to exchange building blocks without changing their surroundings. Thus, apart from identifying the building blocks, in terms of Service Packages and Subsystems, we also identified and described the communication protocols among them. We documented these communication protocols separately from the building blocks. We even had a special architecture group, which approved all interactions between building blocks.

Our building blocks interacted by sending messages, and all messages between any two Service Packages (actually types of Service Packages) were grouped into a set of messages that were handled together. These message-sets correspond to what we now call Interfaces.

We described every message type separate from its sender and receiver. Thus, an Interface was a kind of an object too. As a consequence, Interfaces were management units in their own right. Interfaces formed the skeleton of the system, and they were the system's most valuable asset. Service Packages made the system operate, but they could also be exchanged without changing the surrounding Interfaces. In other words, they were interchangeable. Interfaces, on the other hand, were very stable and changed rarely.

ORGANIZING TO MANAGE THE ARCHITECTURE

To manage this complexity, we learned very early that our organization had to assign responsibilities for a Service Package between two or more developers. However, one developer could very well be responsible for more than one Service Package.

Subsystems contain sets of Service Packages. We made a group manager responsible for each Subsystem and all of the Service Packages within it. The group manager was also the line manager for the people within his group. And, although individual developers might be responsible for several Service Packages, they were usually within the same Subsystem.

The entire organization thus matched the system architecture, and the responsibilities of the individual developers mapped directly onto the system structure.

THERE WERE PROBLEMS OF COURSE...

First, in those days we had to develop everything ourselves! We developed our own operating environment, wrote our own programming language, designed our own database-management system, and developed all of the hardware and software building blocks.

Today, of course, we would try to procure most of the non-differentiating building blocks. To make this work in practice, we further refined our systems architecture into a layered architecture (or, more generally, a System of Interconnected Systems). A layered architecture is a very well-defined, complete system skeleton, in which major parts are isolated from each other by means of explicitly defined interfaces. A layered architecture directly supports building-block interchangeability even as it maintains robustness. Layered architectures also protect your investments, in case you need to change the source of your building blocks, for example.

Second, because we treated Service Packages as atomic, we could reuse only at the Service Package level of granularity. We simply did not have the mechanisms or constructs in place to reuse simple objects or classes. Today we call this coarse-grained reuse. Thanks to the evolution of object technology, we now have all of the basic mechanisms in place to achieve fine-grained reuse. So now we can reuse classes, patterns, and frameworks, too.

...AND WE LEARNED FROM OTHERS AS WELL

We have learned a lot about reuse from others, too, especially from Hewlett-Packard Laboratories. HP Labs have very broad and complementary experience with reuse, unique platform competence, and, last but not least, a number of reuse experts, including the famous "reuse rabbi," Dr. Martin

Griss. Since our merger with Rational, we have gained a substantial experience base in the field of architectures for large complex software systems.

All these combined experiences tell us that reuse simply does not happen
by itself! Rather, achieving reuse is difficult. The only way we have observed
that is repeatable, manageable, and predictable is a systematic approach that
reengineers everything about how you develop systems, with the explicit goal
being to achieve reuse!

Refining Ideas into a General Use Framework

After eight years of research and development, first at Objectory and now
continuing within Rational, we are developing a configurable process for
reuse. Our reuse process will constitute the starting point for an organization to reengineer itself by means of system architecture, development
processes, and organization to achieve reuse. The technology is based on our
use-case driven, OO-based approaches for business and systems engineering.[4]
We have named it Reuse Driven Software Engineering Businesses (RSEB).
A detailed presentation of this technology is published in *Software Reuse*.[5]

RSEB Based on Three Harmonized Cornerstones: A‑P‑O

A is for architecture. To technically define a system architecture, we use a
set of architectural styles that together support reuse through the use of
components. In doing so, we make a clear and very important distinction
between Component Systems and Application Systems. A Component
System is the packaging of a set of related components into a product, and
an Application System is a set of customizable and configurable building
blocks that installers, a production department, or even end-users can use
to assemble a customized application.

An Application System is constructed by selecting, specializing, augmenting,
and integrating components from one or more Component Systems.

The architectural styles we use are:

- *Interfaces* – an implementation-independent public interface of a class
  or subsystem. Interfaces are defined and handled separately from their

realizations, and they can be realized through the use of several interchangeable classes or subsystems. Interfaces thus support robustness and flexibility through interchangeability.

- *Patterns* – defined by two parts. The problem-definition part can be described as an abstract use case. The solutions part can be described as the design of that abstract use case.

- *Frameworks* – an abstract subsystem that typically implements a set of abstract use cases, and that is designed to be reused and extended.

- *Facades* – a complete set of components, such as use cases, classes, diagrams, and descriptions that together show what can be exported from an underlying (component) system. Facades are used, often through restrictions given by a set of visibility rules, to define how an underlying component system can be reused by other component systems or an application system.

- *Layers* – a (subordinate) system representing a well-defined and isolated part of a larger (superordinate) system. A system with a layered architecture typically has two to four horizontal layers.

- *System of Interconnected Systems (SIS)* – a set of (subordinate) systems that are interconnected by means of Facades and Interfaces. In this context, a layered system is one special type of a SIS. A SIS, however, is a more formal and generalized way to define a system architecture.

P is for process. Your development processes should match the system architecture. First, you need a mega process to develop and maintain the total system architecture, including all the different component and application systems. We call this "application family engineering." It involves the development of the overall system architecture, including all component systems, all application systems, and all the interfaces between them.

You also need specific processes for developing the component and the application systems. In the case of a layered architecture, you may also need processes for developing specific systems for cross-business or domain-specific layers, among others.

And, you might also need a specific process to handle the adaptation, integration, and use of, for example, outsourced component or application systems.

O is for organization. Finally, you must implement the process of the RSEB that was designed during process development. This is done by populating the worker roles and by identifying the work products of the RSEB model. Thus for each process—for example, application family engineering, application system engineering, and component system engineering—you identify all worker roles and work products. You then populate the worker roles with suitable resources. The resulting organization is an instance of the RSEB, populated with people and tools who collaborate to develop the specified work products.

WELL-DEFINED APPROACH

The approach we describe here is a systematic way to achieve reuse. It is based on long term, large-scale experiences from building commercial software systems by extensive reuse of components. It combines object-oriented business and software engineering techniques to systematically design an RSEB based on the three harmonized cornerstones: Architecture, Process, Organization.

Applying a well-defined engineering approach like this is the only way we know of to achieve substantial reuse in reality. And some time in the future, when large numbers of companies have successfully done so, the word reuse will eventually become ubiquitous. At that time, *use* will be the word instead, or it may even go without saying—as it did for us at Ericsson back in the '60s!

(Many thanks to Jorma Mobrin at Ericsson for his invaluable assistance with this column.)

REFERENCES

1. I. Jacobson. "A Large Commercial Success Story Based on Objects," *Object Magazine*, May 1996. (See chapter entitled "A Large Commercial Success Story at Ericsson.")

2. I. Jacobson and S. Jacobson. "Reengineering your Software Engineering Process," *Object Magazine*, March/April 1995. (See chapter entitled "Reengineering Your Software Engineering Process.")

3. I. Jacobson. "Concepts for Modeling Large Real Time Systems," Department of Computer Systems, The Royal Institute of Technology, Stockholm, Sept. 1985.

4. I. Jacobson, M. Christersson, P. Jonsson, and G. Övergaard. *Object-Oriented Software Engineering—A Use Case Driven Approach*, Addison–Wesley, Reading, MA, 1992.

5. Ivar Jacobson, Martin Griss, and Patrik Jonsson. *Software Reuse: Architecture, Process and Organization for Business Success*, Addison Wesley Longman, Reading, MA, 1997.

9

IT IS TIME FOR AN OBJECT
MODELING LANGUAGE STANDARD

Ivar Jacobson, MARCH 1997

T HE SUMMER OF 1997 the Object Management Group (OMG) was scheduled to make a decision that could lay the foundation for a series of revolutionary breakthroughs in the world of object technology. That single enabling decision was the adoption of an object-modeling language standard.

The adoption of a standard too early in the development process of scientific or technological undertakings is of course not good. It tends to stifle innovation, freethinking, the flow of ideas and experimentation that are vital to the exploration of the strengths, weaknesses, and boundaries of the thing. However, as a paradigm matures the development and consistent use of standards provides the foundation and framework of consensus required for further advancements, the nurturing of acceptance, and profitable use.

Object-oriented technology has matured for almost 30 years. All modern object-oriented programming languages can trace their origins to Simula, which was developed in Norway in 1967. In parallel, analysis and design methods were developed to bring objects to the specification and design of software systems.

Twenty years ago in 1976 the telecommunications industry agreed on a standard modeling language. I was at Ericsson at the time and contributed to the Specification and Description Language (SDL) adopted by the CCITT. SDL is, in fact, an object modeling language that contains most of the things we consider important in a standard today. In reality SDL is an object modeling standard which has been in place for about 20 years now. Rather impressive, isn't it?

Thus, object modeling is a mature technique. However, over the years the number of different object-oriented methods has exploded. I would estimate there are currently more than 50 published methods and countless unpublished others used internally in organizations. This was known to be the "methods war."

I wrote a guest editorial for *JOOP* in May 1993 entitled "Time For a Cease-Fire in the Methods War."[1] I covered two issues in that article which remain hot topics today, a standard modeling language and a standard development process. In answer to the question of what we could agree on I stated, "All good methods support object modeling. The differences between the leading languages are minor. ... We could use a technique being used to formally specify programming languages. ... You ignore notation differences by specifying an abstract syntax. ... Every methodologist would then be able to specify his own modeling language using this basic technique." Thus on the modeling language I advocated a core meta-model and not a standard notation. I believed it would be too difficult to get a standard notation. Shortly after I wrote that article Grady Booch and I speculated that we could actually predict a standard based on what we were seeing in the industry.

My thinking and understanding have matured since May 1993. I have come to regard the adoption of a standard notation, that is a user language of paramount importance. To agree on a standard core meta-model on which a methodologist adds only his or her own notation, such as I advocated in the *JOOP* article would make the methodologists happy but not the industry. The standard user language must be powerful enough for the majority of software systems being built today and in the near-term. It must be particularly useful in the design of reusable parts such as frameworks, component systems, and libraries. The language should also include mechanisms for limited extensions necessary for special application areas. This is a good approach for a standard language and it was the driving force behind the development of the Unified Modeling Language (UML).

Some time in 1994, Grady Booch and Jim Rumbaugh, who were together at Rational, began to look at ways to merge Booch 93 and Object Modeling Technique (OMT). I continued to play around with the idea of a standard back at Objectory. In the fall of 1995, after I joined them at Rational we added Object Oriented Software Engineering (OOSE) and combined our efforts. Today, we are involved with some of the best minds and most successful and influential companies in our industry in developing the Unified Modeling Language. The UML Partners Consortium was formed in 1996 for defining an object modeling language to submit to the OMG. We met that goal in January of this year.

So, what are the compelling issues demanding a standard at this time?

First, because industry leaders need it now! The UML Partners Consortium is comprised of companies such as Microsoft, Hewlett-Packard, Digital

Equipment, and Oracle, to name just four. They represent billions of dollars of investment in languages, tools and applications. They report that their customers are demanding an easily learned and implemented language, which lends itself to increased productivity and actually supports reuse. The marketplace is faced with developing high quality systems that remain resilient and reliable as they undergo ever-constant changes. The required robustness will come only if there is a language standard in place that will allow communication of generic components at the level of early system definition.

Second, the arcane world of software specification and design must become accessible to the end users. Software architects, at last, will have a "transportable language," understandable between users in different companies, across organizational boundaries and to upper levels of corporate management and leadership. Unlike civil engineering, there are no standardized blueprints in software development. No one would ever begin construction on a building, bridge, or highway without blueprints! However only a very small percentage, maybe as little as 2%, of software developers use blueprints today. I was visiting with a consultant recently who said, "What we really have here is a modern Tower of Babel. We are trying to build these huge systems, structures if you will, and there is no common language for us to communicate to each other exactly what we have in mind." I believe that the adoption of this standard will facilitate an increase in the number of software engineers who use blueprints to close to 100%. It may not happen within five years but it will happen within a decade. 25 years ago I had a dream that someday we would develop a common, basic, simple language to unify widely varying application areas. The UML starts us down that pathway.

Next, issues of productivity must be addressed. The current number of published and unpublished modeling languages has resulted in a nightmare of inefficiency. It is not unusual for different product within the same company to use completely different modeling methodologies. Often significant investments of both time and money are expended in training the methodology du jour. This is exacerbated by the fact that job migration is a fact of life. The UML addresses these resource concerns by providing a universal language on which product blueprints are based. I have heard it jokingly stated, "Managers will finally be able to move personnel from project to project during the specification and design phases as easily as they carry their coffee cups around today."

Finally, reuse will become a reality. This excites me most of all. The great promise of OO technology is the potential to reuse components. Early on developers thought the power would be in reusing code. My own experience from substantial reuse in component-based construction is that if we are to derive maximum benefit and leverage from this technology we must have a mechanism to reuse complete designs. We need to reuse recurring patterns and a framework in the systems designs themselves. Therefore UML provides a non-domain-specific way to capture reusable designs. It enables engineers to capture and communicate in an unambiguous way the underlying "themes."

The Unified Modeling Language addresses a broad spectrum of architectural issues. Our collaboration has been an exercise in balance as we incorporated "best engineering practices," which have real world credentials for producing successful results. We have remained sensitive to the fact that there are loyal users of previous techniques and have distilled the essence of many different methodologies and languages. We have unified the semantics and notation to encompass wide ranging disciplines from hardware to software to business, from Wall Street to the battlefield. The adoption of the UML will greatly increase the number and usability of tools and will encourage the development of add-ons. The UML is nonproprietary. The Partners will respond to feedback, and readers are encouraged to participate in the general discussion forums. Sources of feedback include the OMG Internet newsgroup comp.object, and the Partners' e-mail address at uml_feedback@rational.com. There may be very special applications or intractable problems in the future that cannot be addressed by a language based on a standard developed today. Fine! Then someone will develop "nonstandards" and solve the challenge. That possible eventuality should not prevent us from getting a really good standard today that the user community needs desperately.

It is a rare occasion when one's actions have any real impact on the world. I believe we are standing on the threshold of just such a significant breakthrough in software engineering. The adoption of a standard modeling language at this time in our technological history will have all of the major impacts discussed here and quite possibly some we have not even thought about in our wildest speculations. Maybe, just maybe, we will change the world a little bit.

REFERENCE

1. Ivar Jacobson. "Time for a Cease-Fire in the Methods War," *Journal of Object-Oriented Programming*, 1993. (See chapter entitled "Time for a Cease-Fire in the Methods War.")

10

Only Software and Doghouses Are Built Without Blueprints

Ivar Jacobson, November 1997

A PICTURE IS WORTH A THOUSAND WORDS. The organized pictures known as engineering drawings or blueprints have enabled us to build a technical civilization. The engineering disciplines older than software development have found, through the experience of hundreds of years, drawings that suited their needs, such as the block diagrams, logic diagrams, and other schematics used by electrical engineers. The issue before us is what kind of drawings can take software development to the working level of these other disciplines?

There are two things that will change this situation. The first will organize the pictures for software development, the second will provide a way of preparing and using those pictures. The outcome of the first activity is a standard for blueprints of software. It is called the Unified Modeling Language (UML). The second is the Objectory process.

Models Help us Think

Both words and pictures may be embraced by the still broader term, *model.* A model is an abstraction of something real in the world. We construct models as an aid to our own thought processes. If something is sufficiently

---

* Now the Unified Process.

simple, like building a doghouse, we can do it directly, i.e., without a blueprint-type model to guide us. When that something gets more complicated, like the code for a large software program, we need to abstract it into a model so that we can think about it in the simpler terms of the abstracted elements. Moreover, we need the help of models, because we tend not to be very proficient at being complete or consistent. Automation of model-building helps us to be consistent and complete.

What Is the Real World and What Is a Model?

In the case of software, "real" may be when we get down to the electrical pulses that turn the millions of transistors in a microprocessor off and on. Even so, that is an odd sort of "real." To see them, we have to use an oscilloscope, and what we see on its screen is again, a model. Even the machine code is a model. It is an abstraction from which the digital machinery makes those electrical pulses. Of course, everything upstream from the machine code—source code, design, analysis, architecture, use cases, and requirements—is some kind of a model of the real-world system. Moreover, paralleling this sequence of workflow activities are the development of test plans, test cases, or test models.

Software as Models

Like it or not, software people live in a world of models. The trouble is, most of us don't take our models out of our heads and put them in a form usable by others until the work reaches the source-code stage. Source code is difficult for even other programmers to penetrate, let alone stakeholders less experienced in code. What the field badly needs is a set of models that will (a) help architects and developers themselves think and (b) let others see what they are thinking. Then we have to standardize the set so that more than the handful of people who happen to work in the same neighborhood can communicate with it.

People have been diligently working on the model part of this problem. For example, during the past decade, a number of object-oriented (OO) methodologies have been developing. Three of them: my own Object-Oriented Software Engineering (OOSE), Grady Booch's method, and Jim Rumbaugh's Object Modeling Technique (OMT), came together in Rational

Software Corporation. To broaden this experience further, Rational formed the UML Partners Consortium in 1996 with companies such as Microsoft, Hewlett Packard, Oracle, and IBM. The partners have billions of dollars of investment in software and anticipate more each year. They know they need a standard. Moreover, their application builders, customers, and users are realizing that they also need one.

The modeling techniques employed by our three methodologies and the contributions of many valuable ideas from the group as a whole have resulted in the Unified Modeling Language (submitted September 1, 1997 to the Object Management Group, which is scheduled to act by December).[†]

The participants are convinced of the advantages models provide:

- Models are the means through which developers can communicate the software product to users, customers, and other stakeholders.

- They are the language though which architects, developers, and testers can keep each other informed of progress status.

- Models enable developers to make software architecture-centric, which supports software resiliency and reusability.

- Models allow developers to analyze the users' needs and capture them as use cases; to utilize use cases as a driver for design and implementation; and to test.

- They enable developers to effect changes in one model, then trace those changes through them all.

- Models provide the means to prepare software systems for reuse; the only way to achieve reuse is to model what can be reused.

- Models are equally necessary to future developers to keep a system alive and well (resilient and robust) through many generations.

The fact that UML is unified promises additional advantages:

- All those concerned with software development worldwide, e.g., architects, developers, testers, managers, users, customers, and stakeholders, can comprehend the common models.

- Uniform comprehension minimizes errors of interpretation.

---

† The Object Management Group adopted the UML as a standard in November 1997.

- People can be educated, trained, or indoctrinated once in the UML and use it as a basis of their careers.

- The UML enables people to move around on their own, or to be placed where they are needed at the organization's initiative.

- The large market that unification offers provides tool vendors with the means to finance more effective model-building tools.

What is most important though, is that people across companies can read and understand each other's software. The representation of the software in standardized models is a prerequisite to a worldwide market for reusable components, as well as reuse within a single organization or a group of related organizations.

WHAT IS THE UML?

While the UML is, in one sense, as new as tomorrow, it is, in another sense, decades old. The genesis of my OOSE approach, for instance, goes back to its development within Ericsson in the late 1960s. As early as 1976, the telecommunications industry (including Ericsson) standardized the Specification and Description Language (SDL). SDL is an object modeling language, and to my knowledge, the first standard in this field. The second source was entity-relationship modeling. These two were among the forerunners of the UML currently being standardized. So, the main thrust of the new standard grows out of years of practical experience.

We may think of the UML as providing the users with a vocabulary encompassing three categories: things, relationships, and diagrams.

There are three kind of things: structural, behavioral, and groupings. There are six primary kinds of "structural things": use cases, classes, interfaces, collaborations, components, and nodes. There are two kinds of "behavioral things": interactions and state machines. And there are three kinds of "groupings": models, systems, and packages.

Within the second category—relationships—we find three further classifications: dependency, association, and generalization.

And in the third category, diagrams, UML provides nine types: use case, class, object, sequence, collaboration, statechart, activity, component, and deployment.

You may argue, justifiably, that these are just a lot of words with no explanations, and it's more complicated than it's worth. I sympathize. But we'd need more space to give a more in-depth presentation of the UML. Regarding complexity though, let me offer two defenses.

Software is complicated; it comes in many dimensions; stakeholders want many different views. The UML must support many different kinds of applications: both business and technical. It must be able to deal with systems with huge databases, as well as those with severe real-time.

The attempts to model software development more simply have not been very successful, judging by the failure rates. The simplest way of all, just plain code, runs out of steam when superiors or clients try to figure out what more than a few hundred lines are supposed to be doing.

The new standard supports OO technology and component-based design. The UML, as the "L" in its acronym suggests, is a language. Like other languages, it is widely usable. It is powerful enough to model nearly all of the software systems being built today and in the near future. It models the design of reusable parts such as frameworks, component systems, and libraries. It includes mechanisms for limited extensions into special application areas.

A Breakthrough

I am convinced that this blueprint language will break software development out of the handicraft era and bring it into a modern engineering discipline—the industrial revolution for software. Mostly because the UML is an adopted standard, accepted by all the major players in the field. I expect the consequences to be:

1. The number of developers using any blueprint language will grow from perhaps 2% to 100%, just as electrical engineers worldwide use the same symbols for resistors and capacitors. Although the timescale may be a human generation, software development will no longer be as bottlenecked as it is today.

2. The software we build will be useful in supporting our business goals (thanks to use cases), and resilient to future changes (thanks to architecture). Tomorrow's software will have a dramatically longer life than todays.

3. Reuse will become a reality due to a standard modeling language across applications within a company and across business areas over many companies. The result will be dramatic with regard to costs, quality, and time-to-market.

In Ivar's Words

Q: What initiated the work towards unification of modeling languages and, later on, unified software development processes?

A: Chapter 4 (a guest editorial in JOOP) triggered Grady Booch to call me and ask when we would go ahead and start the work. Grady and I met with Jim Rumbaugh at a breakfast meeting at OOPSLA'93 and tried to get to some outline of work. Not much happened until Jim joined Rational a year later. Grady and Jim announced that they would work on a Unified Method that was both a modeling language and process. I felt that was too much, that it would be better to first work on the language part. When I later in October 1995 joined Rational we agreed to change the effort to focus on the modeling language.

In parallel with these discussions with Grady and Jim, I worked with OMG to standardize on methods. I was asked to do this by senior managers at Ericsson in early 1995. The reason was that Ericsson invested so much in using different modeling techniques like the Objectory approach and wanted to get a standard, a standard that was supported by many vendors. I contacted Richard Soley, whom I knew from my time at MIT in 1983–84, and suggested that OMG would take on the effort of standardizing a modeling language. Richard asked me to get as many other methodologists to support this idea and in particular Grady and Jim. This is how the whole work on standardizing the UML started.

Q: In the UML, there are many types of objects, that is, instances of classifiers. When did you start to perceive that there is a wide range of different objects that all share the fundamental characteristics of object-oriented technology?

A: In my Ph.D. thesis I defined different types of objects. This was then refined in my OOPSLA 1997 paper where I introduced the idea to have several different types of objects when modeling software. This idea then became

more mature in the OOSE book where we talked about class types as you
can see from the following quotes:*

- *Actors as classes: "We regard an actor as a class and users as instances of
  this class."*

- *Use cases as classes: "Each use case is a specific way of using the system
  and every execution of the use case may be viewed as an instance of the
  use case.... These use case instances follow, as do all instances in an object-
  oriented system, a specific class. When a use case is performed we view
  this as if we instantiated the use case's class.... To view use cases as objects,
  classes, and instances is often unnatural to people used to OOP.... The
  purpose of this is that we can use all the benefits of object-orientation...."*

- *Analysis classes, we were talking about three class types: "Many object-
  oriented analysis methods choose to have only one object type, ... We
  have chosen to use three object types ... entity objects, interface objects,
  and control objects."*

- *Attributes as types: "An attribute is described as an association with a
  name and cardinality indicating the attribute's type. Note the similarity
  between this and the acquaintance association. Actually attributes and
  entity objects have many properties in common..."*

- *Design classes: "Blocks are the design objects.... Here it could be possible to use different types of blocks, if preferable, for instance interface
  blocks, entity blocks, and control blocks ...."*

- *Frameworks: "This is a reusable design in terms of ... an abstract
  subsystem.... This abstract subsystem may be adapted to another concrete subsystem." Abstract subsystems could be inherited by a concrete
  subsystem.*

- *Systems and subsystems as types: "Instantiations take place at different
  levels: the delivered system will be instantiated from the designed
  systems...."*
  *"When a system is to be delivered, we say that instantiation will be
  made of a subset of the blocks in the system.... The delivered system*

---

* We used the term object to stand for both classes and/or instances when we did not
need to be precise. However, when we needed to be precise we were so, as you can see
from the quotes. Consistently we used the term object types to stand for types of objects,
classes, and/or instances. When precise we said class types or instances of a class type.

thus consists of a set of block instances which contain those classes, namely the executable code, which have been obtained from the corresponding descriptions. Once the system is installed with the classes that form part of the block instances, the objects that really perform the execution of the system will be created (instantiated)."

- *The idea of viewing the whole architecture as a kind of class: "We can regard the architecture (actually more adequate to say architectural style) as a class. For each specific system we design, we create an instance of that class." A specific system may be a banking system or a telecom system based on the same architectural style.*

Thus the notion of having many types of classes was introduced in the OOSE book. The idea has successively been accepted and extended. Rebecca Wirfs-Brock introduced the term "stereotype" to talk about these different types of classes like boundary classes (called interface classes in my book), control classes, and entity classes. She found the need for more stereotypes than these three, which were used in an analysis model. In a design model she wanted to use seven different stereotypes. She did not use the term stereotype for other types like subsystems, actors, use cases.

Working on UML, Grady, Jim and I have substantially generalized the notion of stereotypes. We have identified what is generic for all stereotypes and how we can attach semantics to each one of them without violating what is common for all or some of them. We have also included as stereotypes model elements such as packages, use cases, actors, relations, operations, etc., thus not just only classical classes.

Q: Much of your discussions are around models of a system, and you seem to have a more stringent understanding of the notion of "model" than most software gurus and methodologists. What is the origin of this fundamental idea? Is there any discipline in particular that you have been inspired by?

A: I really don't know what has inspired me. I think it was some internal paper at Ericsson written by Oleg deBachtin. Oleg was a philosopher. He started as a tool builder for our programming environment, became manager for the team, then he became a doctor in psychology.

Oleg wrote a philosophical paper going back to Immanuel Kant and his "Das Ding an Sich." I don't think I can track Kant's work to what I later did but I know it made me think differently. Most people think of a system as a "thing," whereas the only thing we actually know about this thing is what we tell about it. So the thing is its descriptions, whether this is documents, source code ("understandable" to programmers and compilers), executables ("understandable" to a hardware in some form—"microprograms").

We can continue in this manner to ask similar questions about the design of a software system in terms of subsystems, classes, interaction diagrams, state chart diagrams, and other artifacts. Are they the system? Yes, they are part of it. What about requirements, testing, sales, production, installation, and operation, are they the system? Yes, they are also part of the system.

My conclusion was that a system is actually all the artifacts that it takes to represent it in machine or human readable form to the "machines," the workers, and its stakeholders. The "machines" are tools, compilers, or target computers. Workers include management, architects, developers, testers, marketers, administrators, and others. Stakeholders include funding authorities, users, sales, project managers, line managers, production people, regulatory agencies, etc.

So how I came to the model concept was by saying that one of the most important decisions you have to take about a software development work is what kind of stakeholders or workers you need. Because it is for them that you have to document the system. And this documentation is done in chunks suitable for one or more of these workers. Such a chunk is a model. Some chunks (models) are also just for automated workers like compilers and interpreters.

Q: Some years ago, you applied the use case concept, and other Objectory ideas, to the business process reengineering area. How well has your proposal been accepted by non-IT people? Are use cases used in business engineering so much as in the IT area?

A: Sure, use cases have been universally adopted also for business engineering. Maybe not yet as widely as for software. People who want to do business modeling are typically people who understand software, and who understand that they need more than software modeling techniques. It's very sad that people from business engineering, like Hammer, didn't think about modeling so much, so the stream of people that come from that part is much fewer, most people come to business modeling from the software world. It's a much smaller business, but we have customers with hundreds of licenses of Rose for Business Engineering, for example in one telecom company and in the Swedish pension system.

It is interesting to see that Hammer's business processes were very close to business use cases. New ideas related to Web-design also start finding the customers and for each customer type you find the use cases that the Website should provide to that customer type. This is for instance in essence what David Siegel is doing in his forthcoming book Futurize Your Enterprise.

(Extracts of the answer above are reprinted with permission from Adriano Comai, an Italian IT consultant. It was first published at www.analisi-disegno.com and in the ZeroUno magazine (Italian translation).)

Q: Is it more difficult to persuade IT or non-IT people of the importance to do business modeling as a starting point for a new project or for the evolution of an existing system?

A: The basic problem is that we often think we don't have the time to do business modeling. Time-to-market is today very short... like it's more important that you get something out than that it's a good thing. This means that these approaches of business and system engineering must be very tightly integrated. IT people know that to do business models takes six months, 12 months, and when they start to build the software, the business has changed. So there is some hesitance to start doing business modeling, and there should be with traditional methods. What's unique about the Unified process is that business modeling is part of the process, so if you have six months to develop, then business engineering will be part of those six months.

I can understand that people hesitate to do business modeling; but if we think quality is not so important in order to get it out, then we will always have problems with any structured approach to develop software. But with iterative development we plan and work to get something out with quality, and I think that will help people to accept doing business modeling, continuously, for each release of the software.

(Extracts of the answer above are reprinted with permission from Adriano Comai, an Italian IT consultant. It was first published at www.analisi-disegno.com and in the ZeroUno magazine (Italian translation).)

PART 4:
PROCESS AND TOOLS

———

ANY SOFTWARE DEVELOPMENT TEAM has three cornerstones: the actual individuals participating in the team, their work process, and the development tools they use. These cornerstones must be set up to reach the same goal, namely to produce quality software within time and budget. But what happens when such a team fails? Then we need to change it. But it is hard to change the participating individuals per se. However, if we have a proper process accompanied with a streamlined set of tools in place, it is easier to boost the skills required of those individuals, and, in general, to manage them in a productive manner. Thus, the right process and tools are important—and even essential—to have in place for any serious software development team.

However, it is by no means trivial to put a software development process up on the wall, since there is so much at stake. For example, the process needs to be structured so that it is intuitive and understandable by its stakeholders, that is, the individuals of the development team itself. Moreover, since every development team has its own specific requirements on process, it needs to be structured so that it is easy to change, configure, specialize, and extend. And, the process needs to go hand-in-hand with the tools and be supported by them; that is, the tools should encourage and stimulate individuals to use the proper development process.

This part will explain more about processes and tools, and their relationship.

PART 4:
PROCESS AND TOOLS

———

11

BEYOND METHODS AND CASE: THE SOFTWARE ENGINEERING PROCESS WITH ITS INTEGRAL SUPPORT ENVIRONMENT

Ivar Jacobson & Sten Jacobson, JANUARY 1995

T HE SOFTWARE INDUSTRY MUST ADOPT new engineering practices to mature. For more than seven years, we have worked toward realizing our vision of a Software Engineering Process (SEP) and an integrated Support Environment (SEPSE). We envisioned SEP and SEPSE as the support for the industrial development of software products, at quality and productivity levels well beyond those achieved by current methods and CASE-based practices. SEP and SEPSE will usher in an era of new technologies to enable the software industry to mature and, although we do not claim to have implemented them fully, we believe we have come a long way. This chapter will address these new changes.

SOFTWARE DEVELOPMENT IS STILL A CRAFT

Because software affects practically everything everyone does every day, and because enormous amounts of money are invested in building and maintaining it, outsiders may believe the software industry is one of the most advanced in the world. They might also assume that sound engineering practices are used to develop it.

Unfortunately this is not true! Everyone involved in building software knows that development is still typically based on craftsmanship. Even million-dollar systems are still built with primitive techniques and tools. It is still more the rule than the exception that software producers throughout Europe and North America:

- Shoot from the hip rather than use mature engineering practices.

- Work with poor specifications.

- Ship prototypes as products.

- Shop for "silver-bullet" panaceas rather than systematically reengineering their development processes.

We find that a large percentage of software organizations use simplistic approaches, and we consider it incomprehensible that large software vendors continue to develop software products in such a "cowboy" fashion.

Organizations that want to achieve a much higher level of maturity must leave these ad hoc development practices behind and begin to apply industrial-strength development processes. Only then can they deliver software with the required level of suitability, usability, and quality. Only then can they develop products with the cost and time efficiencies they will need to survive and thrive in the market place.

So, what technologies *are* needed to implement such processes and how should an organization implement them? Well, we believe the answer does *not* lie with the current generation of methods and CASE technologies, regardless of their paradigm. They are entirely insufficient and stand no chance of supporting industrial-strength development.

Instead, we think the answer lies with a mature SEP and an integrated SEPSE. We are also convinced that successful SEP products will be object based. In the interest of brevity, we will state our views on these topics in a simplified and slightly exaggerated way to more clearly convey our message.

A METHOD IS NOT A PROCESS

A method is usually embodied in a textbook and associated with a method-ologist such as Booch, Shlaer, Mellor, Rumbaugh, Wirfs-Brock, or Jacobson.

Methods are personalized; the methodologist takes the role of a guru who tries to convert as many individuals as possible to his or her particular belief.

The method itself is usually a set of interesting ideas and general step-by-step descriptions. However, it typically does not guide developers in how to use it in commercial product development. So, before an entire development organization can use a method, it must undertake a substantial *process-development* effort. Many organizations may be able to do this, but it is a task that falls outside its core business—to develop software products.

This internal process-development effort results in a corporate process handbook and a process model inspired by the method of choice, but that also defines the detailed tasks needed to be performed by the organization to develop its products. Individuals in an organization would use this process handbook to accomplish their everyday development tasks and, therefore, would primarily use the method (textbook) for educational purposes during initial training on their process model.

After two decades of disappointment, first with structured methods and now with object-oriented methods, many methodologists are now calling their methods a process! But of course methods are not a process. And this confusing and inflationary use of the word "process" is in itself evidence of the shortcomings of today's methods.

METHOD SHORTCOMINGS

Apart from this, current methods have crucial, technical shortcomings:

- **Methods are paper products.** Methodologists develop methods by writing a book. Thus, the substance of a method is frozen when the book is published. Incorporating new ideas and modeling constructs requires a new edition. And frequently there is no compatibility between work products of the old book and the new book

- **Most methods are never tried in real projects before publication.** Methodologists add new ideas because they seem to be very good ideas, but they do very little real testing of the ideas in realistic contexts. This is not necessarily a fatal flaw, as long as those who implement the method are aware of this, but many aren't. To be considered mature, a method should be used for several years and on several projects (say, 10 projects over five years).

- **Methods are introductory only.** A method textbook has typically less than 50 pages of real substance (surrounded by an introduction, conclusion, examples, and so forth). This is insufficient both for the commercial use of the method and as a specification for developing supporting tools. Thus, even if a method is very good for educational purposes, it should not be used in any other way! This is true for our own method; we never recommend the use of the OOSE book for commercial development. However, we do recommend people use it to learn the basic ideas before developing a process on the basis of the OOSE method.

- **Methods emphasize new system development over maintenance.** Methods typically begin with a clean slate, describing the life cycle of a software product from nothing to first release. This is not realistic: real products evolve through consecutive releases that are based on new or changed requirements. Methods largely fail to address maintenance in any depth or usable sense.

- **Methods are rich in notations, but lack semantics.** Every method has its own unique notation. Unfortunately, the notations have become the center of the methods war. Simple notations are often regarded as inferior, which has lead to overly rich notations that are not necessarily appropriate for the application domain being modeled. The opposite is true for semantics. Most methods provide semantics that are too loosely defined, which not only makes it difficult for tool developers to offer powerful semantics-checking to help automate development, but also makes it difficult to provide animation and simulation. From a usability point of view, this is backward: We would be better off with a semantically rich method that uses simple notations to capture the complexity of the given application domain.

CASE TOOLS DON'T MATCH METHODS

CASE tools are built to support and automate the use of methods. Surprisingly, most CASE tool vendors do not have a direct association with a methodologist. Instead, most base their development efforts on the method textbook, with very little direct cooperation from the methodologist. Thus, there is a big gap between a method and the tools intended to support and automate it.

As we've said, tool developers frequently discover that the method description is not entirely clear, consistent, or formal. CASE developers are left to improvise and so they fill the blanks, in a more or less ad hoc manner, to:

- Make method decisions on their own.

- Formalize loosely defined concepts.

- Invent missing workflow steps.

The result is that CASE tools end up supporting an automated *dialect* of the method rather than the original method.

Compare this approach with other areas of software development. For example, to develop a banking system, software developers would have to consider the business process and their supporting information systems concurrently, recognizing their interdependence. The system developers learn from the process developers and vice versa. The resulting support systems tightly match the supported processes and are highly suitable and usable.

The same principles should apply to the methodologists and CASE tool developers. Unfortunately, this is rarely true.

The consequence of this lack of cooperation is that CASE tools actually solve a nonproblem. They try to support methods and method elements, some of which were not even thoroughly tested and lack a well-defined software-engineering process. The resulting suitability and usability of CASE tools is generally low.

SECOND-GENERATION METHODS

The notion of "second-generation methods" is primarily marketing hype, but in theory it means methods based on other methods. The driving force behind this new trend is the *method comparison*. Now we actually have two opposing powers behind the evolution of methods: the methodologists and the comparers of methods!

Comparing methods is a very difficult task. To manage this complexity, those who compare methods use simplifying techniques. One of the most common is the "methods overview," which compares methods against a global features checklist. A natural assumption is that the method with the most features checked is the best!

Methodologists consequently add new modeling constructs and process components, without thoroughly verifying or testing them in realistic contexts, to fill up the checklists and make the method appear to be better than before or better than another method. These "method patches" are released as "second-generation methods," typically in the form of a new edition of the book.

Obviously, this trend will not lead to better, more usable methods, but to method elephantiasis. This we don't need!

WHAT WE DO NEED

A software engineering process, unlike a method, is a commercial product developed by practitioners within a commercial organization that markets, sells, and supports these kinds of products. More technically, the SEP is a process framework that must be tailored to each organization. It has an underlying architecture of communicating process components and modeling constructs. It defines these concepts, their semantics, and their syntaxes rigorously and in detail. These features mean the SEP can be used by large organizations developing commercial software products.

A SEP is not only a process, but also an integrated support environment, the SEPSE. The SEPSE is integral to the SEP in the sense that it is one aspect of the SEP and cannot be meaningfully separated from it.

In Watts Humphrey's words: "A Software Engineering Process is the total set of activities needed to transform a user's requirements into software"[1] (see Fig. 11-1).

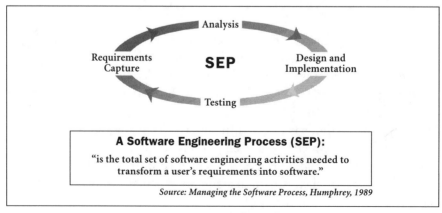

Figure 11-1. The SEP.

Although this definition is a bit superficial, it clearly states that a software-engineering process must support *all* the engineering activities needed to build a software product. A SEP must be based on a holistic approach, in terms of the supported development life cycle and its traceability relations.

To further clarify, let's look at the characteristics of a SEP from three points of view: the user organization, the users, and the development organization.

THE SEP USER ORGANIZATION

A SEP supports the entire life cycle including new development and maintenance. It supports workflows such as requirements capture and analysis, design, implementation, and testing. All activities that must be performed can therefore be defined and described in their correct context.

A SEP offers detailed support across all life cycle activities including configuration management, version control, metrics, project management, concurrent engineering, reviews, and quality assurance. This means that the SEP not only provides tool support for these tasks, but also supports the establishment of these activities and the performance of them over the course of a product's entire lifetime.

A SEP supports organizations that have multiple roles and multiple users. It offers specific, differentiated support to project managers, function managers, analysts, system architects, designers, programmers, component designers, testers, and so on. It also defines how these different roles interact with each other in their performance of various tasks.

A SEP is designed as a process framework that is tailored to meet the precise needs of different organizational cultures, different applications, and different human resources. It is streamlined to improve developer productivity dramatically. Implementing a SEP into an organization may therefore also have the (sub) goal of bringing the organization to the highest possible level process maturity, Level 5 on the Software Engineering Institute's Capability Maturity Model.

A SEP is best inserted into an organization via business process reengineering (BPR) techniques or other equally powerful change-management techniques.[2] This is because its insertion demands implementation tasks such as planning, training, and configuring, as well as the release of the specific SEP. It also requires a pilot project.

THE SEP USERS

Both the process and the underlying architecture of a SEP can be tailored to support several methods and notations. So, developers working in Booch-like, OOSE-like, or OMT-like fashions can still do so. A SEP, therefore, can bridge different methods and notations and protect modeling investments, regardless of which method and architecture domain were used to build the model. SEPs do this by using a common, standardized method framework consisting of metaprocesses and metamodels.

A SEP is also an enabling technology and a prerequisite to achieving systematic reuse. It helps users reuse the work products of other developers, projects, and products both within a development organization and even across an entire line of business.[3]

THE SEP DEVELOPMENT ORGANIZATION

A SEP is designed by process developers using BPR-type modeling techniques. SEP developers use such techniques to formally define roles and deliverables as well as the interactions among them (see Fig. 11-2).

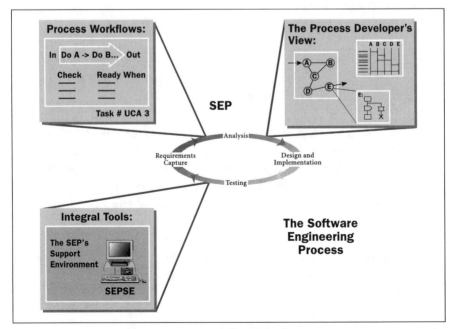

Figure 11-2. The SEP views.

124

A SEP has two different types of descriptions: design descriptions (which are primarily intended for those developing the SEP), and workflow descriptions (intended for those using the SEP). These two descriptions correspond to the way we document information systems, namely by means of design documents and user manuals.

The design descriptions include formal models (object, interaction, and state-transition diagrams). They constitute techniques SEP developers need to create the SEP and its supporting tools.

The workflow descriptions are defined and developed by the SEP development team to be used by the application developers to follow the process.

THE SEP SUPPORT ENVIRONMENT

A SEPSE consists of a set of integrated tools such as single editors, object-modeling tools, and project management tools. Its development takes two efforts: one to develop the necessary tools and the other to integrate them. To facilitate integration, every tool is based on a common open (de facto) standard for method interoperability and control and data integration.

The most important features of a SEPSE are:

- **Its online support for the enactment of a SEP-based work flow and modeling.** A SEPSE is imperative to achieve dramatic improvements in both productivity and quality.

- **Its tools are integral to the SEP.** SEPSE tools are developed concurrently with the SEP, with a purposeful interdependence. This lets the SEP and SEPSE affect each other's limits and possibilities, thus enabling optimization of the SEP.

- **It is fully configurable to the SEP.** SEPSE tools are designed as a metasystem that implements a method framework and its underlying metamodels and metaprocesses.

INVESTMENT AND PAY-OFF DIFFERENCES

There are substantial technical differences between developing a SEP/SEPSE and developing a method/CASE-based technology. One of the more obvious can be described in terms of money (see Fig. 11-3)!

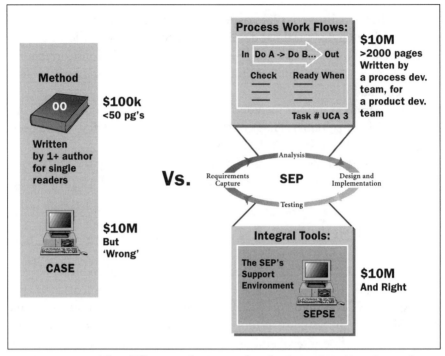

Figure 11-3. The differences between developing a SEP/SEPSE and a method plus associated CASE tool.

The "development cost" of a method is equal to the cost of writing the associated textbook. We estimate this cost to be on the order of $100,000 (US). The development cost of an SEP, in contrast, is at least $10 million, based on our experience developing the Objectory SEP. The difference is that a SEP is a commercial product, the result of a regular product-development effort by at least 10–15 process developers. SEP developers work in project form over many years, periodically releasing new versions of the process via normal product planning and product release cycles.

The cost to develop a CASE tool and a SEPSE are closer. Our experience-based estimate is that the cost to develop a mature, marketable, commercial product is on the order of $10 million, plus an additional $2 million or so annually for maintenance and new releases. The big difference here is that with a CASE tool this investment is misdirected at a nonproblem, and consequently does not pay off. A SEPSE investment will have a good payoff because a SEPSE has a very high level of suitability and usability by offering support for, and being an integral part of, a SEP.

Making SEP/SEPSE a Reality

How do we make SEP/SEPSE technologies a reality? The development of SEP/SEPSE is a standard product-development effort. These products will only come about through enterprises that take on the entire effort and financial risk of developing and industrializing SEP/SEPSE.

This task is much better suited to the process developers and practitioners of our industry than methodologists. We therefore encourage industry practitioners to take charge of the development of these new SEP/SEPSE technologies. This will only happen if, at the same time, the methodologists take charge of their responsibility to push our technologies forward, and thus play a more significant role in the evolution of the software industry than to become so-so SEP/SEPSE developers!

The methodologists should develop new method elements, such as modeling constructs and process components, to be used for future SEP/SEPSE enhancements and developments. This is exactly what the industry needs to be able to deliver software products with the required level of suitability and usability. It is also exactly what software development organizations need to develop these products at a cost and speed that will keep them competitive.

Conclusions

In this chapter, we have discussed the immature status of the software industry. We have presented our visions regarding the software engineering process, with its integrated support environment, and discussed this vision in relation to the method- and CASE-based technologies used by many software development organizations today. We have also presented our views on how the software industry could go about implementing this vision as a means to ripen and mature the industry.

Our most important conclusions are:

- The software industry needs mature software engineering processes.

- The era of methods is over; methods are textbooks only and should be dealt with accordingly.

- The era of CASE is over because CASE tools solve nonproblems looking for a process.

- SEPSE tools supported by a SEP are the industrial-strength tools the industry needs.

- Process developers and practitioners in cooperation best do the development of the SEP/SEPSE technologies.

- We must liberate the methodologists from having to become so-so SEP/SEPSE developers.

- We must also offer the methodologists the freedom to shift focus toward advancing technologies and thus play a more important role in the evolution of the software industry.

We are convinced that SEP/SEPSE-based technologies actually and eventually will allow us to build large, complex, high-quality software much more efficiently than ever before. As this happens, we will see a dramatic change in the marketplace leading toward an industrialized and more efficient way of developing software products. Only then will our industry reach a maturity level where any outsiders' intuitive assumptions about our industry finally are true.

REFERENCES

1. W. Humphry. "Managing the Software Process," Software Engineering Institute, 1989.

2. I. Jacobson, M. Ericsson, and A. Jacobson. *The Object Advantage—Business Process Reengineering with Object Technology*, AddisonWesley Longman and ACM Press, Reading, MA, 1994.

3. Ivar Jacobson, Martin Griss, and Patrik Jonsson. *Software Reuse: Architecture, Process and Organization for Business Success*, Addison Wesley Longman, Reading, MA, 1997.

12

REENGINEERING YOUR SOFTWARE ENGINEERING PROCESS

Ivar Jacobson & Sten Jacobson, MARCH-APRIL 1995

S UCCESSFUL COMPANIES SEEKING new technologies to better support the development of mission-critical business processes will find an obvious candidate in object technology. Object technology has become synonymous with new, more competitive software-engineering practices. This is due in part to its potential to improve software reuse; in part to its ability to bridge the "semantic gap" between the business and IT domains; and also, in part, to the expectation that it will be the fundamental construct and paradigm in the coming era of open distributed computing.

Unfortunately, these high expectations for object technology are often left unfulfilled. This is because many companies underestimate the time and effort it takes to manage the transition successfully. A successful transition to object technology calls for a detailed, well-managed project; planning to have changes in business development, organizational development, and individual development all take place concurrently; and the implementation of new technologies and tools.

In this chapter we will introduce the principles and application of a technique that meets the requirements of such a project by taking a reengineering approach. The technique is a specialization of a general technique for business process reengineering with object technology.[1,2]

THE REENGINEERING TECHNOLOGY FRAMEWORK

A reengineering project using this technique (see Fig. 12-1) starts with a *reengineering directive*, a top-management directive that clearly states that reengineering is needed and why. The reengineering directive states that now is the time to act, and it presents arguments, supported by evidence, as to why the current software engineering process (SEP)[3] must be reengineered. It also serves as the first input to the reengineering team: a group of staff assigned by the company to run the entire reengineering project.

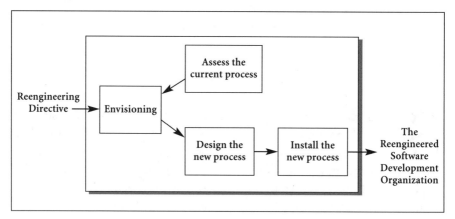

Figure 12-1. Reengineering a SEP.

The arguments of the reengineering directive, which must be very persuasive if they are to recruit the entire development organization successfully, are based on an analysis of: (1) new business requirements on the SEP, (2) deficiencies in the current SEP, and (3) consequences of *not* reengineering the SEP (the "inaction cost"). A typical example could be:

Our company's business processes change faster and have a shorter lifespan than ever before. This requires us to build our supporting IT systems faster than we currently do. We must therefore, within three years, reduce our average development cycle time, from requirements to system in production, to nine months.

The reengineering project then starts with an *envisioning* activity. The purpose of the envisioning activity is to formulate a vision of the new, reengineered SEP and its support environment, the SEPSE.[3] This results in requirements on the reengineered SEP including issues like:

- The workflows of the new SEP, such as requirements capture, analysis, and design.

- The deliverables of the new SEP, including documents and models (in this case object models).

- Reuse strategies and goals (e.g., "Reuse more than 80% of all specifications, models, and source code").

- The set of tools and integration technologies needed for the SEPSE.

- Metrics and measurable objectives for the new SEP/SEPSE.

During the envisioning activity, you may have to alternate between evaluating and testing new technologies such as object modeling tools and tool integration platforms, and refining the vision of the new SEP/SEPSE to find the best possible fit. This leads to a better understanding of the available technologies and where the reengineering project is going. It also ensures that the vision of the new SEP/SEPSE is realistic and can be implemented.

In parallel with the envisioning activity, you may also want to assess the current SEP, or, in other words, reverse-engineer it. The assessment will use a combination of standard assessment techniques, such as interviews and different inquiry methods, and will help the reengineering team build a common understanding of the current SEP: its cycle times, bottlenecks, and so forth. The current SEP may, for instance, be based on a structured analysis/structured design approach or an information engineering approach. The assessment also helps the reengineering team formulate adequate requirements for the new SEP.

When the specification of the new SEP/SEPSE has been completed and approved and the reengineering team has decided to proceed, the design work can start. Designing the new SEP/SEPSE, (see Fig. 12-2), is the most central activity of the entire reengineering project.

The design activity starts with the development of a process model, which describes the new software-development organization and the processes it offers from an outside point of view. The most interesting process in this model is the new SEP. Large software-development organizations, however, may very well offer several other processes, such as "tendering," "error handling," and "support." Here though, we will focus entirely on the new SEP.

The description of the SEP will vary in style and context, depending on the actual development organization and its specific situation and needs.

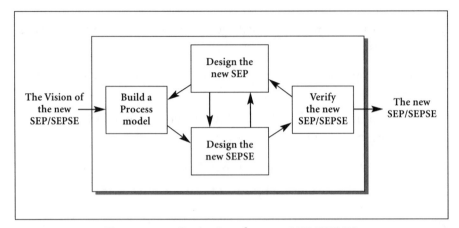

Figure 12-2. Designing the new SEP/SEPSE.

Things like the nature of the application domain (transaction processing, decision support, real-time), market segment (telecom, banking, process control), implementation technique (stand-alone, client/server, mainframe), and so on will all affect how this is done. But all SEP descriptions will most likely describe a common set of core workflows including requirements capture, design, implementation, and testing.

When the process model has been finalized and approved, the actual specification and design work begins.

The new SEP is designed by means of an object model defining all the components needed to build the SEP. These components are modeled as objects, representing both the various work roles of the new SEP and the various deliverables created and handled by the new SEP. Examples of work roles are a "requirements collector," "product orderer," "requirements analyst," "designer," and "tester." Examples of deliverables are "requirements specification," "use case model," "analysis model," "design model," "implementation model," which includes the source code, and "beta product." The object model also describes how the objects must interact to realize the SEP.

Concurrently, the new SEPSE is designed by integrating a set of tools, or tool components, on a suitable integration platform (e.g., Microsoft's COM platform). To achieve the best possible fit between the SEP and the SEPSE, it is crucial that they be allowed to affect one another.

Designing and implementing the new SEP/SEPSE need not be a major greenfield development effort. Such a clean-slate effort is too large, complex, and time consuming for any organization outside the software industry to justify, because it is outside its core business. Instead, you should procure the set of needed process and tool components, and then configure and integrate them to build the new SEP/SEPSE. This can be achieved using mature "framework-based" SEP/SEPSE technologies.[3] By framework based we mean complete generic designs that can be specialized to build organization-specific designs by means of configuration, parameterization, and extension.

Using a framework-based technology as the starting point represents a quick and straightforward way to implement the reengineered SEP/SEPSE, and it will also require a substantially smaller effort than the greenfield approach.

The resulting reengineered SEP has two types of descriptions: formal and workflow. The formal type, the type we have discussed so far, is intended primarily for the reengineering team itself. It is based on an object model complemented with interaction diagrams, state diagrams, and other specifications. The workflow type is intended for the developers, i.e., analysts, designers, programmers, and testers, who will participate in the SEP in their daily work.

The last design activity is to verify the new SEP/SEPSE, or rather the beta version of it, before it can be installed for general use throughout the company. This is normally done through one or more pilot projects in which the entire SEP/SEPSE is used and tested. If you find that the beta version does not fulfill the requirements, you must further iterate between design activities and piloting activities until you have verified that the reengineered SEP/SEPSE meets its goals. Now the first version of the SEP/SEPSE can be released by the reengineering team.

As Figure 12-1 shows, the next step is to install the new SEP/SEPSE within the targeted development organization. This is done through staffing, SEP workflow descriptions, SEPSE tools, training, and mentoring. In other words, the installation process requires a team of trainers, mentors, and consultants, supported by members of the reengineering team, to deliver a package of services to the staff of the new development organization. The entire installation process must, of course, be very well planned and executed to guarantee a successful transition to the new SEP/SEPSE.

When the installation has been finalized, the company has a reengineered software-development organization. This means that the company now also has a new and dramatically improved capability to develop the IT systems it needs to fulfill its business goals.

EXPERIENCES AND CONCLUSIONS

We have introduced object technology into several large organizations in Europe and North America for eight years now.

The framework-based SEP/SEPSE technology that has been used is Objectory, and a wide range of different approaches have been taken. In many cases, the SEP/SEPSE products were delivered to organizations without any training or mentoring, leaving the organization to find its own ways to succeed; in many other cases, organizations introduced the SEP/SEPSE products together with some initial training and mentoring services; but also, in several cases, organizations have introduced the SEP/SEPSE products as part of a total reengineering effort.

The conclusion, based on our accumulated experiences from these projects, is that organizations are far more successful with their transition to object technology when they take the reengineering approach as opposed to the other more traditional and commonly used approaches. We have also seen that the reengineering approach reduces the risk of failure to virtually zero.

In other words, by using a reengineering technique, such as the one described in this chapter, you stand a dramatically better chance of reaping the benefits of objects.

EDITOR'S NOTE

The SEP as mentioned here is for example manifested by the Rational Unified Process (RUP) product. RUP is a Web-enabled, searchable knowledge base that describes the development process through guidelines, templates, and tool mentors for a number of critical software-development activities. RUP is structured around the notions of *workers* (developer roles), *artifacts* (work products), and developer *activities* (refer to chapter entitled "Designing a Software Engineering Process"); these are then combined into workflow descriptions that capture the dynamics of the development process. Please refer to www.rational.com for more information on RUP.

References

1. I. Jacobson, M. Ericsson, and A. Jacobson. *The Object Advantage—Business Process Reengineering with Object Technology,* Addison–Wesley/ACM Press, Reading, MA, 1993.

2. I. Jacobson. "Business Process Reengineering with Object Technology," *Object Magazine,* 4(2): 16–22, 1994. (See chapter entitled "Business Process Reengineering with Object Technology.")

3. I. Jacobson and S. Jacobson. "Beyond Methods and CASE—The Software Engineering Process with Its Integral Support Environment," *Object Magazine,* 4(8): 24–30, 1994. (See chapter entitled "Beyond Methods and CASE: The Software Engineering Process with Its Integral Support Environment.")

13

DESIGNING A SOFTWARE ENGINEERING PROCESS

Ivar Jacobson & Sten Jacobson, JUNE 1995

I N OUR PREVIOUS CHAPTERS, "Beyond Methods and CASE: The Software
Engineering Process with Its Integral Support Environment" and
"Reengineering Your Software Engineering Process," we presented our
vision of SEP/SEPSE, the Software Engineering Process and its integral
Support Environment. We also discussed how to best introduce SEP/SEPSE
into an organization through reengineering.

In this chapter, we present what we believe is a new, revolutionary way
to design and use a SEP. This approach is an object-oriented business-
engineering technique based on use cases and objects.[1] It is vastly different
from the way most software development organizations work with methods
today.

Here our focus is the SEP, but in a forthcoming chapter titled "Designing
an Integrated Software Engineering Process Support Environment," we will
present related SEPSE tool design techniques.

WORKING WITH A SEP

Working with a SEP in an organization requires a set of different, collaborative roles and responsibilities, as illustrated in Figure 13-1.

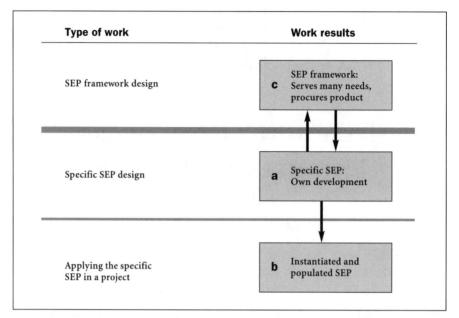

Figure 13-1. Working with a SEP in a development organization.

Our starting point is with an internal group that designs a SEP specific to the organization's needs and requirements (Fig. 13-1, box a).

First, the group develops a use-case model of the SEP itself. This outside view defines the SEP as a single use case, in the context of the organization and its external actors, i.e., users such as beta-customers or customers (Fig. 13-2). The organization could very well have other use cases, such as tendering or error handling, but here our focus is the SEP.

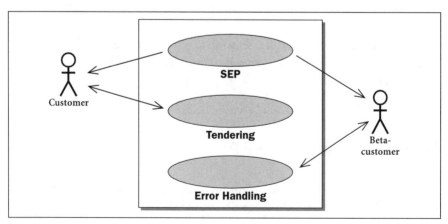

Figure 13-2. The outside view, i.e., a model of the software development organization and its users.

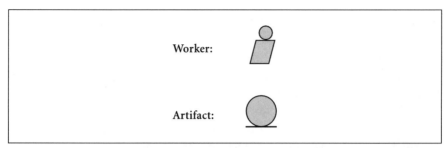

Figure 13-3. The two object types used to model the inside view of the development organization.

Next, the group develops object models representing inside views of the SEP. These object models capture the different workers (resource types) and artifacts (work products) of the SEP and the relations among them (Fig. 13-3). A worker represents a position that can be assigned to a person or a team within the organization. Artifacts represent work products that are created, changed, or used by workers. Workers are responsible for handling the artifacts. Such a worker-responsibility-artifact combination is, for example, when a Requirements Analyst worker is responsible for a use-case model artifact and, e.g., for maintaining and version-controlling the model.

We use associations to indicate such relationships. For example, Figure 13-4 shows a sample object model for the responsibilities during "requirements analysis." In this example, the Product Orderer is responsible for a Feature List, and will request the Requirements Analyst to develop a Requirements Specification based on this list. Upon request, the Requirements Analyst is responsible for developing both a Requirements Specification and a Use-Case Model based on the input from this list.

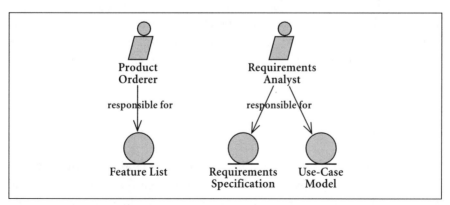

Figure 13-4. A model of the objects responsible for requirements analysis.

An object is given responsibilities that are suitable to allocate to the worker the object represents. This provides for a seamless mapping between object classes and workers as well as between object instances and individuals participating in the SEP. Individuals, in fact, may also have capabilities matching more than one worker, allowing them to populate several object instances in the SEP. In other cases—although it should be avoided—an object instance may also be populated by an inseparable group of individuals.

Attributes and attribute types can be used to model object properties such as object state, revision states, references to other objects, and instance identity. State-transition diagrams can be used to describe the object's life cycles.

An object's responsibilities can also be described informally in the SEP. For example, a Designer's responsibilities are to know when an analysis model is done and ready to use, know when the analysis model changes its revision state, perform design, know when an implementation is done, and receive a change proposal. A Designer also collaborates with other objects by means of informing when a design is done, requesting an implementation to the design model, proposing change, and disclosing when the design model has changed its revision state. At any point in time, a Designer has a specific state, which represents where it is in its life cycle.

The description of a worker's total responsibility consists of two different parts, representing two different views of the worker. One part constitutes a formal description of the responsibilities of the worker (as discussed above); the other part consists of activity descriptions of the worker. The activity descriptions define, in detail, how the worker's responsibilities are to be carried out. A worker, therefore, offers process support directly targeted for the resource type it represents. A process participant, i.e., an individual populating an instance of a worker, will therefore get a detailed activity description matching his or her responsibilities. This liberates individual process participants from having to deal with the entire process and lets them concentrate on their own responsibilities. Indeed, the entire SEP is of little if any interest to individuals other than the SEP designers themselves.

Generalization-Specialization

A specific SEP (Fig. 13-1, box a) is actually a class and could therefore be instantiated and used by more than one organization or more than one project, as long as they share the same needs. Generalization and specialization of a specific SEP allows one to adapt it to many organizations with entirely different needs (Fig. 13-1, box c). Generalization results in an abstract, generic, reusable SEP framework. In the future, development organizations could buy such frameworks from external vendors and then specialize them to suit their specific needs, offering substantial improvements in lead-time, quality, and cost.

To generalize a specific SEP to a SEP framework, one creates more generic superclasses for each class. In Figure 13-5, Designer (in C++ and RDBMS) is generalized in two steps, first to Designer (in C++), then to Designer. As illustrated, one might then define other alternative specializations of these classes, such as for Java and ODBMS.

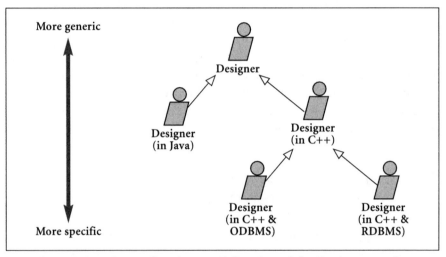

Figure 13-5. Generalization-specialization of the Designer worker using inheritance.

Both specific and framework-based SEPs are products and must be handled accordingly. SEP designers must therefore release and support their SEP products under strict configuration management and version control.

SEP PROJECT DYNAMICS

A project is an instantiated and populated SEP (Fig. 13-1, box b). It begins when qualified individuals populate the instantiated object model; that is, when the project manager allocates human resources using work orders or contracts. In addition, the project manager also identifies the required artifacts, which may either already exist, such as the requirements specifications and the project plan, or that must be created by the SEP, such as analysis models and design documents.

The projects plan should define, among other things, a schedule for the population of all the objects, their responsibilities, and individual time constraints for things like start times, review times, and expected completion. As a project progresses, some instances of workers will be staffed and others will complete their life cycles. So, the number of collaborating worker instances (individuals and teams) will vary over time just as they do in an executing object-oriented system.

At the same time, the project will create new artifact instances. These become a set of persistent deliverables, i.e., the real assets produced by the project. To facilitate the persistence of artifacts, the project must have a repository.

As we described in previous columns, the process of instantiating and populating a specific SEP is a reengineering effort. Such reengineering efforts would of course also promote substantial reuse and consequently save significant amounts of time and money if the organization started with a SEP framework to design the specific SEP.

TAILORING THE PROCESS— USE OF SEP FRAMEWORKS

SEP designers at a software development organization can start from scratch by defining a new, specific SEP, an envisioning activity that is done by describing the specific SEP use case in detail. The SEP designers can then design the SEP by means of object modeling. However, to do this cost-efficiently, we envision that they will specialize the objects, i.e., classes, contained in a suitable SEP framework, which is procured from an external framework vendor.

SEP framework designers, on the other had, work for a framework vendor. They design a generic SEP that reflects their best understanding of the common needs of a vertical market, such as developers of banking or process-control systems; or an entire horizontal market, such as developers of PC-based client/server systems. The more horizontal the targeted market, the more generalized, or abstract, the SEP framework must be.

Therefore, we also envision that SEP frameworks representing several levels of abstraction will be offered on future SEP markets. Furthermore, the Unified Process is currently targeted for a fairly horizontal market, but can be further specialized for more vertical markets.

Experiences

We have used these techniques to define and design SEP framework components since 1987.[2] Among other things, this work has resulted in Objectory (consequently, now called the Rational Unified Process), which is a framework-based commercial product offering a set of SEP/SEPSE components.

When we started this work, we built a model of a generalized SEP consisting of more than 20 collaborating objects. We called those objects "factories" because at the time we were using the software factory metaphor to express our vision of a SEP framework. The factories were specialized by means of inheritance and fully described using a formal specification language, SDL.[3]

Based on our own very positive experiences, we are convinced these techniques will revolutionize the way most successful organizations work in the future.

We also believe they will change the way organizations design and build automating tools, from today's CASE, process-enactment, and workflow tools to tomorrow's SEPSE tools. The driving force is the potential of SEPSE to offer substantially higher levels of usability and productivity than today's tools can offer. This is sufficient material for another column, however, so we will come back to it another time.

The Object Advantage

Objects have some very powerful features that bring important benefits to SEP design:

- Designers, engineers, and managers can all understand object models.

- Object models are flexible and can directly map to artifacts.

- With objects, you can build a very detailed process model.

- Objects are very suitable for modeling collaborative processes.

- Objects have well-defined interfaces, so responsibilities can be easily integrated.

- Object models capture concurrency among process components.

- Objects capture semantics very naturally, prerequisite to automation via SEPSE.

- Version control of object process components is straightforward.

- Objects are easy to specialize and generalize via inheritance.

REFERENCES AND SUGGESTED READING

1. I. Jacobson, M. Ericsson, and A. Jacobson. *The Object Advantage—Business Process Reengineering with Object Technology,* Addison–Wesley/ACM Press, Reading, MA, 1993.

2. I. Jacobson. "Object-Oriented Development in an Industrial Environment," Proceedings of OOPSLA'87, *SIGPLAN Notices,* 22 (12): 183–191, 1987.

3. C.C.I.T.T., Facscicle vi. 11, "Functional Specification and Description Language," (SDL), Rec. z.100–z.104, Geneva, 1984.

4. I. Jacobson et al. *Object-Oriented Software Engineering—A Use Case Driven Approach,* Addison–Wesley, Reading, MA, 1992.

14

DESIGNING AN INTEGRATED SOFTWARE ENGINEERING PROCESS SUPPORT ENVIRONMENT

Ivar Jacobson & Sten Jacobson, SEPTEMBER 1995

IN OUR PREVIOUS CHAPTERS, "Beyond Methods and CASE: The Software Engineering Process…"[1] and "Designing a Software Engineering Process,"[2] we have presented our vision of the software-engineering process (SEP), its support environment (SEPSE), and an object-oriented business-engineering technique[3] for designing and working with a SEP. Now we describe how to combine this approach with a similar object-oriented software-engineering technique[4] to design and implement a SEPSE.

Among other things, this approach provides seamlessness and full traceability from the SEP business models to the SEPSE models (see Figure 14-1 for an example). This revolutionary approach to SEPSE design leads to an integrated tool environment that stands a good chance of delivering the productivity, quality, and lead-time improvements that generations of CASE tools have long promised.

In this chapter, our focus is SEPSE design techniques, but we will briefly outline some important aspects of SEPSE implementation.

We also hope to scotch, once and for all, the myth that an efficient support environment can be built without a well-defined software engineering process.

SEPSE Design Starts from SEP Models

As we illustrate in Figure 14-1, you can use techniques based on use cases and objects to develop a business model of a software-development organization. Developing this model involves identifying:

- The set of business processes the organization offers to its users, including the SEP and other processes such as tendering and error handling.

- The organization's users, customers, and beta-customers.

- The work roles, or workers (such as Product Orderer and Requirements Analyst in Figure 14-1), and artifacts (work products such as Requirements list and Use-case model in Figure 14-1) handled through or produced by the business process and relations among them. The set of SEP workers and their responsibilities is the starting point for defining a corresponding set of SEPSE use cases. For each worker, you identify a directly corresponding user, or SEPSE actor. For each worker responsibility, you define use cases the SEPSE must offer. And for each artifact, you define its direct representation as a SEPSE entity object.

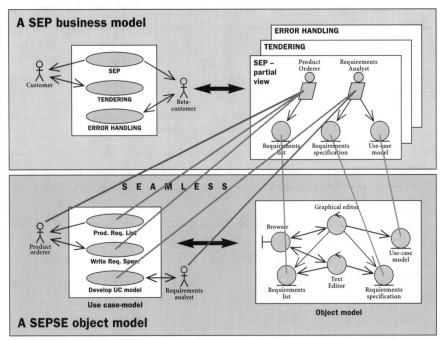

Figure 14-1. The relations between SEP and SEPSE models.

In Figure 14-1, the SEPSE actors are Product Orderer and Requirements Analyst. The actors' responsibilities, as defined in the corresponding SEP workers, translates to the SEPSE use cases: produce a requirements list, write a requirements specification, and develop a use case model. Defining these SEPSE use cases correctly is a very important design task. As Figure 14-2 illustrates, the principle is that the total set of responsibilities of an SEP worker, in this example the responsibilities R1, R2, and R3, results in a corresponding set of SEPSE use cases, in this case UC1, UC2, and UC3.

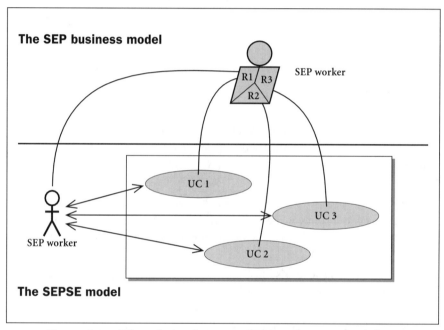

Figure 14-2. The relation between SEP worker responsibilities and SEPSE use cases.

The goal is to define SEPSE use cases that automate the SEP in the most efficient way. To achieve this, you must either have a good knowledge of available SEPSE implementation technologies or use prototyping. It is also important that the SEP and SEPSE designs are allowed to mutually affect each other.

Once use cases are defined, you proceed to develop the SEPSE object model. The result is an ideal SEPSE object model, as depicted in Figure 14-3. In this example, the SEPSE actor System Designer is associated with a set of SEPSE objects that support three example use cases: develop analysis model, develop design model, and write source code.

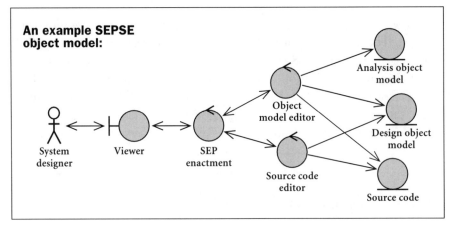

Figure 14-3. An example SEPSE object model.

The SEPSE objects here map directly to SEPSE components including a viewer, SEP enactment tool, object-modeling editor, and source-code editor. The artifacts in this example are an analysis-object model, design-object model, and source code. The SEP enactment tool represents a unique SEPSE feature as it coordinates the right set of collaborating modeling tools and artifacts for any given SEP task, i.e., it drives the integrated SEPSE environment for the SEPSE user, or SEP participant. For example, when the System Designer has generated source code from a design model, the SEP enactment tool will recognize this and provide an appropriate editor loaded with this source code.

By developing these kinds of object models for every SEPSE use case, you define all the responsibilities the SEPSE objects, i.e., the integrated tools, must fulfill. As we have discussed previously, the starting point for a SEPSE design may be a SEP framework, not a specific SEP. If so, the result would be a SEPSE framework that could not be implemented, instantiated, and used as such. Rather, such a framework would serve as the starting point for building a specific SEPSE to fit the needs of a specific SEP.

The task of building and instantiating a specific SEPSE should be undertaken by a reengineering team that has the responsibility of building specific SEPs/SEPSEs for a development organization.[5] The reengineering team need not start with a clean slate, but instead could specialize and integrate procured, framework-based SEPSE components.[*]

---

[*] This is how the Rational Suite of development tools emerged. Please refer to www.rational.com for more information.

SEPSE DESIGN FEATURES

Designing and implementing a SEPSE as described leads to a highly usable, efficient, integrated tool environment that becomes an integral and inseparable part of the SEP.

Two important features of such a SEPSE design are usability and ease of collaboration, i.e., multirole support.[†]

The usability of SEPSE tools is guaranteed to be very high because all SEPSE users, modeled as actors, and all SEPSE functional requirements, modeled as use cases, are derived directly from the SEP business model. This is exactly the approach you would use to develop any mission-critical information system that supports a specific business process.

Examples of collaboration, or multirole aspects, explicitly defined by a SEP/SEPSE design are worker responsibilities, traceability links, work-product ownership, work-product version control, interfaces, and relations between SEP workers.

Using a SEP model for SEPSE design allow us to define, for example, how one worker may base his own work on the work of another, avoiding unclear responsibilities and relationships that could easily deadlock a project, causing undesirable delays.

Figure 14-4 shows how the workers *use case designer* and *object designer* collaborate efficiently. The use case designer develops a use case description, including a set of interaction diagrams, for a specific use case and, as a result, also creates a set of object specifications based on these use case descriptions. When implementing the corresponding object, the object designer uses these object specifications to write the source code. In other words, the use case designer specifies the object and has full ownership of the object specification, and the object designer implements the object and has full ownership of the object implementation.

By releasing and storing both object specifications and object implementations, with full version control, in, e.g., a common repository, the use case designer can release many object specifications and the object designer can implement the corresponding objects without anyone blocking the other with a clear definition of their respective responsibilities.

---

† This can also be recognized as one of the fundamental ideas behind the Rational Suite of development tools, and its slogan: unifying software teams. Please refer to www.rational.com for more information.

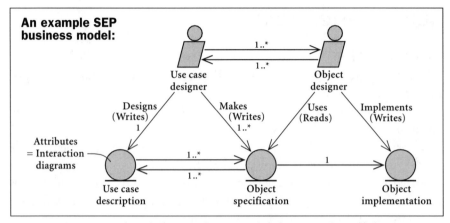

Figure 14-4. A detailed SEP object model showing the collaboration between a use case designer and an object designer.

The SEPSE models will also define and enforce consistency between object specifications and implementations.

SEPSE IMPLEMENTATION

Implementing a SEPSE involves fulfilling requirements derived from two orthognal aspects: the SEPSE design and the available implementation technologies (such as tools, tool components, and integration platforms). A common misconception is that tool builders can use a single, generic process description to build tools suitable for different development organizations building any type of application. This is a total misunderstanding!

You must begin with a well-defined SEP if you are to build a truly usable SEPSE, much as you must have a clear understanding of a specific business process to build an efficient information system to support it. SEPSE development is just a special case of information system development.

To implement a SEPSE design, you compose different technologies of your choosing, including available tools, tool components, an integration platform technology, a system architecture, a version control system, and a common archive or repository.

Today, this primarily involves integrating available tools on top of a common operating system, with or without specific tool-integration mechanisms. Because there is no widely accepted integration standard, this requires a lot of "glue" software and transformations between different tool representations.

A SEPSE implemented this way typically use a simple file format to share information among tools. In these systems, the file level rarely represents anything at a finer granularity than a subsystem, or even a complete system.

We believe this cumbersome and coarse-grain approach will be replaced by a more efficient object-oriented approach such as the one we describe. In the future, SEPSEs will be implemented by configuring and assembling object-oriented frameworks, i.e., abstract subsystems or "microtools." SEPSE frameworks, which correspond directly to SEPSE objects, will virtually plug into and integrate with other SEPSE frameworks in a highly standardized integration infrastructure, such as the Object Management Architecture of the Object Management Group (OMG). Furthermore, underlying metamodeling techniques will support the need for flexibility, portability, and customizability. Future metamodel-based SEPSEs will, for example, let users either choose among different modeling constructs (or methods if you will) or define their own including notations and semantics.‡ A global, object-oriented repository that supports a granularity as fine as a single object or lower will support information sharing, version control, and configuration management.

Progressive tool vendors are already partly using this forward-looking scenario.

Some Key Aspects of SEPSE Implementation

There are a few key aspects of our SEPSE implementation techniques and technologies that are worthy of elaboration. By limiting the aspects we mention here, we do not mean to imply that all other aspects of building an efficient SEPSE are less important, only that they are not our focus here.

Usability

A SEPSE must have a truly *usable* user interface, in a wider sense than just a GUI. Use cases have proven to be a very powerful way to enforce use-centered, not user-centered, UI design. We believe future SEPSEs must have

---

‡ This is exactly what can be done in the Rational Suite SEPSE since it is based upon the Unified Modeling Language (UML); users can easily extend the modeling language by introducing their own stereotypes. Please refer to www.rational.com for more information.

a single homogenized user interface, like a central *superviewer*, that uses dynamic links to relate relevant tools and pieces of information for any given SEP task. Navigation, seamlessness, and traceability will be supported by hyperlinks and traceability links implemented with tool components such as browsers, diagram editors, and query editors. Such a superviewer could also be called an "active form," akin to compound-document technologies such as OLE and OpenDoc.

CONSISTENCY AND COMPLETENESS

Because our approach begins with a well-defined and semantically rich SEP, the resulting SEPSE rests on a full-set underlying semantic model to support checking for consistency, completeness, and syntactical correctness.

MULTIROLE SUPPORT

Because the SEP design defines all aspects of worker collaboration, the implementation of these in the SEPSE is straightforward. One aspect of this is support for configuration management and version control. Another aspect is support for ownership by means of, e.g., security and authorization control, which can be implemented directly, say, in an OMG Common Object Request Broker Architecture (CORBA)-based SEPSE using the OMG's common object services for security.

LAYERED ARCHITECTURE

Figure 14-5 shows a SEPSE architecture that integrates tools of tool components using available integration-platform technologies. No such standards have yet achieved widespread acceptance in the market, but some—including HP Softbench, DCE Toolkit, OMG's CORBA, OLE, and OpenDoc—could be suitable infrastructures for building SEPSEs.§ In any case, the architecture would be layered and form the operating system from middleware to common

---

§ Some versions of the Rational Suite SEPSE are built upon Microsoft's COM component technology, which is a refinement of "OLE" as mentioned here; please refer to www.rational.com for more information.

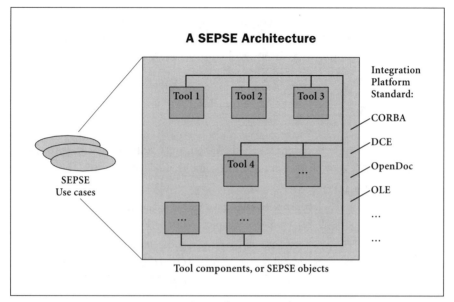

Figure 14-5. The architecture of a SEPSE.

facilities, to the specific SEPSE objects. Well-defined interfaces would con-
nect the layers. Object-modeling techniques allow us to formalize and enforce
these architectural layers by means of explicit contracts.

A GLOBAL OBJECT-ORIENTED REPOSITORY

This is one of the most complex issues of a SEPSE implementation, calling
for, among other things, a common, underlying object-oriented semantic
model for sharing information between SEPSE components. We will not deal
with this in any depth here, but rather just mention that a SEP/SEPSE model
will serve as a very powerful input to defining such a semantic model.

SEPSE EXPERIENCES

We have used this approach to develop and implement SEPSE components
since 1987. Among other things, this work has resulted in Objectory SE, a
framework-based support environment that offers a set of tightly integrated
SEPSE components supporting the Objectory SEP.

Having experienced the power of this approach, not the least in building many user-specific SEPSEs, we feel that this is the way industry leaders will go to develop competitive, integrated support environments in the future.||

REFERENCES

1. I. Jacobson and S. Jacobson. "Beyond Methods and CASE," *Object Magazine*, 4(8): 24–30, 1995. (See chapter entitled "Beyond Methods and CASE: The Software Engineering Process…")

2. I. Jacobson and S. Jacobson. "Designing a Software Engineering Process," *Object Magazine*, 5(3): 79–81, 1995. (See chapter entitled "Designing a Software Engineering Process.")

3. I. Jacobson, M. Ericsson, and A. Jacobson. *The Object Advantage—Business Process Reengineering with Object Technology*, Addison–Wesley/ACM Press, Reading, MA, 1993.

4. I. Jacobson et al. *Object-Oriented Software Engineering—A Use Case Driven Approach*, Addison–Wesley, Reading, MA, 1992.

5. I. Jacobson and S. Jacobson. "Reengineering Your Software Engineering Process," *Object Magazine*, 5(1): 12–16, 1995. (See chapter entitled "Reengineering Your Software Engineering Process.")

|| The bottom line is that the Rational Software Corporation used the approach as outlined here when they designed the Rational Suite of development tools; please refer to www.rational.com for more information.

15

BUILDING YOUR OWN
PROCESS BY SPECIALIZING
A PROCESS FRAMEWORK

Ivar Jacobson & Sten Jacobson, NOVEMBER–DECEMBER 1995

E VERY SOFTWARE-DEVELOPMENT organization is unique and, consequently, there is no such thing as a single method that fits the needs of every organization. In fact, we are convinced that every single product line needs its own unique method to accomplish its task in the best possible way. This is true, at least, once the development organization has "matured," that is, once it has completed an initial learning phase.

Indeed, a mature organization will not settle on a specific method. Instead, it will rely on a well-defined process to maximize its performance.

WHAT IS THE DIFFERENCE BETWEEN
A METHOD AND A PROCESS?

A method as we described in the chapter entitled "Beyond Methods and CASE: The Software Engineering Process..."[1] is a set of notations and general systematic descriptions of some development tasks such as object-oriented analysis and design. Typically, it is described in a textbook that describes the state of the work of its originating methodologist, the guru. However, a method typically does not guide developers on how to use it to develop a commercial product. A process, on the other hand, is a rigorously engineered product designed by software-engineering practitioners for use in commercial development organizations. It defines how individuals with different competencies undertake all the separate, well-defined roles and responsibilities necessary to develop software. And it defines exactly how those roles and tasks (or workflows) should collaborate.

A process has an underlying architecture of collaborating workflows and modeling constructs. Its concepts, semantics, and syntax are defined rigorously and in detail.

Henceforth we will move away from talking about "method" and "methodology" in favor of "process," which we will use in the specific sense of "software-engineering process" or SEP. And since we always assume that a SEP support environment (SEPSE), in the form of a set of integrated tools or tool components, is an integral part of a SEP, our use of "process" will also encompass the complete SEP/SEPSE.*

A COMMERCIAL SOFTWARE DEVELOPMENT ORGANIZATION IS A SOFTWARE ENGINEERING BUSINESS...

A very powerful way of describing a commercial software development organization is to regard it as a "system" of a "software engineering business," as we will call it here. Furthermore, by using an object-oriented business modeling technique[4] a software engineering business can be described as a system consisting of a set of collaborating objects grouped into subsystems. Hence, a software engineering business is an engineered system described in terms of an object model.

Examples of software engineering business objects are system analyst, use case designer, requirements specification, and design model. These objects are actually classes that can be generalized, specialized, instantiated, and populated using straightforward OO techniques.

Examples of software engineering business workflows are requirements analysis, design, implementation, and testing.

---

* A process is always developed concurrently with tool support: see the SEP/SEPSE approach as discussed in the chapters "Beyond Methods and CASE: The Software Engineering Process,"[1] "Designing a Software Engineering Process,"[2] and "Designing an Integrated Software Engineering Process Support."[3] To develop a process without tool support is just an academic activity.

…And a Specific Process Is a Development Case of the Software Engineering Business

A process represents one way of using the software engineering business, i.e., the system. More clearly, a process is a specific business use case of the software engineering business!

This is a very powerful way to look at the process of a software development organization—as a use case of the software engineering business.

We have used this approach ourselves for more than eight years now, and, when doing so, we use a specialized business use case concept called the "development case." A development case represents one path through the collaborating workflows of the software engineering business. In other words, a development case is a specific process optimized for fulfilling the specific tasks, as required, of a software engineering business; a development case is a tailored version of the process.

Can Any Process Be Defined as a Development Case of a Software Engineering Business?

Yes and, in fact, so can any method or methodology discussed in the industry today! Different methods such as OMT, OOSE, Booch, Fusion, and Shlaer/Mellor can be defined as development cases of a software engineering business. But that is not all! By implementing a method as a development case, you empower the method to become a full-fledged process.†

The different methods—and different processes in general—may of course use slightly different sets of workflows, at least on the object level. At the same time, however, a given software engineering business could very well offer several different development cases, representing different paths through its workflows, very much the same way as a software system can offer many different use cases from its set of objects.

On a more detailed level, but still within one development case, there is also a great deal of variability allowing every single instance of a process to

---

† The ideas from many approaches, such as from OMT, OOSE, Booch, Fusion, and Shlaer/Mellor, have been integrated in the Unified Process.

make its own unique choices by means of, say, specific documents, notations, and work steps to be used.

AS WITH OBJECT-ORIENTED SYSTEMS GENERALLY, A SOFTWARE ENGINEERING BUSINESS CAN BE GENERALIZED INTO A REUSABLE FRAMEWORK

As we stated initially, every organization and product line is unique; at the same time they all have a lot in common! Solving this dilemma calls for a technique that allows us to reuse all the common assets of a software engineering business, at the same time as we can build specific, or concrete, software engineering businesses without compromise.

So far, we have discussed how a software engineering business can be regarded as a system with a set of collaborating workflows. Now, to solve our little dilemma, we would like to bring this one step further by describing a solution, i.e., a technique, that allows us to define a wide range of specific software engineering businesses capable of offering an even wider range of specific development cases.

This is achieved by developing a software engineering business "framework" that can be specialized to become different concrete software engineering businesses.

Such a framework consists of a generalized, or abstract, software engineering business that consequently consist of a set of abstract classes and subsystems. This software engineering business framework is, in other words, an integrated set of generic workflows that offers a highly modularized, very flexible starting point for building concrete software engineering businesses.

Building a concrete software engineering business in this way is much more efficient than starting with a clean slate,

Powerful object-oriented concepts, such as patterns, frameworks, and layered architectures, offer all the technical tools needed. Concrete software engineering businesses are designed by means of specializing the framework; and this is done, technically, by means of inheriting and extending the abstract classes and subsystems of the framework.

CAN I BUILD ANY CONCRETE SOFTWARE ENGINEERING BUSINESS FROM THE FRAMEWORK?

Yes! With a software engineering business framework like this, one can define a wide range of substantially different processes. We have in fact seen that it is quite feasible to build a single framework that can be specialized to offer development cases that support, and in fact also empower, many different methods, in that they can offer, e.g., OMT-like, OOSE-like, and Fusion-like processes.

Specializing a software engineering business framework this way is a very straightforward task. It always starts by defining a specific development case, i.e., the required process that at the same time constitute the requirements specification for the concrete software engineering business.

As different lines of business mature, we also expect to see industry-specific process frameworks, say, for developing insurance or banking systems, and domain-specific process frameworks for the development of client/server or network-management systems. Building concrete software engineering businesses based on such frameworks is even more efficient!

WE HAVE EXPERIENCED THE POWER OF PROCESS FRAMEWORKS!

Over the years, we have defined a large number of development cases for many different organizations, i.e., software engineering businesses. We did this using Objectory, which is architectured to explicitly support both the definition and implementation of specific development cases.

To facilitate a quick start for organizations still at an early point on their learning curve, we also used a set of predefined default development cases such as "PremiumAnalysis and Design," "LiteAnalysis and Design," and "Requirements Analysis." These development cases represent different software engineering business stereotypes and they can in many cases constitute a good starting point and a reasonable trade-off between detailed specific needs and time.

Defining a specific development case is normally and best done up-front, when a new organization or a new project is about to start. Because the whole approach is very straightforward, it has proven to be a very natural way of working even for novices. Defining a specific development case this way also means that the organization is prompted to make several important process/method design decisions up-front, where they belong, as opposed to letting projects get stuck or delayed due to too many deviations caused by unresolved process issues.

As this approach is well-defined and repeatable, it also offers the necessary predictability for project planning, time and cost estimation, and, most importantly, full management control!

REFERENCES AND SUGGESTED READING

1. I. Jacobson and S. Jacobson. "Beyond Methods and CASE—The Software Engineering Process with Its Integral Support Environment," *Object Magazine* 4(8): 24–30, 1995. (See chapter entitled "Beyond Methods and CASE: The Software Engineering Process...")

2. I. Jacobson and S. Jacobson. "Designing a Software Engineering Process," *Object Magazine*, 5(3): 79–81, 1995. (See chapter entitled "Designing a Software Engineering Process.")

3. I. Jacobson and S. Jacobson. "Designing an Integrated SEPSE," *Object Magazine*, 5(5): 93–96, 1995. (See chapter entitled "Designing an Integrated Software Engineering Process Support Environment.")

4. I. Jacobson et al. *Object-Oriented Software Engineering—A Use Case Driven Approach*, Addison–Wesley, Reading, MA, 1992.

5. I. Jacobson and S. Jacobson. "Reengineering Your Software Engineering Process," *Object Magazine*, 5(1): 12–16, 1995. (See chapter entitled "Reengineering Your Software Engineering Process.")

6. I. Jacobson, M. Ericsson, and A. Jacobson. *The Object Advantage—Business Process Reengineering with Object Technology*, Addison–Wesley, Reading, MA, 1994.

7. J. Odell. "Introduction to Method Engineering," *Object Magazine*, 5(5): 68–72,91, 1995.

In Ivar's Words

Q: Why can't we use your books to design real software ?

A: The Unified Process book is a textbook to be used for education. It is intended to introduce people to the software engineering process; it presents a number of modeling techniques and a number of method components. But to use it for real product development it needs to be "productified" (or "processified"). This is when you take a method from being a textbook to being a SEP/SEPSE. You can either do it by yourself or buy it from a SEP/SEPSE vendor.

The situation we have today in the software world is that people and organizations rely too much on individuals, whether these individuals are excellent programmers or methodologists. This is an obvious sign of the immaturity of our business compared to other engineering disciplines such as mechanical, construction, or civil engineering. We must all work toward changing this situation. This change should be lead by practitioners and "pragmaticians" and not by individuals writing books. I said at a panel at OOPSLA'94 "It is time for you, the practitioners to take the command and leave us, the methodologists, behind you in creating your standards and your engineering approaches to software engineering. Release us, the methodologists, from this work and let us do what we are good at and what we have been good at in the past, to push the technology forward." At the same panel, in which Booch, Henderson-Sellers, Mellor, Rumbaugh, and Wirfs-Brock also participated, I also said: "Object modeling has been carried out for more than 20 years today. There is a 15-year-old international standard, CCITT-SDL, that specifies many of the things you use today to do object modeling, such as interaction diagrams and state transition diagrams. So it is time to create a standard for object modeling. But this new standard will be developed by practitioners and not by methodologists."

In an interview in a Swedish software paper a couple of weeks ago I said: "One must beware of having a simplified view on competition between the different object-oriented methods. This is not a horse race. ... Different from a horse race, ... the competition between object methods will not finish with a winner and the rest being loosers. The users and their management will most certainly take the command and they will not let a bunch of gurus control them. The users will want to have access to a variety of techniques, e.g., from Shlaer/Mellor, from Rumbaugh, from Coleman, from Booch, and maybe from myself. Not until we have got there, can we say that the software industry have gained some extent of maturity." And a way to get there is to push the SEP/SEPSE idea forward.

Q: What should software methodologists do then?

A: I think we should continue to push new technology. Let me give my personal view on methodologists.

We should write papers, books, and give tutorials and presentations to stimulate the flora of software engineering ideas. Some may have more impact than others on what people will be using. But no single individual will alone form a standard being used by the software industry for the whole life cycle. Knowing that—and I think everyone agrees to this—I suggest that methodologists should not spend their valuable time in integrating all men's goods into their own context. There is a tendency now, related to the idea of second-generation methods, to write books and integrate good ideas from other methodologies. In some situations it may be worthwhile to do so (if the book is going to be used at universities for basic education). But in most cases it just creates confusion and references would be more proper. Particularly when people just rewrite what already has been well written just to make it fit in their own book. I have also seen a tendency to integrate stuff in methods books just to cover all areas of software engineering. People who have very little experience more than theoretical include some pages on things like version control and configuration management, testing, metrics, project management, reviewing, etc. Again it may be well motivated for textbooks in basic software engineering. But I don't think it is fair to say that these superficial descriptions of other people's work should be part of the adopting methodologist's own work. Beware of "method elephantiasis"!

Instead, I think that practitioners should put it all together. These are the only people who have real experience and they are less biased to any particular idea. The result of their work should result in a SEP/SEPSE according to our vision.

Q: What do you think about "second-generation methods"?

A: The term is used to denote that a second-generation method is based on a first-generation method. Is that good? No, because,

1. *Is there any method that is not based on any other method? My early object-oriented design method developed in 1967 was heavily based on a design method (at least ten years old at that time) used within Ericsson to design telecommunication systems. I used ideas like object diagrams, interface specifications (to define interfaces between objects), interaction diagrams and the documentation templates. Furthermore the whole design process in 1967 was based on this earlier method. Basically new was primarily that the 1967 method was adapted to software systems and not systems implemented with electromechanics!*

   You can take any other method and you will find similar relationships to earlier works. One of the most popular methods, OMT, is probably an even better example of a method based on methods. The uniqueness of that method is how it has been composed of other people's work.

   To further develop methods based on other methods is most natural and that will continue to happen.

2. *If we adopt the term second-generation method, what will then a third-generation method be? Would the second generation be the last generation? I don't see what the next generation in this dimension would look like.*

3. *We already have a need to express versions or generations of a method. Booch talks about his second-generation method. Rumbaugh will now come out with his second-generation OMT. This use of the term second-generation makes sense. Personally, I use the term generation to talk about an evolution that is incompatible to an earlier issue. My second-generation OOSE method was developed 1978, the third in 1987 (OOPSLA'87), and the fourth in 1992 (the OOSE book). Later generations were incompatible with earlier. I use versions to talk about changes that are compatible with an earlier issue. Versions are primarily related to products, such as software engineering processes, and not to textbooks like method books.*

4. *Finally, it is by no means proved that a "second-generation method" would be better than what it is based on. I have seen examples where*

a method based on other methods has patched ideas from other methods without in depth working through all the difficulties in doing so, such as removing unnecessary seams, resolving semantic incompatibilities.

Q: What will happen to the CASE industry? Will it die?

A: No, certainly not, but I believe it will be restructured. CASE vendors must make a choice. They cannot any longer just ship tools and have their customers just rely on a number of textbooks or develop their own process. They have to go into another business and I can see two choices. Larger successful CASE-companies will move into the SEP/SEPSE area and provide their customers with both process and tool support. Smaller companies with a very good tool technology could focus on developing tool components, which then are used and integrated by others to build SEP/SEPSE environments.

Q: What do you think about beta-testing when is comes to development processes?

A: We have learnt that beta-testing can be just a review of the process. For example, this is how the Rational Unified Process is "tested" before general availability. Instead we think that thanks to the iterative approach, one of the first iterations will exercise the whole process and make that a kind of "test" that is specific to the organization employing the process.

PART 5:
USE-CASE
ENGINEERING

———

USE CASES ARE POWERFUL since they serve many essential purposes during software development. First, use cases help us define contracts regarding the software that is to be developed; contracts that need to be signed by the ones who ordered the software development effort. Then their use cases drive the whole development effort. That is, they are useful as planning instruments; they help us define crisp areas of responsibilities within the development team; they help us design and architect the system by proposing classes and sub-systems; and they help us test a system by proposing various test cases.

And there is more! In this part we learn about the fundamental notion of use cases, and their usefulness in general. We can read about how to realize use cases by analyzing and designing them in object models of a system; and find some discussions regarding the formalization of use cases.

PART 5:
USE CASE ENGINEERING

—

16

BASIC USE-CASE MODELING

Ivar Jacobson, JULY-AUGUST 1994

HE USE-CASE MODEL is a means to communicate requirements between customers and developers and to structure object models into manageable views. We advocate that developers model use cases explicitly at the very start of a software development project. In every project, no matter what method, use cases must be identified—eventually, more or less clearly—if the project is to be successful. At the latest, they are identified during integration testing or when the user manual is written—activities that are, by nature, use-case oriented. However, by identifying them early, during system specification, the entire development will benefit.

In this article, I describe the use-case construct and different modeling techniques associated with use cases during different activities in the development work. The description is general in the sense that the techniques are applicable to most object modeling techniques and not delimited to a particular object-oriented design method.

INTRODUCTION

System development is a process of model building. This is true also for object-oriented development, which typically begins with a requirements model and ends with an implementation model. Object models include details such as the internal structure of the objects, their associations to each other, and how the objects dynamically interact and invoke behavior of one another.

This information is of course necessary to design and build a system, but it is not enough in order to communicate requirements. It does not capture task domain knowledge, and it is difficult to verify that an object model really corresponds to the system that should be built.

The very first system model we build must therefore be comprehensible both to people inside the development organization—analysts, designers, implementers, and testers—and to people outside—customers, users, and sales people. Object models are too complex for this purpose: A real but still rather small system (one that takes two to five man-years to build) consists of about 100 objects. A larger system (10–100 man-years) consists of several hundred or several thousand objects. And some systems have 10,000–100,000 objects!

We therefore do not think the very first model of a complex system should be an object model. Instead, it should be a model that describes the system, its environment, and how the system and its environment are related. In other words, it should describe the system as it appears from the outside; i.e., a black-box view.

Use cases are a way to structure this black-box view. A use case is just what it sounds like, it is a way to use the system. Users interact with a system by interacting with its use cases. Taken together, a system's use cases represent everything users can do with it. For a more comprehensive presentation of use cases, see Jacobson.[1]

"Use cases" resemble "use scenarios" as used by some authors in the object-oriented world. However, there are several differences, syntactic as well as semantic. Scenarios normally mean use-case instances, and there is no equivalent to use-case classifiers that in turn describe a wide range of related and similar use-case instances. Use cases are thus treated more formally and are described in a model of their own, as well as in interactions between objects in different object models. Scenarios are normally described as interactions between objects only.

Use cases are the "things" a developer sells to customers. It is essential that the buyers and builders of a system agree on this black-box view. If we can identify, early on, all the ways the system will be used and then control development so that the system offers these ways, we will know we are building the right system.

Use Cases Understood Intuitively

Use cases have two important roles:

1. They capture a system's functional requirements.

   A *use-case* model defines a system's behavior (and associated information) through a set of use cases. The environment of the system is defined by describing the different users. The different users then operate the system through a number of use cases.

   A use-case model does not replace object models. Instead, one or more object models are developed orthogonally to the use-case model. The use-case model is an external view of a system; the object model is an internal view of the same system.

2. They structure each object model into a manageable view.

   Although it is easy to build object models for "toy" systems, object models for authentic systems are unavoidably complex, as mentioned above. We have seen hundreds of examples of how object modeling can be applied to systems such as cruise control, conference management, home heating systems, etc. The problem with all these examples is that they do not reveal the complexity of real systems development, such as applications for banking, insurance, defense, and telecommunication. Methods that may seem to work well for these simple applications do not necessarily scale up.

   To manage complexity of a real system, it is practical to present its object models in a number of different views. In our approach, one view is drawn for each use case, and for each view, we model only those objects that participate in that use case. A particular object may of course participate in several use cases. This means that a complete object model is seen through a set of object model views—one per use case. We can now find all the responsibilities[2] of an object by looking through all use cases in which this object has a role. Every role of an object means a responsibility for the object. The total responsibility of an object is received by integrating all its responsibilities. If the model is a design model, then we can implement the responsibilities of each object straightforwardly. In the simplest case, a design object will be class coded in, e.g., C++.

In this article, unfortunately, we also have to use a simple application—an automated-teller machine (ATM)—as an example of how to capture functionality in a use-case model.

AN EXAMPLE

At an ATM, a customer can perform simple banking transactions, such as withdrawing money, without visiting a cashier. To accomplish this, the ATM must communicate with a central bank system to update the account balance before it dispenses cash (see Fig. 16-1). The central bank system stores all the information about customers, their accounts, and the personal identification number (PIN) associated with each card. When a customer performs a transaction at the ATM, the central bank system has control over verifying the PIN code and updating the account balance.

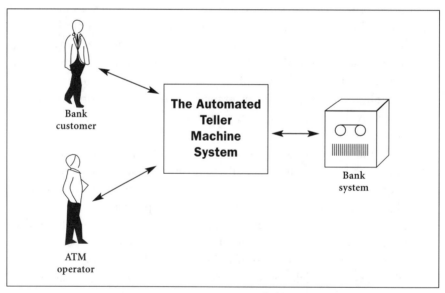

Figure 16-1. Overview of the ATM.

Customers can also deposit money or transfer funds between accounts at an ATM. In both cases, the ATM must inform the central bank system so that it will know the correct balance of all accounts.

When the ATM must request some information—e.g., the PIN—from the customer, it displays a message on a screen. The customer answers the request through a keypad. Finally, at the end of any transaction, the customer receives a receipt with the information about the transaction and his account balance. (We realize that security is a very important issue in a system like this, but we will not address this aspect to simplify the explanation of the system.)

USE-CASE MODELING

In this section, we present the constructs used to build a use-case model. We will interleave precise definitions of their syntax and semantics with their application to the ATM example.

A use-case model is a model with two types of classifiers, *actor* classifiers and *use-case* classifiers. See Figure 16-2. for a schematic example.

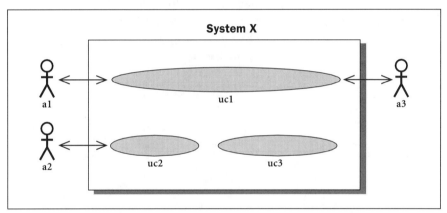

Figure 16-2. A use-case model (a1–a3 are actors, and uc1–uc3 are use cases).

Attached to each actor classifier is a *name*. Actor classifier names are unique.

Attached to each use-case classifier is a *name*. Use-case classifier names are unique within the scope of the system.

An actor classifier has an association to at least one use-case classifier, and a use-case classifier has an association to at least one actor classifier. These associations are denoted *communication* associations.

An instance of an actor can create instances of use cases (actually of use-case classifiers), and a use-case instance obeys its classifier. A communication association between an actor classifier and a use-case classifier means that stimuli can be sent between instances of the actor classifier and instances of the use case or of the use-case classifier itself. The latter case is relevant when new use-case instances are created.

Actor Pragmatics

Actors are objects that reside outside the modeled system; use cases are objects that reside inside the system. Actors are what interacts with the system and are created outside the control of our modeling tools. They represent everything that has a need to exchange information with the system. Nothing else outside the system has any impact on the system. Actors may be implemented both as humans and as other systems.

We make a distinction between actors and users: a user is not a formal concept. A user is a human who uses the system, whereas an actor represents a specific role a user can play. Actors are classifiers; users are some kind of resource that manifests instantiations of these classifiers. An instance of an actor classifier exists only when the user does something to the system. The same user can thus act as instances of several different actors.

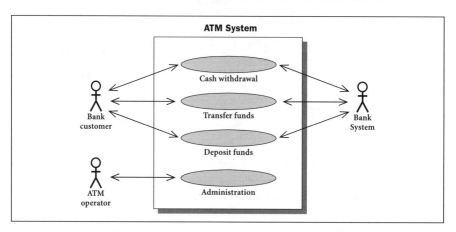

Figure 16-3. Example of a use-case model.

For example, in modeling our ATM system, we can identity three types of actors (Fig. 16-3). The primary actor is the bank customer, who will perform transactions; we are building the system for this type of actor. Then there is the operator, who will maintain and support the system. Finally, there is the bank computer, which must be informed of transactions that bank customers perform.

Thus, there are three different actors:

- Bank customer
- ATM operator
- Bank system

Example: Use-case model.

There are three actors and four use cases shown in Figure 16-3.

Cash withdrawal is an example of a use case for a bank customer. A bank customer must be able to withdraw money from his account. Other use cases that might be interesting are Transfer funds and Deposit funds. Are these use cases not too small? Should these all be one single-use case? Probably, but in the example we have to treat them as separate use cases to demonstrate use case modeling for real systems. The ATM operator wants to perform the use case Administration. The bank system must interact with the first three use cases, which also interact with the bank customer.

Use-Case Pragmatics

When an actor uses the system, the system performs a use case. The collection of the use cases is the complete functionality of the system. In the same way as with actors, the use case is a classifier that can be instantiated. When a use case is performed, this classifier instance exists as long as the use case is operating.

What Is a "Good" Use Case?

A good use case when instantiated is a sequence of actions performed by a system that yield a measurable result of values for a particular actor. Let us look more closely at two key words here:

> *A measurable result of values.* This key word is important in obtaining use cases that are not too simple. A use case shall make sure that an actor can perform a task that has an identifiable value. It can be considered possible to put a price or a value on a successfully performed use case. In certain circumstances, it is possible to implement a use case as a planning unit in the organization that includes the actor. For example, a user of a CASE tool for method support can be offered the use cases Identify object model and Specify an object.

> *A particular actor.* This key word is important in obtaining use cases that are not too large. It is important to begin with individual (human)

EXAMPLE: CASH WITHDRAWAL USE CASE.

A NORMAL COURSE

A greeting message is waiting on the display:

The customer inserts his card into the ATM (see Fig. 16-4).

The ATM reads the code from the magnetic tape on the card and checks to see if it is acceptable.

If the card is acceptable, the ATM asks the customer for his PIN code.

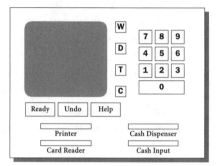

Figure 16-4. The bank customer/user interface.

Waiting for PIN code:

The customer enters his PIN code.

If the PIN code is correct, the ATM asks the customer to select a type of transaction.

Waiting for transaction type:

The customer selects the cash withdrawal function, and the ATM sends the PIN code to the bank system and asks the bank system for the customer's accounts. The account numbers that are received are displayed to the customer.

---

actors, i.e., instances of actors. A good hint when determining suitable actors is to name at least two different people who would be able to perform as the individual actor. Assume that you are developing a CASE tool. It can be a developer, i.e., someone who develops systems using the CASE tool as a support. It can also be a system administrator, i.e., someone who manages the CASE tool. Each of these two actors will have their own demands on the system and therefore will require their own set of use cases.

Thus, we can look at use cases as long transaction objects with states that we can manipulate by communicating with them. The main difference between

Waiting for the customer to decide:

The customer selects an account and keys the amount to be withdrawn.

The ATM sends a request to the bank system for the withdrawal of the amount from the specified account.

The bills are prepared to be dispensed.

The card and bills are ejected from the ATM to the customer.

The receipt is printed and given to the customer.

ALTERNATIVE COURSES

The card is not acceptable:

If the card is not acceptable because the magnetic tape on the card is not readable or if it is of the wrong type, then the card is ejected with a bip.

Incorrect PIN code:

If the PIN code is incorrect, a message is displayed to the customer, who is given a chance to enter the correct code.

Not allowed to withdraw:

If the bank system does not accept the withdrawal, a message informing the customer is displayed in 10 seconds and the card is ejected.

Cancel:

The customer can always cancel the transaction at any moment when he is asked for some information. This will result in an ejection of the card and the end of the transaction.

what we usually think of as an object and a use case is that objects can communicate with other objects within the same system, whereas a use case can communicate only with actors outside the system, not with other use cases.

Where Do Use Cases Come From?

Use-case modeling is preceded by an envisioning activity in which users participate to find the uses cases and the associated user interfaces. It is very appropriate to carry out the envisioning work as a series of workshops in which user interface designers are observers and users are the center of interest. Users are observed in the workplace; they are interviewed and asked to describe in an episodic way different use scenarios, i.e., use-case instances.

As a means to better understand the users' needs, sketches of the user interface evolve and, when these have become stable and not before, prototypes can be developed.

Work on use-oriented design, usability testing, etc. is very important in understanding the envisioning work. Here I would like to refer to *Scenario Based Design*.[3]

USE-CASE CLASSIFIERS

A use-case classifier can be modeled as a state machine. An instance of a use case traverses states of this machine during its lifetime. A state represents here the potential of the use case (instance). Which continuation the use case will follow from its current state is dependent on which stimulus it will receive. A received stimulus from an actor (instance) will cause the use case to leave its current state and perform an action; which one depends on the state-stimulus combination. The action includes manipulation of internal attributes of the use case and outputs to actors. These can be the ones that created the use case or other actors that have been involved during the course of the use case. The action is finished when the use case again has entered a state (possible the same one) and is awaiting another stimulus from an actor.

Traditional information systems have use cases that are simpler and are usually not modeled as state machines. If these use cases can be viewed as having only one state, then the state machine model may seem unnecessarily complex. In these cases, a simpler model could be used.

Hence, the use-case model is represented by several actors and use cases. When the system is in operation, instances are created from the classifiers in this model. Each use-case classifier has a description, which is crucial for understanding the system requirements and for finding the actual objects in the system. For the time being, we recommend that you describe the behavior of use cases informally, in structured English. In a forthcoming article, we will formalize the description of use cases and actors as well as their interactions and interfaces. For further discussion see chapter entitled "Formalizing Use-Case Modeling."

The Cash withdrawal use case is depicted in Figure 16-4. As seen in this example, a use case has a number of alternative courses that may carry the use case through a different flow. As many as possible of these alternative courses should be noted when the use case is specified.

Best Applications for Use Cases

Use cases play many different roles in modeling complex real systems. Complex systems are software systems, e.g., for financial applications, geographical-information systems, process-control systems, telecommunication systems, CAD/CAM, and more traditional information systems. Complex systems are also enterprise models, e.g., for banks, manufacturers, insurance companies, and telecommunication administrations.

For what kinds of development work are use cases particularly well suited? A list of the applications mentioned so far follows:

Use cases are tools for modeling the system from an external viewpoint—a black-box view. This view is essential so that people who request the system will be in agreement.

Use cases can be used to structure a complex object model into manageable views.

Use cases bind together different models of a system; for instance, the use case model with analysis object model and the analysis object model with the design model.

Use cases are tools for organizing the developer's work, from sales to requirements analysis, design, implementation (optionally including the operating system and the computer architecture), testing, and operation.

Use cases are test cases in the integration test of a system. The test planning can start when the use cases are identified.

Use cases are also the source when writing the user manual. Thus the work with the manual can start when the use case model is developed.

These are other interesting uses of use cases:

Use cases are powerful reengineering tools.[4] It is difficult to capture the functionality of an old software system, even of an object-oriented one. But it is normally rather easy to recreate a use-case model and map it onto the old design. Several projects have been carried out using this approach, as reported in Jacobson and Lindstron.[5]

Use cases can be used to dimension the processor capacity of a system.

The number of required processor instructions per use case can be measured, and the requested capacity for a given mix of use cases can be calculated.

Use cases can be treated as execution objects in a software implementation; they may be atomic change objects in a running system, or atomic restart objects at error situations, etc.

Use cases (and in particular interaction diagrams) are used to identify efficient access patterns for the database design.

USE-CASE INTERACTION: POINTS OF DISCUSSION

Because the use-case model should express only an external view of the system, we made several important decisions about what can and cannot be expressed in the model:

1. Internal communication among occurrences inside the system must not be modeled. So, use-case instances that are the only objects in this model do not communicate with one another. Otherwise, we would have to specify interfaces among use cases.

2. In the implemented system, instances of use cases will obviously effect one another. However, the use-case model provides no means to model such relations. These relations are certainly very important, but they are internal details that should not to be expressed here. Other models, i.e., the object models, will allow us to express such relationships.

3. Use-case models will not express concurrency. Instead, we assume that use cases are interpreted for one instance and one action at a time; you may say that the system is sliced into use cases and that use-case actions are atomic and serialized.

4. The use-case model can express only classifier associations. For more information refer to chapter entitled "Basic Use-Case Modeling (*continued*)."

In this way, we get a use-case model that can be used to understand the requirements of the system and that people who order the system and people who develop the system can agree on. In some cases, it would be very interesting to simulate the system at an early stage. With the above assumptions made, the use-case model cannot be used. Instead, we suggest an early object model for this purpose. In OOSE (see *Object-Oriented Software Engineering—A Use Case Driven Approach*[6]), we suggest the use of the robust-object model.

RELATED WORK

The use-case construct has been in use for many years. It was first presented to the object-oriented community in 1987,[7] but it (or a similar construct) has been used for the development of object-based systems since 1967. (See Jacobson[8–10] for earlier articles on this topic.)

The CRC-card approach discussed by Cunnigham[11] uses a similar idea called execution scenario in a refreshingly informal way. A system's design evolves by going through a number of execution scenarios and identifying classes participating in each scenario. Each class gets a card, on which is written the name of the class, its responsibilities, and its collaborators. This approach is excellent for teaching object-oriented thinking (the subject of Beck and Cunningham's article[11]), but in our view it is too simple to develop and maintain real systems—even if some people use it for that purpose today.

Responsibilities on the system[1] (viewed as an object) are close to use cases. A particular responsibility on an object is that part of a use case that is requested by the object.

Scenarios[12] are intended to serve as use case instances. The definitions, however, are very loose. Scenarios are described by event traces, which are similar to interaction diagrams (presented in Jacobson[7]). This is a more practical notation than timing diagrams, as sketched in Booch.[13]

Use scenarios[14] are also use-case instances. Scripts, in the same reference, are an alternative concrete syntax for interaction diagrams.

Threads[15] can be viewed as a generalization of use cases. Interesting work is being done on threads—particularly, a notation for a thread that is being developed.[16]

Others[17,18] have introduced similar ideas—threads of execution, mechanisms, and scenarios—but the definitions, when they exist, are weak. Booch[18] now has adopted use cases and interaction diagrams, but objects are found first and use cases as object interactions later.

By now, it may be clear why we have chosen the term *use case* instead of a term like *use scenario*. Use case is more precise, as is test case. We want to discuss all the ways a system is going to be used, and we want to do that in a more and more formal way as we proceed to develop more and more detailed models of the system. When the system is implemented, we want to be able to track a use case down to the code that implements it. Even in an operating system, we want to be able to associate a use-case instance to executed instructions.

REFERENCES

1. I. Jacobson. "Toward Mature Object Technology," *Report on Object Analysis and Design*, 1(1), May 1994. (See chapter entitled "Building with Components: Toward Mature Object Technology.")

2. R. Wirfs-Brock, B. Wilkerson, and L. Wiener. *Designing Object-Oriented Software*, Prentice–Hall, Englewood Cliffs, NJ, 1990.

3. John Carrol, Ed., *Scenario Based Design*, IBM, Yorktown Heights, NY.

4. I. Jacobson. "Industrial Development of Software with an Object-Oriented Technique," *Journal of Object-Oriented Programming*, pp. 30–41, Mar./Apr. 1991. (See chapter entitled "Industrial Development of Software with an Object-Oriented Technique.")

5. I. Jacobson and F. Lindstrom. "Reengineering of Old Systems to an Object-Oriented Architecture," OOPSLA' 91, ACM Press, pp. 40-350, 1991.

6. I. Jacobson, M. Christersson, P. Jonsson, and G. Övergaard. *Object-Oriented Software Engineering—A Use Case Driven Approach*, Addison–Wesley, Reading, MA, 1992.

7. I. Jacobson. "Object-Oriented Development in an Industrial Environment," Proceedings of OOPSLA' 87, Special Issue of *SIGPLAN Notices*, 22(12): 83–191.

8. I. Jacobson. "On the Development of an Experience-Based Specification and Description Language," IEEE Proceedings of Softwared of Engineering for Telecommunications Switching Systems, July 1983.

9. I. Jacobson. "Concepts for Modeling Large Real Time Systems," Department of Computer Systems, Royal Institute of Technology, Stockholm, Sweden, Sept. 1985.

10. I. Jacobson. "FDL: A Language for Designing Large Real Time Systems," Proceedings of IFIP'86, Sept. 1986.

11. K. Beck and W. Cunningham. "A Laboratory for Teaching Object-Oriented Thinking," Proceedings of OOPSLA'89, Special Issue of *SIGPLAN Notices* 24(10): 1–6.

12. J. Rumbaugh, M. Blaha, W. Premerlani, F. Eddy, and W. Lorensen. *Object-Oriented Modeling and Design*, Prentice–Hall, Englewood Cliffs, NJ, 1991.

13. G. Booch. *Object-Oriented Design with Applications*, Benjamin/Cummings, 1991.

14. K. Rubin and A. Goldberg. "Object Behavior Analysis," *Communication of ACM* 35(9): 48–62, Sept. 1992.

15. R.J.A Buhr and R. S. Casselman. "Notations for Threads," Tech. Report SCE-92-07, Department of Systems and Computer Engineering, Carleton University, Ottawa, Que., Canada, February 1992.

16. R.J.A Buhr and R. S. Casselman. "Architectures with Pictures," *Proceedings of OOPSLA'92*, October 1992.

17. P. Coad and E. Yourdon. *Object-Oriented Analysis*, 2nd ed., Prentice–Hall, Englewood Cliffs, NJ, 1991.

18. G. Booch. *Object-Oriented Analysis and Design with Applications*, Benjamin/Cummings, 1994.

17

BASIC USE-CASE MODELING
(continued)

—

Ivar Jacobson, SEPTEMBER-OCTOBER 1994

A USE-CASE MODEL should present an external view of a system. Therefore, as discussed in my previous chapter "Basic Use-Case Modeling,"[1] we have made several important decisions about what can and cannot be expressed in the model. These are summarized here:

- Internal communication among use-case instances must not be modeled.

- Conflicts between use-case instances must not be expressed in the model. These could be expressed in an object model of the entire system, realizing the whole set of integrated use cases.

- Use-case models will not express concurrency.

- The use-case model can express classifier relationships.

In this way, we get a use-case model that can be used to understand the requirements of the system and to reach an agreement between people who order the system and people who develop the system.

By now, it should be clear that use-case modeling is a technique that is quite independent of object modeling. Use-case modeling can be applied to any technology—structured or object-oriented. It is a discipline of its own, orthogonal to object modeling. However, the semantics of a use-case model draws strongly on the semantics of an object model. And there is a clear mapping from a use-case model onto an object model.

In this chapter, we will continue to present the basics of object modeling. In particular, we will present classifier relationships between use cases. These ideas were first introduced in my 1987 article for OOPSLA[2] and, in more elaborate form, in my 1992 book.[3]

RELATIONSHIPS BETWEEN USE CASES

Real systems may contain a large number of use cases. From our experience, a smaller system (2–5 man years) might include something like 3–20 use cases. A medium-sized system (10–100 man years) might include 10–60 use cases. Larger systems such as applications for banking, insurance, defense, and telecommunication may contain hundreds of use cases.

To produce an intelligible use-case model, we need a way to relate the use cases to one another, avoid redundancy between use cases, and describe use cases in a layered way.

We do this with *generalization* and *extend* relationships between use cases.

THE GENERALIZATION RELATIONSHIP

When developing real applications with several use cases, it is normal to find use cases with similar descriptions. To avoid redundancy and to enhance reuse, we need means to extract the similar descriptions and to share these between different use cases. We say that these shared descriptions are descriptions of abstract use cases and that the original use cases—those that share descriptions—are concrete use cases. The numbers we gave above all refer to concrete use cases.

In the ATM example described in Jacobson,[1] it is obvious that several use cases will share the sequence that checks the card and the PIN code. It will also show up when the bank customer makes cash withdrawals or transfers or deposits funds.

We call that part of a use case we extract an *abstract* use case, because it will not be instantiated on its own but is meaningful only to describe parts shared among other use cases. Use cases that really will be instantiated are *concrete* use cases.

Example

Here we might identify an abstract use case that checks the card and its PIN code. This abstract use case, called Card transaction, is used by concrete use-case sequences as a subsequence.

Formally, a generalization relationship between two use cases, for instance Cash withdrawal and Card transaction (see Fig. 17-1), means that a use-case instance that is created and obeys the concrete classifier. Cash withdrawal will, as instructed by this classifier, obey an abstract classifier Card transaction. Only concrete use cases can be instantiated, whereas abstract use cases cannot.

We break out abstract use cases like the one in Figure 17-1 so that we only have to design them once and then reuse them in other use cases. Experience shows that you should wait to identify abstract use cases until you have described several concrete use cases. Abstract use cases should evolve from concrete use cases, not the other way around.

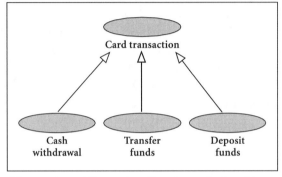

Figure 17-1. The generalization relationship to describe sharing between use cases.

We describe abstract use cases as we do other use cases, such as the previously described Cash withdrawal. The modified use-case classifier Cash withdrawal will then specify how it uses Card transaction. It will also describe what it uses of the abstract use case classifier.

The generalization relationship is very close to an inheritance relationship, but because the semantics of this kind of inheritance have not been formally defined, we give it another denomination. Generalization between use cases can also be multiple generalizations (compare with multiple inheritance). Several common parts may have been extracted out of a concrete use case into a number of abstract use cases, since several use cases share these parts. In other words, a specific concrete use case can then use all these abstract use cases.

In use-case sharing, the entire abstract use-case classifier is always used. The shared use-case classifier need not be one single action description or part of an action description, although this is often the case. Instead, we may have a situation in which the generalization relationship means that the shared action descriptions are interleaved into a concrete use-case classifier (see Fig. 17-2).

For example, in the description of the abstract use case B, p and q are parts of action descriptions that will be interleaved with r and s in describing the concrete use case A. The notation pu and qu means "use" p and q, respectively.

So an instance of the use-case classifier A will, as it obeys A (after obeying o), be instructed to use p and then continue to follow A's part r, etc. Within a use case

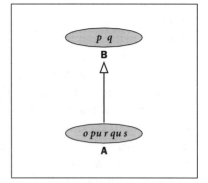

Figure 17-2. The concrete use case A uses an abstract use case B and decides how to interleave the parts from B.

description, there may be several different atomic sequences, such as o pu r qu s, wherein o normally is initiated by the reception of an input stimulus.

THE EXTEND RELATIONSHIP

The extend relationship lets us capture the functional requirements of a complex system in the same way we learn about any new subject: First we understand the basic functions, then we introduce complexity. In use-case modeling, we first describe how to enhance them to allow more advanced use cases, some of which may depend on the basic ones. The extend relationship not only supports the development of an intelligible structure, it is also useful to introduce new use cases to an existing system. (The pragmatics of this relationship are discussed in my 1986 article.[4])

The use case classifier where the new functionality should be added should be a complete, meaningful course of events in itself. Hence, its description is entirely independent of the extended course. In this way, the description pays no attention to any courses that can be inserted, and this complexity is thus avoided. We describe the first basic use case classifiers totally independent of any extended functionality. Similarly, we can add new extensions without changing the original descriptions.

Example

Suppose we want to collect statistics on how often Cash withdrawal is used. To do this, we could extend the use case Cash withdrawal. Every time you execute Cash withdrawal, another use case counts and accumulates the number of times this transaction has been used. (See Fig. 17-3.)

In this way, you gain two things. First, the original use-case description is easy to understand because it is not loaded down with the extension. Second, the extension is very clearly separated from other behavior descriptions.

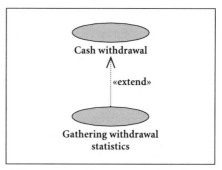

Figure 17-3. A common situation is having one use case collecting statistics regarding another use case, thus extending the other use case.

An extend relationship from one use case to another—for instance, from Gathering withdrawal statistics to Cash withdrawal—means that a use-case instance that obeys classifier Cash withdrawal will, as instructed by the other classifier, interrupt the interpretation of Cash withdrawal and instead obey Gathering withdrawal statistics. Later, the instance can again obey its original classifier.

Thus, extend is used to model extensions to other, complete use cases. We use extend to model:

- Optional parts of use cases.

- Complex and alternative courses.

- Subsequences that are executed only in certain cases.

- The insertion of several different use cases into another use case, e.g., Card transaction or a menu system with options.

To get an appreciation for the extend relationship, we would like to present some experimental use of it. We studied a very large application (more than 100 man years) that had been designed using an object-based approach. The existing design consisted of a number of objects interconnected through well-defined interfaces.

We studied two alternatives:

1. Redesigning the system without the extend relationship. In this case, we had to first design about 80% of all known functional requirements in the first release and were then able to add the remaining 20% without having to modify the first release.

2. Redesigning the system with extend relationship (and its corresponding programming language support tools).[4] In this case, we had to first design about 20% of all known functional requirements in the first release and were then able to add the remaining 80% as extensions, without changing the first release. With the right programming tools, it would be possible to add more than half of the extensions without even having to test for damage to the first release.

This experiment shows that using extend gives us an opportunity to reduce software development costs dramatically, since it allows us to add even larger increments to a system without changing what already exists. This means, in other words, that we can reduce the complexity of maintaining a software system and thus greatly reduce the costs for the continuous development of the system. Even if the extend relationship is not supported in the programming environment but is used only in analysis, it gives us a more structured ("structured" is used here in the conventional sense) way to understand a system's requirements. To a much greater degree than would otherwise be possible, extend lets us introduce requirements in layers: First basic functionality and then more advanced functionality, without having to modify the basic functionality.

THE GENERALIZATION VS. THE EXTEND RELATIONSHIP

As with the generalization relationship, the extend relationship may also be viewed as a type of inheritance relationship. But there are important differences between the generalization and extend relationships.

Suppose you have three use-case classifiers: Cash withdrawal, Gathering withdrawal statistics, and Supervising withdrawal behavior. We have introduced a new extended use case, Supervising withdrawal behavior, which allows the designers of the ATM system to learn more about how people really use their system.

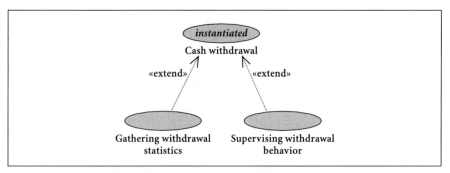

Figure 17-4. Cash withdrawal will be instantiated only.

Only Cash withdrawal will be instantiated. The other two classifiers include extend relationships to Cash withdrawal. An instance of this classifier will, during its lifetime, obey behavior as specified by its classifier and extend it as specified by the other two classifiers. These extensions may be conditional—inserted only when a specific condition is valid (See Fig. 17-4).

Why not employ generalization relationships instead of extend relationships? There are two ways to do this:

1. Cash withdrawal uses Gathering withdrawal statistics and Supervising withdrawal behavior (See Fig. 17-5).

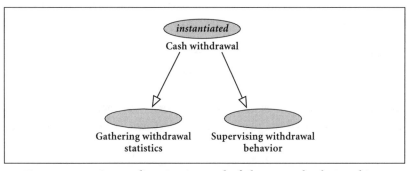

*Figure 17-5. Generalization instead of the extend relationship—
alternative 1.*

That would mean that Cash withdrawal had references to the extensions, which would spoil the whole extensibility idea—i.e., that Cash withdrawal can be understood and developed independent of Gathering withdrawal statistics and Supervising withdrawal behavior.

2. Gathering withdrawal statistics and Supervising withdrawal behavior uses Cash withdrawal. This would not only require the use cases

Gathering withdrawal statistics and Supervising withdrawal behavior but also a use case corresponding to a combination of these (see Fig. 17-6.).

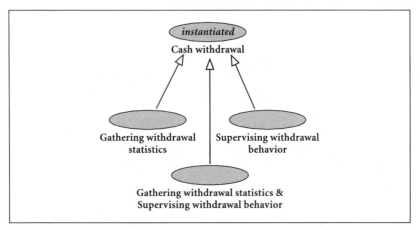

Figure 17-6. Generalization instead of the extend relationship— alternative 2.

This is necessary to express the flexibility offered by the extend relationship, namely, that Cash withdrawal can be extended by any combination of Gathering withdrawal statistics and Supervising withdrawal behavior. With many extensions this would be an unmanageable technique.

In fact, in most cases the choice between generalization and extend is quite obvious and causes no problems. Generalization is found through extraction of common sequences from several different use cases, whereas extend is found when new courses are introduced or when there are extensions to an existing use case that the user wishes to perform in some specific cases.

SUMMARY

Use-case modeling is and important tool for developing an outside view of a system. Combined with other techniques for human-computer interaction, it will help you to build systems with high usability. Furthermore, it is a powerful means of communication between different kinds of people participating in the development work, such as orderers, users, requirement analysis, designers, and testers.

In the future, you will see a lot of work on use-oriented design—both in research and applications development. This whole area will grow tremendously, and it will grow rather independently of the growth of object technology.

I will also describe how use cases and objects are related to one another; that is, how every use case in a system is realized by a set of interacting objects, along with different useful techniques to model this relation. For further discussion on use-case modeling, large systems, and formalization of use cases refer to chapters entitled "Use Cases and Objects," "Use Cases in Large-Scale Systems," "Systems of Interconnected Systems," and "Extensions: A Technique for Evolving Large Systems."

EDITOR'S NOTE

The generalization relationship as discussed here was originally called a "uses association"; and the extend relationship was originally called an "extends association." It can be noted that the semantics of these relationships have been slightly refined due to the development of the Unified Modeling Language,[5] although their essence is made quite clear already in this article.

There also exist other relationships between use cases that are not mentioned in this article, such as the include relationship.[5] This relationship can for simplicity be thought of as a reversed extend relationship that provides explicit and unconditioned extensions to a use case. Moreover, the behavior sequence and the attributes of an included use case are encapsulated and cannot be changed or accessed—only the result (or function) of the included use case can be exploited; this is a difference as compared to using the generalization relationship. However, in this book we will not dwell into too many details about these relationships; instead we refer to the UML documentation set[5] for details.

We end with a word of caution: the more relationships introduced into a use-case model, the higher the risk of getting functionally decomposed and too abstract use cases. This is a threat to the understandability, maintainability, and general usability of the use-case model, and should thus be done with care.

REFERENCES

1. I. Jacobson. "Basic Use-Case Modeling," *Report on Object Analysis and Design,* 1(2): 15–19, 1994. (See chapter entitled "Basic Use-Case Modeling.")

2. I. Jacobson. "Object-Oriented Development in an Industrial Environment," Proceedings of OOPSLA '87, Special Issue of *SIGPLAN Notices,* 22(12): 183–191, 1987.

3. I. Jacobson, M. Christersson, P. Jonsson, and G. Övergaard. *Object-Oriented Software Engineering—A Use Case Driven Approach,* Addison–Wesley, Reading, MA, 1992.

4. I. Jacobson. "Language Support for Changeable Large Real Time Systems," OOPSLA '86, ACM, Special Issue of *SIGPLAN Notices,* 21(11), 1986.

5. *The Unified Modeling Language for Object-Oriented Development,* Documentation set, ver. 1.1, Rational Software Corp., September 1997.

18

USE CASES AND OBJECTS

Ivar Jacobson, NOVEMBER-DECEMBER 1994

U SE-CASE MODELING is an analysis technique for eliciting, understanding, and defining (primarily functional) system requirements. Use cases help you focus on the usability of a system; that is, on *what* the users want the system to *do* for them. A use-case model (together with business object definitions) is therefore the best foundation we know of for writing a contract between customers and developers.

The use-case model defines system requirements but does not deal with internal system structure. In theory, this means that, based on a use-case model, any sound design method—structured or object-oriented—can be used to construct the system as long as the product can perform all the use cases well (correctly, with flexibility, good UI, etc.).

Object orientation represents the best practice for building high quality systems efficiently. The purpose of this chapter is, therefore, to show how the use-case model can be mapped to an object model. We do this without assuming any particular method for the object design process, though we will use the notation of UML[1] as we are most familiar with that notation. If there is no risk for confusion, we use the term *object* when speaking of instances as well as of classes.

USE-CASE MODEL VS. OBJECT MODEL IN THE SOFTWARE DEVELOPMENT PROCESS

In the previous chapters "Basic Use-Case Modeling"[2] and "Basic Use-Case Modeling (*continued*),"[3] we have already defined the use-case model as consisting of actors, use cases, and the relations between them. *Actors* are objects that reside outside the modeled system; use cases are objects that reside inside the system. Actors represent everything that has a need to exchange information with the system, including what are usually referred to as the *users*. When an actor uses it, the system performs a *use case*. The collection of use cases is the complete functionality of the system. A good use case, when instantiated, is a sequence of actions performed by a system, which yields a measurable result of values for a particular actor. (It is interesting to note, even if it is outside the scope of this chapter, that the semantics of a use-case model draw strongly on the semantics of an object model.)

There is a clear mapping from a use-case model onto an object model. In this mapping, each use case is performed by a number of participating objects wherein each object plays a specific role in the realization of the use case. This means that all the behavior defined for a use case is distributed to these different objects, which cooperate to realize the use case. Different objects take on different roles; some are aimed more at interacting with the user, others represent business objects, others still serve to bind together a use case.

Furthermore, each object may also participate in several use cases, possibly playing different roles in different use cases. When defining each object class, the roles must, therefore, be integrated from all the use cases in which the instances of the object class participate.

Design can be described as a process of hypothesis generation and validation. That is, given a use case, you (1) generate a hypothesis, using, for instance, the design principles of OOSE[4] with one ore more possible objects, and (2) in some way, validate the hypothesis against the original use case to determine if it is good implementation with respect to some criteria. There is a "gap" between a use case in the use case-model and its actual design and implementation in terms of interacting objects. This gap is "filled" with details of, for instance, how conflicts between use cases are solved, how currency is dealt with, and, at the lowest level, how use cases are implemented in code.

Design is the challenging process of defining suitable software architecture. It involves identifying the right classes and their roles or responsibilities and collaborations.[5] Some people claim that this is a simple task of planning out the classes from a two-page written specification. Not so! Finding the right classes is an elaborate process of looking for the essence of the software, asking the question, "What is it that we *really* want to build for our users?" The use cases thus serve as the most important input when finding the object classes. How to proceed when building for the right software architecture and the classes thereof will not be discussed here (see Jacobson[4]). We will assume that you, one way or another, will identify the objects you want to have to realize your use cases, and we will describe these use cases then represented in terms of your objects. We use two types of notations to map use cases to object models: class diagrams and interaction diagrams.

Class Diagrams

For each use case, you need to prepare a class diagram that shows the classes participating in the use case and their relationships. Use the use-case description and your selected design method to identify candidate classes and their relationships to realize the use case. Then use a class diagram to describe the result.

Example

Assume that for the use case Cash withdrawal, you have arrived at a class diagram (see Fig. 18-1).

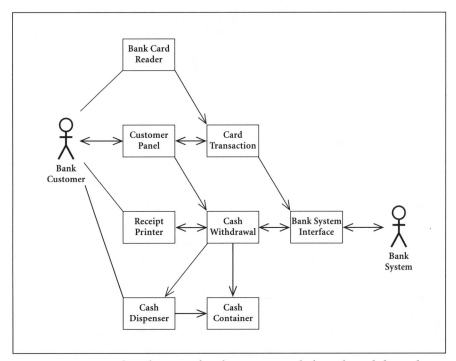

Figure 18-1. Class diagram for the use case titled Cash withdrawal.

As you can see, two actors and eight classes participate in this use case realization. Here is a brief description of the eight classes. The descriptions are not complete, but they will give you an idea of what each class will do:

- *Bank Card Reader* will implement the card driver, a mix of hardware and software, for reading back cards.

- *Card Transaction* will perform all the operations on the card information and will initiate the Customer Panel.

- *Customer Panel* will perform all communications with the customer; i.e., display messages from the ATM and receive information entered by the customer.

- *Receipt Printer* will print receipts for the customers.

- *Cash Dispenser* will perform all operations on the real bills; i.e., count and dispense money to the customer.

- *Cash Withdrawal* will coordinate the withdrawal transaction. It will initiate all the necessary communication with the customer as well as the Bank System. It is also responsible for checking that there is enough cash in the ATM and a sufficient balance in the customer's account.

- *Cash Container* will hold a counter for each type of bill in the ATM. In this way, Cash Withdrawals can find out exactly how many bills there are of each type in the ATM.

- *Bank System Interface*, a communication protocol, will transform the internal messages in the ATM to electrical signals sent to the Bank System.

To simplify the presentation, we have not separated out the interface hardware from the software in the example above. We have, furthermore, only shown the normal flow of events, not the exception handling.

In this system, we have decided to use two processes. The first will handle objects that interacts with the Bank Customer, i.e., Bank Card Reader, Card Transaction, and Customer Panel. These objects will be able to receive stimulus from the Bank Customer even if there is a transaction going on inside the ATM. The second process will handle the other five objects, which perform the transaction and dispense the money.

INTERACTION DIAGRAMS

An interaction diagram adds more detail and shows how participating objects (that is, instances of classes) interact to realize the use case. There are two types of interaction diagrams: sequence diagrams and collaboration

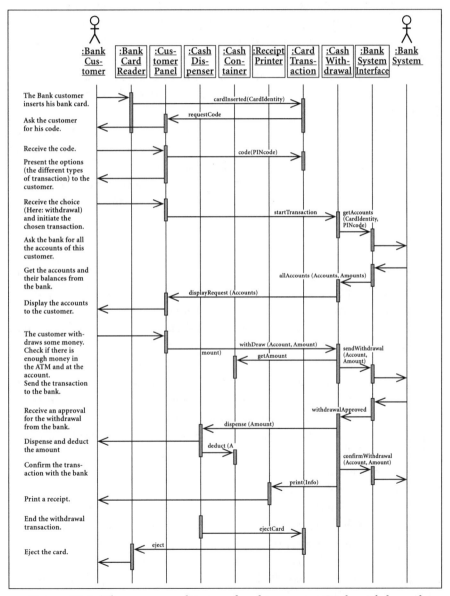

Figure 18-2. The sequence diagram for the use case Cash withdrawal.

diagrams; these two diagram types are isomorphic but are used in slightly different contexts. However, in this chapter we focus on sequence diagrams.

In a sequence diagram, a participating object is represented by a vertical column (also called a "lifeline"[1]) (Fig. 18-2). The order in which the lifelines are placed is not significant, but they should be positioned for maximum clarity. If several instances of the same class participate in the same use case, an individual lifeline can represent each of those instances if this lends clarity to the diagram. A lifeline most often represents an instance but might also represent a class. Often, you also wish to add one or more lifelines to represent the actors of the environment—such as, for example, the leftmost and rightmost lifelines indicating Bank Customer and Bank System shown in Figure 18-2.

Interaction takes place when objects send stimuli (such as messages) to one another. As you draw the interaction diagrams, you also define all the stimuli sent, including the parameters. The main purpose of this activity, which we call use-case design, is thus to identify the interfaces of the objects.

EXAMPLE

We now look at the design of the use case Cash withdrawal. You distribute the text representing the behavior of the use case over the objects participating in the use case; this text becomes margin text in the sequence diagram. The resulting sequence diagram is shown in Figure 18-2. How we arrived at this diagram is in itself a very interesting story, but we will not cover that problem in this chapter. Here, we will assume that your method has helped you to do that work, and we will show how you can represent your design.

In the sequence diagram, you see that almost all events are directly triggered from an operation on the window. The diagram contains no complex sequences partly because this is a toy example and partly because we have only described the normal course of events. All handling of errors and exceptions is shown in other sequence diagrams to improve the clarity of the documentation.

At the left edge of the sequence diagram, you usually describe the behavior sequences that the objects will carry out; these are called *activations*. On the lifelines, activations are represented by rectangles. The descriptions of the activations provide the basis on which to identify and describe the objects' operations later on. It is not always practical to make descriptions of all activations. The structure of the margin text might easily get too complex and make it difficult to understand to which activation a certain text paragraph belongs. When you use sequence diagrams in a real design model, you should use program constructs that exist in the chosen programming language—e.g., for-loops in C++—to ease migration to the actual implementation later.

A use case usually can take alternative courses based on the user interaction and on the system state; this is described as alternative paths in the use-case description. There is no point in trying to show all these variants in a single sequence diagram, since it would become too messy. It is better to make several sequence diagrams for a use case, wherein each diagram shows clearly what happens when an alternative course of events is performed.

You can also describe parallel sequences (e.g., when several processes participate in a use case) in a sequence diagram by using fork-like constructs.

Generally, the concepts used here are generic terms. When we specialize to a specific implementation environment, we use its concepts. For example, when working in Smalltalk, we could talk about methods instead of operations.

There is an alternative way for sequence diagrams to describe how a use case is performed in terms of object interactions. That technique was introduced by the author[6] in 1985 and means that you, in principle, annotate the associations in the class diagram with stimuli name and the order in which these stimuli are being sent. That technique is particularly useful for simpler use case designs, and is used by Coleman[7] under the name "object interaction graphs," but it does not scale up to design larger use cases. The UML defines a similar but more expressive diagram called a "collaboration diagram."[1]

Sequence diagrams have been used for many years in the telecommunications world to describe communication among hardware units. The author introduced these diagrams in 1968 for object-based design of software systems and in 1987 to the object-oriented community.[8] The concept of sequence diagrams has been further developed within Objectory AB and as message sequence charts within CCITT.[9]

References

1. *The Unified Modeling Language for Object-Oriented Development*, Documentation set, ver. 1.1, Rational Software Corp., September 1997.

2. I. Jacobson. "Basic Use-Case Modeling," *Report on Object Analysis and Design*, 1(2): 15–19, 1994. (See chapter entitled "Basic Use-Case Modeling.")

3. I. Jacobson. "Basic Use-Case Modeling (*continued*)," *Report on Object Analysis and Design,* 1(3): 7–9, 1994. (See chapter entitled "Basic Use-Case Modeling *(continued)*.")

4. I. Jacobson, M. Christersson, P. Jonsson, and G.G. Övergaard. *Object-Oriented Software Engineering—A Use Case Driven Approach,* Addison–Wesley, Reading, MA, 1992.

5. R. Wirfs-Brock, B. Wilkerson, and L. Wiener. *Designing Object-Oriented Software,* Prentice–Hall, Englewood Cliffs, NJ, 1990.

6. I. Jacobson. *Concepts for Modeling Large Real Time Systems, Department of Computer Systems,* The Royal Institute of Technology, Stockholm, September 1985.

7. D. Coleman, P. Arnold, S. Bodoff, C. Dollin, H. Gilchrest, F. Hayes, and P. Jeremaes. *Object-Oriented Development—The Fusion Method,* Prentice–Hall, Englewood Cliffs, NJ, 1994.

8. I. Jacobson. "Object-Oriented Development in an Industrial Environment," *Proceedings of OOPSLA '87,* Special Issue of *SIGPLAN Notices,* 22(12): 183–191, 1987.

9. CCIT, Message Sequence Chart, Recommendation Z. 120, International Telecommunication Union, Geneva, 1993.

19

A CONFUSED WORLD OF OOA AND OOD

Ivar Jacobson & Magnus Christerson, SEPTEMBER 1995

G OOD METHODS ARE BASED on good practices. A software engineering method can be seen as an experience in developing software. Our own work has evolved over almost 30 years. Hundreds
of experienced software developers have had a major impact on the object-
oriented software engineering (OOSE) method[1] and the Objectory process,
and consequently the Unified Process.

When you learn, as we have, from so many people and projects, you
become nondogmatic and humble when faced with real-world problems. You
understand that there is no single way to do something. And you realize that
if you are to help many different organizations and applications, you must
develop a process that can be configured to different needs and preferences.

These lessons pertain to the application of OOSE to analysis and design.
Our practitioner customers often communicate confusion about object-
oriented analysis (OOA) and object-oriented design (OOD). In particular,
our coworkers and we hear questions such as:

- What is the difference between analysis and design? Do you need both?

- Isn't analysis a kind of design?

- How is analysis related to use-case modeling?

- Why do we need more than one object model?

- Doesn't analysis encompass the domain as well?

- Does analysis include simulation?

- Do you need to manage an analysis model separate from a design? Or does the analysis model evolve into a design model?

- Where do we find frameworks and patterns?

There is no simple answer to these questions. In this chapter we will try to review analysis and design in terms of what you really need, from a pragmatic point of view. A lot of confusion has been introduced because the purpose of analysis and design has not been clear.

WHAT IS OOA?

A number of methods have been proposed for performing OOA. Although the approaches vary, all of them aim at developing an object model of the system to be built. This object model will specify the functionality of the system in terms of interacting objects.

HOW DO YOU DO OOA?

There are basically two main approaches to reaching an analysis object model:

- From the real world
    This strategy starts with identification of entities from the real world of the problem domain and assignment of data and behavior to these entities. This approach is also called data-driven OOA. Methods like the object modeling technique (OMT),[2] Fusion,[3] and Booch[4] have historically used this approach.

- From use cases
    This approach starts with a separate activity, identifying the use cases or the scenarios of the system and then deriving objects from these. Given a use-case description, you derive the objects that can provide the use case. As some have described it, the objects "fall out" of the use cases in a simple and natural way. This approach is also called behavior-driven OOA. Methods like OOSE and responsibility-driven design[5] use this approach. We believe that defining the requirements is best done

through use-case modeling. There is a growing consensus among object methodologists that this approach is preferred over the earlier one (see Jacobson and Christerson[6]). Use-case modeling is done to capture and understand the requirements of a new system (i.e., what is to be built) before you build it. During requirements capture you identify all the needs the system should satisfy. In use-case modeling this is done by finding the users (actors) of the system and all its use cases. Defining the system boundary is a key decision in this activity.

At the same time you identify, use case by use case, the required user interfaces and then you harmonize them over all use cases. It is important that you capture the content of the user interfaces during analysis. Graphical user interface (GUI) builders require that you define both contents and layout at the same time, but if you don't use these tools, layout details can wait until design. One way to make use cases concrete is to build UI prototypes that users can validate. Prototyping is thus an aid in analysis, but it doesn't replace analysis.

ISN'T OOA SOME KIND OF DESIGN?

Absolutely. A good study done in 1993 reached this conclusion.[7] What is called OOA is actually not much of an analysis. As it is described in most object-oriented methods, what we call OOA actually includes some elements traditionally thought of as "design": You perform OOA to reformulate the requirements, expressed either as use cases or as a list of requirements, into a system design in terms of interacting objects. In other words, once you have understood the requirements you proceed to structure them into an *analysis model* that serves as the internal structure of the system to be designed. In our earlier work[1] we have chosen to call this *robustness analysis* because the purpose is to develop an object model that promotes reuse and is robust in the face of changes. In the Unified Process,[8] this workflow is called "analysis."

Some organizations have decided to find a more adequate term for this activity. Thus, Ellemtel, an Ericsson R&D company, is using the terms *ideal design* and *ideal object model* and distinguishes that from *real design* (normally called OOD) and *real object model*. We would personally be very happy if we could agree on these terms instead of the ones now being used, but we won't pick a fight to get there.

WHAT ABOUT THE BUSINESS APPLICATION DOMAIN? HOW DO YOU KNOW THE USE CASES?

It is essential to understand the business domain to define the right requirements. To perform use-case modeling, it is important to understand the problem domain. To understand the problem domain, some people suggest that during the analysis you also build a business domain model. A domain model is a model of the system's environment—its business context. This model can de done using two different approaches, both assuming that you capture requirements by means of use cases:

- Identify the key concepts in the business domain and make a domain object model that defines the business objects of the system to be built. Then use these domain objects to identify a terminology to describe your use cases.

- Make a business model of the business processes you are going to support with information technology (IT). Briefly, our approach[9] is first used to model the business in terms of use cases, which actually means to identify how customers can use the business. This will systematically uncover your true business processes. Then build a business-object model that corresponds to the required business use cases. This business-object model should contain two basic object types: objects that correspond to deliverables, products, etc., and objects that correspond to human resources. The former correspond to domain objects; that latter correspond to actors that will be supporting the system by use cases in an information system.

The first alternative may look faster, but it is riskier. It is ad hoc and provides no systematic way to find the domain objects; you must pick them from your experience base. If you are working on a team, you will have to negotiate with people who have different experience bases.

Of course, we recommend the second alternative. It provides a systematic way to find the domain objects and the use cases of the IT support you are going to develop. In addition, it provides a systematic way to find objects that you can use within a business domain. This is extremely valuable when designing IT support for a business with many business processes. Using use-case modeling combines a data-driven and a behavior-driven approach. If you don't use this approach already, we encourage you to study it carefully.

WHAT ABOUT SIMULATION?
DOESN'T ANALYSIS INCLUDE SIMULATION?

Simulation (if done) can be done in all activities—requirements capturing, analysis, and design. Simulation is done to test the feasibility of a certain problem. It may be to evaluate a business process, an algorithm, a robotic system, a missile system, etc. Since a use-case model does not allow you to reason about concurrency, conflicts between different processes, and conflicts in accessing different resources, these problems have to be dealt with elsewhere. These are dealt with very well in analysis, where you describe each use case in terms of interacting objects.

WHAT IS OOD?

All methods proposed for OOD aim at defining a system design in terms of an object model. Independently of how you have reached analysis objects, all methods mold these analysis objects into design objects, i.e., the objects that really get implemented.

The important function of a design model is to help you understand how the real system will be built or is built. In other words, how is the design model mapped to code? Hence, design is an abstraction of your code. A design model uses constructs for classes and their relationships, packaging classes and the subsystem into larger subsystems. Moreover, a design describes how the classes and the subsystem do something useful together—how they interact to realize use cases. These are basically the most important aspects of design.

During analysis we ignored implementation issues. During design these issues become very important. You can use various stereotypes for solutions to these common problems. Examples include persistence and mapping to relational databases, proxies in concurrent processes and objects that are transmitted across address spaces, controlling transactions, etc. In many of these cases you can utilize frameworks for implementing these objects. The design should reflect how class libraries and frameworks are used. Furthermore, to lower the life cycle cost you need to have support for plug-gability over time. This means that is should be possible to exchange some subsystems independent of other subsystems. This can be accomplished by defining interfaces between subsystems (see Jacobson et al.[10]) Design should therefore express and formally define subsystems independently. Interfaces are also used to allow several people to work on the same system with minimal interaction.

Interfaces are the best way to coordinate and synchronize the work between individual developers and between groups of developers. What groups can use what interfaces? What do the interfaces look like in detail and how do they work? The larger the project, the more you need formal interfaces.

For a good design, it is crucial that you identify not only objects but also their dependencies. Dependencies reveal the implication of change—a change in one object will potentially change dependent objects. Clearly, we want dependencies that make the system easy to maintain and change. Circular dependencies, for instance, are usually not easy to maintain and to change.

How Do You Accomplish Maintainability and Reusabilty?

The first thing to do is to get the structure of your object model right. In OOSE we have a specific workflow, called robustness analysis, which we use to develop a good and maintainable analysis object structure, both static and dynamic. The purpose of robustness analysis is to derive the objects to offer the use cases. The focus is on identifying the approximately right objects—objects that will be tolerant to change and especially promote reuse.

When defining the objects, our guideline is to use three stereotypes: boundary objects, control objects, and entity objects.[1,8] These objects should be application- or domain-specific objects, but not cross-domain objects. This is an empirical guideline for the design of systems that can be enhanced with new functionality more easily. It is also a kind of layered approach, with each object type corresponding to a layer. There is yet another important reason to partition functionality according to our three stereotypes. Most methods are either data-driven (like OMT or Booch) or behavior-driven (responsibility-driven design). And it is true that some applications may be more data-intense and others have more behavior. However, the trend is that applications may be more complex in both ways. Entity objects are there to support complex data structures, whereas control objects take care of the more complex behavior. Entity objects and control objects are both first-class objects. Thus they communicate with one another to realize a use case. Moreover, entity objects have other relations similar to the ones you find in traditional modeling, such as aggregates. Control objects normally have no other relationships than com-munications. Having both types gives you the best of both worlds.

Some objects, typically entity objects, can be made reusable within the same business domain. For these objects, extra development effort will improve their reuse.

> *For a good design, it is crucial that you identify not only objects but also their dependencies. Dependencies reveal the implication of change—a change in one object will potentially change dependent objects.*

Separating out use-case-specific behavior into control objects and presentation specific behavior into separate boundary objects promotes this reusability aspect. This is because other applications can use these objects in some other way. If you really would like to understand this idea, read the new revised printing of *Object-Oriented Software Engineering*.[1] This is just a simple example of how reuse can come into play during develop-ment. Other reuse aspects include architecture, layering, organization, etc. We will come back to reuse issues in a separate chapter entitled "Succeeding with Objects: Reuse in Reality."

During robustness analysis you should be able to try out several different structures. Changing an analysis model should be easy, and thus iterations are encouraged.

WHEN SHOULD YOU MOVE OVER TO DESIGN?

It is tempting to go into detail about the application in the analysis model. This is dangerous and will cost you time (and money!). Often the design gives you constraints that you just have to follow. For example, if during design you want to use a framework and have not considered this in analysis, the time you have spent with details in analysis will have been wasted. This is why we suggest that you finish analysis when you have found all ideal objects and assigned them their responsibilities. So it is important to get the focus of the development efforts right: find the "ideal" objects and don't bother about details until you have the overall picture clear. Design is about getting these details right. During design you use detailed description techniques like state diagrams and sequence diagrams for some objects and use cases.

Some criteria of what not to do in analysis:

- Make analysis dependent on the implementation environment.

- Unless you want to simulate your analysis model for some reason, don't try to identify all methods on the objects or use state diagrams or sequence diagrams; however, we are encouraged to use collaboration diagrams in a slightly informal manner during analysis.[8]

It is very important to strike the balance of work between analysis and design. You will get this with experience. If you do not have experience, our advice is to take a part of the application (or make a small prototype) and run it all the way through to implementation and try to hit on most of the critical aspects. With this method your project will typically take a couple of weeks. Cheating and taking shortcuts is dangerous because the experience you get may be false and nonrepresentative.

During design you should not need to iterate because of the requirements, but only because of the implementation environment.

DOES THE ANALYSIS MODEL BECOME DESIGN MODEL, OR SHOULD THEY BE SEPARATE?

Designing real applications is very complex. The design should start from something clean. This clean picture is the analysis model. Many people do an analysis model for the first development cycle of a new product. This is a key milestone in their projects.

When you start to work on your design you can either continue in the same model as you did analysis and add design details in this model, or you can keep the analysis model as is and start designing in a separate model. What is the right way? Let us review some facts. The analysis model is used to:

- Find the ideal structure of the system, a structure that must not be violated in design unless there is a very good reason.

- Introduce new people to the system, which is greatly simplified by a clean model.

- Reason about the basic impact of a new requirement, also easier with a clean model.

An analysis model is thus valuable both in the first development project and also during later life cycle projects. Software development projects in the software life cycle spend most of their time understanding what somebody else did. Usually design introduces a lot of details that you may not want to see to understand the system on a high level. First you want to understand the high-level logical structures before you delve into details.

So should you have one or two models? It really is a tradeoff over the software life cycle. By having two different models, maintained throughout the lifetime of a system, different problems are solved using different models. Surely there is value in having different models to gain better understanding. But they need to be consistent with each other. It is very seldom that you will get a chance to update them after your project is finished. It simply must be part of the development project.

Getting the first outline of a design model can be done simply as a generation of the analysis model into a design model. This generation can be more or less advanced depending on how many predefined frameworks you have for some objects. Automating the update of the analysis can be done if you decide a mapping of how a design solution is abstracted in analysis.

SEAMLESSNESS BETWEEN ANALYSIS AND DESIGN?

The use case realizations are the same in both OOA and OOD, in the sense that they realize the same use cases. However, the allocation of behavior to objects can be different in OOA and OOD, since their models have different purposes. However, the objects in OOA should be traceable to objects in OOD. Since we have similar use case realizations across models, that in turn are based on use cases in the use-case model, the use case driven approach provides seamless traceabilities between models. Each use case corresponds to a view of an object model (in both analysis and design) that is complete, in the sense that it includes all of the objects that together realize the use case. Of course there are other views of the object models as well, such as static views including inheritance hierarchies or interesting aggregates.

WHERE DO YOU FIND FRAMEWORKS?

A framework is a subsystem in the form of a pool of classes designed to be reused and extended. In OOSE and Objectory a framework is an abstract subsystem that can be reused to design a concrete subsystem. There are different kinds of frameworks.

Domain frameworks are frameworks that are business-specific to your own domain (e.g., insurance, banking, healthcare, and telecommunications) and are used during analysis. Our construct for finding these abstract subsystems is the service package. A service package is a management unit of a set of related classes. These frameworks should be used during analysis.

Utility frameworks are generic over many domains, such as frameworks for user interfaces and standard communication protocols, frameworks for distributed systems in general and client/server applications in particular, frameworks to manage persistent objects, etc. These frameworks should be introduced during design and be part of the design environment you have selected, i.e., part of the design language and an extension to the selected programming language. They should be procured from those who specialize in such frameworks.

WHERE DO YOU FIND PATTERNS?

A pattern is used to express a standard solution for a common problem. For instance, the way we divide objects in terms of boundary objects, control objects, and entity objects is a pattern of how to design changeable and reusable object-oriented systems. A pattern is a design of an abstract use case. You use abstract use cases to model concrete use cases. Most methods now recommend mapping a use case onto interacting objects using sequence diagrams. If the use case is an abstract use case, this mapping will result in a candidate pattern. If the abstract use case is heavily reused in the use-case model, then you have probably found a pattern.

Patterns can be found in different layers of a system. Patterns at low layers are those that are like utility objects, they can be reused over many different applications. Most of the patterns in Gamma et al.[11] are utility patterns. Higher-layer patterns are domain specific, but not application specific. They are reusable over many different applications within the same business domain.

CONCLUSION

A lot of confusion exists around the concepts of OOA and OOD and related concepts. We have discussed some of this confusion and, understanding the issues and taking a pragmatic view, found there are answers: either one clear answer, an answer that may be discussed, or an "It depends..." answer. There is enough agreement, though, that we can have meaningful discussions on the basics and start to harmonize in the fields of OOA and OOD.

REFERENCES

1. I. Jacobson, M. Christerson, P. Jonsson, and G. Overgaard. *Obect-Oriented Software Engineering*, AddisonWesley Longman, Reading, MA, 1993.

2. J. Rumbaugh, et al. *Object-Oriented Modeling and Design*, Prentice–Hall, Englewood Cliffs, NJ, 1991.

3. D. Coleman, et al. *Object-Oriented Development—The Fusion Method*, Prentice–Hall, Englewood Cliffs, NJ, 1994.

4. G. Booch. *Object-Oriented Design with Applications*, 2nd ed., Benjamin-Cummings, Reading, MA, 1994.

5. R. Wirfs-Brock. *Designing Object-Oriented Software*, Prentice–Hall, Englewood Cliffs, NJ, 1991.

6. I. Jacobson and M. Christerson. "A Growing Consensus on Use Cases," *Journal of Object-Oriented Programming*, 8(1): 15–19, 1995. (See chapter entitled "A Growing Consensus on Use Cases.")

7. G. M. Hoydahlsvik and G. Sindre. *On the Purpose of Object-Oriented Analysis*, Proceedings of OOPSLA'93.

8. G. Booch, I. Jacobson, and J. Rumbaugh. *The Unified Software Development Process*, Addison Wesley Longman, Reading, MA, 1999.

9. I. Jacobson, M. Ericsson, and A. Jacobson. *The Object Advantage*, Addison Wesley Longman, Reading, MA, 1994.

10. I. Jacobson, S. Bylund, P. Jonsson, and S. Ehnebom. "Using Contracts and Use Cases to Build Pluggable Architectures," *Journal of Object-Oriented Programming*, 8(2): 18–24, 76, 1995. (See chapter entitled "Using Interfaces and Use Cases to Build Pluggable Architectures.")

11. E. Gamma, R. Helm, R. Johnson, and J. Vlissides. *Design Patterns—Elements of Reusable Object-Oriented Software*, Addison Wesley Longman, Reading, MA, 1995.

20

USE-CASE ENGINEERING: UNLOCKING THE POWER

Ivar Jacobson & Sten Jacobson, OCTOBER 1996

USE CASES AND USE-CASE MODELING techniques are becoming an integral part of object-oriented system development. Although the literature contains many articles and papers on the basics of use-case modeling, there is little on how to apply it to support the entire development life cycle. In this column, we present a way to do that by exploiting some of the more advanced—and perhaps less well-known—use-case properties. Armed with this knowledge, you can go beyond simply capturing requirements, and unlock the power of use cases to both bind and drive all phases of system development.

We call this integrated approach *use-case engineering*—"use-case" because it is use-case centered, and "engineering" because it is both systematic and manageable (two requirements of a mature engineering discipline). The underlying techniques are not new. Many (and others like them) have been around for decades. What makes use-case engineering so powerful is the seamless way these techniques are integrated.

Use-case engineering has its own life cycle, which parallels system development, with three cornerstones:

- Analyze the use cases.

- Design the system to implement the use cases.

- Test that the use cases have indeed been fulfilled.

ANALYZE THE USE CASES

In this activity you capture, clarify, and validate the system's use cases through a *use-case model.* (Our use case and object-modeling terms are defined in the Unified Modeling Language.) The use-case model consists of actors and use cases. An *actor* represents anything that interacts with the system, human or machine. A *use case* is a sequence of actions offered by the system, which produces a (measurable) value to a particular actor. In other words, a use case is a way for an actor to use the system.

To describe use cases we use *structured text* to produce a description that is entirely text based. It has well-defined pre- and postconditions, and may also include structured statements such as "when…" and "if…" You can further formalize the description by introducing sequence and state diagrams, for example, but formalism should be used carefully. Users, orderers, project managers, and system designers must be able to understand the use-case description. Too much formalism can compromise that goal.

A typical use case has one basic sequence of actions and several closely related alternative sequences. Depending on how an actor initializes a use case and the system's state at that time, the use case can execute any one of these sequences. The execution of one specific sequence is an *instance* of the use case. A use-case instance is called a scenario.

One of the most important results of use-case modeling is that you allocate responsibilities between the actors and the use cases. In essence, you delimit the system. The resulting border is the interface between the user and the system—a powerful starting point for user interface design (see sidebar).

The final step in analyzing the use case is to validate the use-case model. This is done typically in audits and model reviews attended by development groups, as well as others whose feedback is important, such as users, project managers, and line managers. The result is an approved use-case model.

DESIGN TO IMPLEMENT THE USE CASES

System design starts from the approved use-case model. The design work is also based on object-modeling techniques and typically encompasses a mix of top-down (subsystem and architecture) and bottom-up (class) design activities.

To design use cases you must first identify a set of collaborating classes for each one. You then group these classes into subsystems (in large systems you would first design a set of collaborating subsystems). Next, you iteratively integrate all of these specific use-case designs into a single, homogenized design model. This is a complete model of the system and as such offers all the behavior specified in the use-case model. Many of the subsystems (classes) typically participate in several use cases, so the total responsibility of a subsystem (class) is the integration of its different roles in different use cases. Thus, a design based on use cases produces a model where each subsystem (class) offers the total set of responsibilities needed to fulfill its role in the system.

To capture subsystem (class) collaboration and behavior, we use *interaction diagrams*—both sequence and collaboration diagrams—and *state diagrams.* Both diagram types have several styles and dialects. As long as their semantics are the same, or at least compatible, you can use either of them.*

For large system designs, such as those that involve an overall system architecture, interaction diagrams are used to design and describe the subsystem interfaces. These interfaces describe the public interfaces of the subsystem and can be defined using the CORBA/IDL syntax, for example.

TEST THAT THE USE CASES ARE FULFILLED

Test cases are derived from use cases, either explicitly or implicitly. In actuality, those who have developed and tested a real system have identified its use cases, whether they formally labeled them as such or not. Hence, the idea of testing based on use cases is not new.

What *is* new with use-case engineering is that testing is performed systematically and with full traceability back to the approved use-case model. Because a use case may have several possible instances (sequences of actions), all of which must be tested, you will have many test cases for every use case.

You can identify and briefly test cases as soon as you have an approved use-case model. With the design model approved, you can even generate the test cases from its interaction diagrams and/or state diagrams.

---

* However, now that the Unified Modeling Language is available, we recommend you using that language in the first place.

Because the test cases are the basis for the complete integration and system-test specifications, testing activities "close the loop." You now should be able to systematically verify that you have built the system correctly.

BENEFITS OF USE-CASE ENGINEERING

It helps project managers by binding together the stages of the development life cycle. Use-case engineering can be a project manager's best friend. Not only do use cases drive all development activities, but they also offer full traceability between those activities as well as an explicit means to plan, execute, and monitor them. Specifically, they let you:

- Capture system requirements.

- Identify and define all class relations on a per-use-case basis.

- Easily derive test cases for use case testing and system certification.

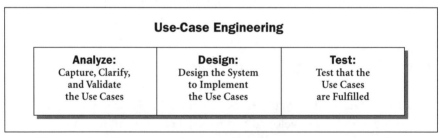

Use-Case Engineering		
Analyze: Capture, Clarify, and Validate the Use Cases	**Design:** Design the System to Implement the Use Cases	**Test:** Test that the Use Cases are Fulfilled

Figure 20-1. Use-case engineering has three cornerstones: analyze the use cases, design the system to implement the use cases, and test that the use cases have indeed been fulfilled.

Planning is also easier with use-case engineering. Project managers can plan many activities on a per-use-case basis. They can view the use-case model as the starting point for calculating the required calendar time and resources needed for every project activity. They can further identify, define, and refine requirements of many of the project activities directly from the use cases.

The project manager can also assign well-defined responsibilities to each project member: one or more use cases, and one or more activities related to those use cases, to each member. For example, the project manager can make one project member responsible for three use cases in analysis, another

---

BETTER USER-INTERFACE DESIGN: ANOTHER BENEFIT

User-interface design starts from the point the system has been delimited by means of identifying its actor and use of cases.

Identifying the interfaces for all the use cases in the first activity. In the beginning, this is a brainstorming or CRC card–like activity (we use sticky notes on a wall). You start with a specific actor and identify all the necessary interfaces, use case by use case. You then continue with the next actor, and the next ... until all actors are done. The result is a first cut of the systems user-interface description.

Your next step is to make these interface descriptions precise and concrete enough to build a prototype. This prototype is used for usability testing, an interactive process in which real users work with the prototype and the user-interface designers, to optimize the system's usability before implementing the system.

Usability testing may cause you to redefine how responsibilities are allocated between the users (actors) and the system (use cases). However, this iteration often produces a more efficient user interface.

---

member responsible for designing one use case, and another for writing complete test specifications for a set of use cases.

Whatever way the project manager chooses to allocate responsibilities, project activities are well defined and clear to all the project participants. The input is always a specific version of a specific use case, whether it be a requirement-analysis description or a complete use-case design. Therefore, issues such as version control and configuration management also have a direct relationship to use cases and become an integral part of use-case engineering.

It supports iterative development. Use case engineering lets you apply use cases to support iterative development, and to define a systematic way of capturing and designing a suitable system architecture as clearly as possible.

You define each iteration by a set of prioritized use cases (the highest priority defines the first iteration). This also means that you capture and design the first version of the system architecture in this first iteration of development. You simply base the architecture on the most important use cases, those identified and described within this first iteration.

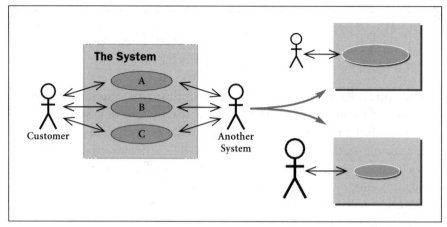

Figure 20-2. The system border is set through allocation of responsibilities to actors or use cases, respectively.

Moreover, one iteration is a slice of all the development work, from analysis to design and testing. Basically, this means that you work through the complete development life cycle for every iteration of your project. This "trailblazer" approach leads to a substantial reduction of the risks involved regarding, for example, technical limitations in the implementation techniques, or the uncertainty of early time and resource estimates.

It has broad application. You can apply use-case engineering to design hardware/software, pure software systems, and for business process reengineering and continuous improvement.

Whatever the application, you will have a systematic approach to building *truly usable systems*—from computer-based systems that offer users increased personal productivity to a business that offers its customers some increased value.

The most recent evolution of use-case engineering is our joint work with one of the world's leading experts on reuse, Dr. Martin Griss from HP labs. In this work we integrate our approaches for business and systems engineering into a mature overall process for large-scale reuse in developing families of related applications. We call this technique the "Reuse Driven Software Engineering Business."[1]

With use-case engineering use cases are much more than just another modeling construct. Use-case engineering offers a way to reap the full benefit of use cases in every phase of engineering one's system.

EDITOR'S NOTE

The notions of "analyze" and "analysis" as discussed in this chapter can be thought of as including both requirements capture and analysis,[2] although this is left out here to simplify the presentation.

REFERENCES AND SUGGESTED READING

1. Ivar Jacobson, Martin Griss, and Patrik Jonsson. *Software Reuse: Architecture, Process and Organization for Business Success*, Addison Wesley Longman, Reading, MA, 1997.

2. I. Jacobson, G. Booch, J. Rumbaugh. *The Unified Software Development Process*, Addison Wesley Longman, 1999.

3. I. Jacobson et al. *Object-Oriented Software Engineering—A Use Case Driven Approach,* Addison–Wesley, Reading, MA, 1992.

4. I. Jacobson. "Basic Use-Case Modeling," *Report on Object Analysis and Design*, 1(2): 15–19, 1994, continued in 1(3): 7–9, 1994. (See chapters entitled "Basic Use-Case Modeling" and "Basic Use-Case Modeling (*continued*).")

5. I. Jacobson. "Formalizing Use-Case Modeling," *Journal of Object-Oriented Programming,* June 1995. (See chapter entitled "Formalizing Use-Case Modeling.")

6. I. Jacobson and M. Christerson. "Use Cases in Large-Scale Systems," *Report on Object Analysis and Design,* 1(6): 9–12, 1995. (See chapter entitled "Use Cases in Large-Scale Systems.")

7. I. Jacobson and M. Christerson. "A Growing Consensus on Use Cases," *Journal of Object-Oriented Programming,* March–April 1995. (See chapter entitled "A Growing Consensus on Use Cases.")

21

FORMALIZING USE-CASE MODELING

Ivar Jacobson, 1995

A S I WROTE IN THE CHAPTER entitled "A Growing Consensus on Use Cases,"[1] there is a growing acceptance of use cases. This is good news. It is also good news that, so far, methodologists have introduced new use-case concepts very carefully. This means there is a good chance we can achieve a standard use-case modeling technique, at least for basic use-case modeling. I have presented my proposals to this standard in several articles and the book *Object-Oriented Software Engineering—A Use-Case Driven Approach.*[2–5]

As use cases become increasingly popular, interest in further developing the basic ideas will grow. Thinking on use cases will develop in both "soft" (process- or human-related) and "hard" (model- or language-related) directions, and this new thinking will come from people with different knowledge bases, such as computer scientists, software engineers, user-interface experts,[6] sociologists, and psychologists. At the Objectory Corporation (and now the Rational Software Corporation), we have developed use cases in both soft and hard directions: We have used use cases to model businesses,[7] and we have extended the modeling language to support recursive use-case modeling.[8,9] Recursive modeling facilitates a powerful architecture, which we call *systems of inerconnected systems.*

In this chapter, I focus on use-case modeling languages, touching only briefly on process issues. In particular, I want to describe our approach to formalizing use-case modeling. To explain what should and should not be in a use-case model, I first summarize the design rationale for a basic use-case model.[3,4] Then I discuss different formalization levels and go into detail about some of them.

BASIC USE CASES: DESIGN RATIONALES FOR THE MODELING LANGUAGE

Use cases serve many roles in the various software development activities, from envisioning to requirements capture, user-interface analysis, ideal and real object modeling, testing, and so on. For a more complete list of roles see Jacobson[3] or, better, Jacobson and Christerson.[10]

The whole idea behind the use-case model is to capture a system's functional requirements before design work starts. To understand the rationale for a use-case modeling language, therefore, one must first understand who the use-case model's stakeholders are.

THE STAKEHOLDERS OF A USE-CASE MODEL

A use-case model is developed during requirements analysis by people who often have a lot of experience, either in designing certain types of systems or in the business area being modeled. These analysts do not necessarily know any particular implementation technique more than superficially.

The resulting use-case model is used by many groups. It is used as a model of "What" as an outside view of the system, by:

- Orderers, to validate that the use-case model specifies all the needs of the supported business (i.e., all the needs of the people who will use the system).

- User-interface analysts and designers, to specify user-interface support for each use case.

- Function managers and project leaders (or process owners and process managers, in a process organization), to review and supervise development at different levels.

- Technical writers, to structure the overall work on the user manuals at an early stage.

It is used as a model of "How," as an inside view of the system, by:

- Designers of corresponding analysis and design object models, one for each use case, to harmonize the design over all use cases and to resolve conflicts among use-case instances.

- Integration testers and system testers, to identify test cases at an early stage.

EXPRESSABLILITY OF A USE-CASE MODEL

Requirements analysts must be able to create a use-case model that users can read. The What model, the outside view, is the model that all its stakeholders can understand. In my experience, the best use-case models talk about system's functions (used here in its everyday meaning), not its form. It should express who the users are and what their needs are.

In a use-case model, users are actors and needs are use cases. Thus, actors and use cases are the only ocurrences, phenomena, or objects in a use-case model—no more, no less. This simplicity is one reason use-case models are so easy to understand and why they have become so popular.

We have made three other important decisions about what cannot be expressed in a use-case model:

1. Internal communication among occurences inside the system cannot be modeled. Use-case instances are the only types of objects inside the system. Therefore, they cannot communicate with one another. Otherwise, we would have to specify use-case interfaces, which would result in an internal view similar to an object model.

2. Conflicts among use-case instances cannot be modeled. Obviously there will be such conflicts in an implemented system, and these relationships are certainly very important, but they represent internal details. Such relationships should be expressed in the object models.

3. Concurrency cannot be modeled. We assume that use cases are interpreted one instance and one action at a time. In effect, use cases are atomic, serialized slices of a system.

Given these restrictions, one cannot use a use-case model to simulate a system at an early stage. Instead, I suggest using an early object model for this purpose. In Jacobson et al.[2] we suggested the simulation of a system using a robust-object model that has the class behavior specified. Objects are very nice simulation instruments, as the designers of Simula discovered back in the early 1960s.

Many people have asked me why I have not developed a formal specification language for use-case modeling. In fact, I almost did. In my thesis[11] I described a formal language to specify (an early form of) use cases. The language was object-oriented, which means that I described use cases formally in terms of communicating objects. This is how I believe formal (mathematical) system specifications should be done. However, this is not use-case modeling with only use cases and actors, as described previously. This is more like using a formal object-specification language similar to Object-Z[12,13] to specify use cases. I used an object language for the same reason I believe in object modeling in general: Objects are practical for the design of complex software. Whether you design with a programming language or a specification language is of no importance.

I believe, therefore, that simulation should be carried out by using a formal object model, not a formal use-case model. Simulation can still be done use case by use case, since an object model will have at least as many views as there are use cases. There may be more views than use cases, but there is at least one view for each use case. This means that there is a full seamlessness between use cases in a use-case model and use cases in an object model.

Formally specifying every use case can be valuable for other purposes, including test-case generation. Here too, however, I believe that each use case should be specified in terms of formally specified objects.

Having said this, I still think it is valuable to formalize use cases and actors in the use-case model. Organizations that use formal techniques to specify requirements, such as for protocols, may want to extend their use-case models with more formal techniques. The question is, how far can use cases be formalized? My answer has been consistent for many years: as far as possible without violating the three rules stated above.

LEVELS OF FORMALISMS

Use-case modeling has been formalized to different levels. Here I give an overview of these levels only, relying on your intuition to supply some of the details. Remember that here I am not discussing how to map use cases to objects.[2,5] This is a very important subject, but a quite different one. After describing the basic constructs, I sketch the four principal formalisms: classifier relationships, interaction diagrams, interfaces, and state diagrams.

BASIC CONSTRUCTS

A use-case model is a model of a system. It consists of actors and use cases (Fig. 21-1).

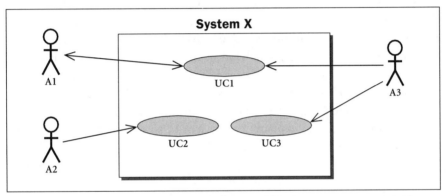

Figure 21-1. A use-case model of system X (A1–A3 are actors and UC1–UC3 are use cases).

Actors and use cases have unique names within the scope of a system. Each actor has a communication association to one or more use cases, and vice versa.

Actors and use cases are considered to be classifiers that can be instantiated.* A communication association between an actor and a use case means that an instance of the actor will communicate with an instance of the use case during its lifetime.

For each combination of actor and use case there must be a description of its dynamic behavior, how the actor instance interacts with the use-case instance. We call these use-case descriptions, even though they also describe actor behavior. At this basic level, the behaviors of actors and use cases are described informally, in structured English.

Because actors and use cases are classifiers, these descriptions describe alternative, exceptional behavior. Furthermore, to each use-case description you may want to attach a description of different use-case instances or scenarios,

---

* In the UML, "a classifier is an element that describes behavioral and structural features."[14] Note that only certain kinds of classifiers, such as actors and use cases, can be instantiated.

which will probably be used during development only to explain different uses or different people's perceptions of uses (as suggested by Rebecca Wirfs-Brock in private conversations). Finally, in some cases you may want a static description for each actor classifier and each use-case classifier.

Classifier Relationships

These basis modeling constructs can be enhanced with classifier relationships. Since one actor can inherit another actor, one actor instance can use the same use cases as another actor instance. A use case can have a generalization relationship to another use case, which means that their classifiers share behavior in an abstract use-case classifier; or, a use case can have an extend relationship to another use case, which means the behavior of the former use-case classifier is extended to the latter classifier. The distinction between these two relationships is tricky to explain in a few words, so please refer to Jacobson[4] and Jacobson and Thomas.[1]

Interaction Diagrams

Dynamic behavior, as captured in a use-case description, can be formalized by using interaction diagrams[2,5] (Fig. 21-2).

An interaction diagram describes the interaction among (usually) object instances. Here the objects are actors and use cases. Each use-case description can have several interaction diagrams. Rebecca Wirfs-Brock has suggested that an interaction diagram describes a "conversation," a term that I think is well in line with the semantics of these diagrams. Each such conversation has a unique name within the use case.

In this case, an interaction diagram describes the sequence of interactions among use-case and actor instances. An actor sends a stimulus to a use case, which receives the stimulus and performs an action. The action involves manipulating the internal attributes of the use case and then sending one or more stimuli to the original actor or to other actors. Structured English is used to describe an action. An interaction diagram can describe different paths the conversation will follow. Thus there are constructs to describe iteration, repitition, branching, and parallelism.

Each interaction diagram that describes a conversation can be associated with pre- and postconditions. A precondition, for instance, might be

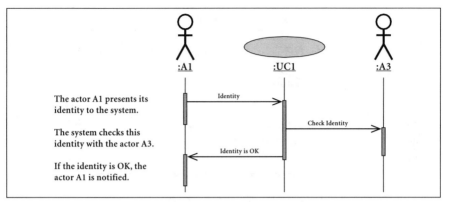

Figure 21-2. A sequence diagram describing the behavior of the use case UC1 in system X.

"The actor A1 has logged on to the system," and a postcondition might be "The actor A1 has been notified if its identity is OK or not" (see Fig. 21-2).

Each use case may also have pre- and postconditions. In a telecommunication system, for example, the Local call use case might have the precondition that the calling subscriber has acquired a subscription. A postcondition would be that the subscriber still has a subscription. In other words, the subscriber cannot lose a subscription in the middle of a call. Among other things, pre- and postconditions let you slice a system into independent use cases.

INTERFACES

Larger systems usually have several actors and a lot of interactions with each one. The number of different types of stimuli to and from the system may be very large—say, more than 1000. An interface (or several interfaces) is a nice technique of describing a large number of stimuli between the actors and the system.[15]

An interface specifies an object's interface in detail. The "realizes" relationship specifies the object that is realizing an interface, and the "uses" relationship specifies the object that uses the object realizing an interface, e.g., through communication (Fig. 21-3). Thus, an actor or use case that realizes an interface will realize all the stimuli defined in the interface, and an actor or use case that uses an interface will know that there is either a use case or an actor that realizes it.

We achieve a much more intelligible interface when we structure an interface in terms of objects (actually classifiers) and direct a stimulus to one object

227

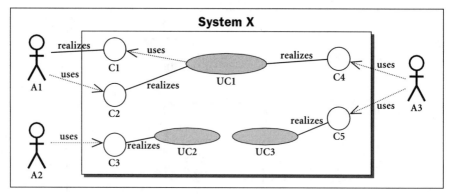

Figure 21-3. Interfaces in system X.

only. An actor provides an interface that one or more use cases use, and a use case provides an interface that one or more actors use. If they are carefully designed, several use cases can jointly provide a single interface. In such cases the use cases would also share a function, so an abstract use case should probably have been found.

Graphical user interfaces (GUIs) and communication protocols are two examples of interfaces that are very well described as objects. A GUI can first be described at an abstract level as a set of interfaces. The realization of an interface receives a stimulus and retransmits it to the associated use-case instance. One can describe (and put requirements on) the objects behind an interface by using state diagrams or preconditions and postconditions.

STATE DIAGRAMS

In many cases, the static classifier descriptions of actors and use cases can be modeled well with state diagrams.

A classifier can be thought of as a state machine. For example, a use-case instance traverses several machine states during its lifetime. Here a state represents the potential of the use-case instance. Which continuation the use case will follow from its current state depends on which stimulus it receives. A stimulus received from an actor instance will cause the use case to leave its current state and perform an action, depending on the state-stimulus combination. The action involves the manipulation of internal attributes of the use case and its outputs to actors. These can be the ones that created the use case or other actors that have been involved during the course of the use case.

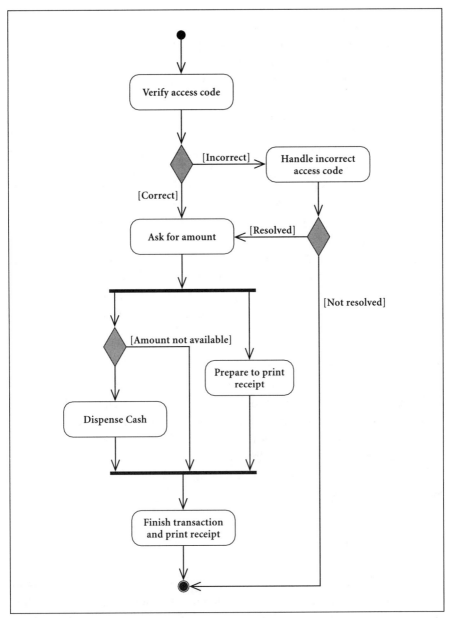

Figure 21-4. The use case Withdraw money of an automated teller machine (ATM) modeled with an activity diagram.

The action is finished when the use case has again entered a state (possibly the same one) and awaits another stimulus from an actor.

In many other cases, particularly for use cases that primarily save and retrieve information, the classifier can be described as a set of actions, each one initiated by a stimulus. In these cases each action is associated with pre- and postconditions, to determine the state of the use case before and after the action.

What kind of state diagram should be used? Jim Odell gives a good overview of different ways to make state diagrams.[16] My own preferred notation is the CCITT/SDL,[17] extended in Jacobson et al.[2] and in the UML.[14] Which one you will prefer is a matter of habit and taste.

In Figure 21-4 we use a variant of a state diagram called an *activity diagram* to model the use case Withdraw money when a customer performs a cash withdrawal. The diagram is fairly intuitive; each state represents an action of the use case.

Another technique that has become popular lately is to use a modified version of Harel's hierarchical state diagrams[18] as is also included in the UML.[14] This technique is particularly valuable when describing complex state machines, such as use cases with several actions going on in parallel.

EXPERIENCES

In its current form, use-case modeling has been used extensively for nearly 10 years. We have become more and more convinced that use cases should be treated as a subtype of a more generic phenomena of which "normal" objects (as used in object modeling) are a subtype. Thus, use cases are classifiers that can be instantiated and that may have inheritance-like relationships to one another.

CONCLUSION

Here I have presented the design rationale for use-case modeling and overviews of the different ways to formalize the modeling language. This, of course, is not the last word on this question. We continue to gain experience as people use our technology, and I am sure you, dear reader, have a number of proposals to further the thinking behind use cases. I welcome all the publicity about use cases, and feel free, if you like, to present your suggestions directly to me.

References and Suggested Reading

1. I. Jacobson and D. Thomas. "Extensions: A Technique for Evolving Large Systems," *Report on Object Analysis and Design,* 1(5): 7–9, 1995. (See chapter entitled "Extensions: A Technique for Evolving Large Systems.")

2. I. Jacobson, M. Christerson, P. Jonsson, and G. Övergaard. *Object-Oriented Software Engineering—A Use Case Driven Approach,* Addison–Wesley, Reading, MA, 1992.

3. I. Jacobson. "Basic Use-Case Modeling," *Report on Object Analysis and Design* 1(2): 15–19,1994. (See chapter entitled "Basic Use-Case Modeling.")

4. I. Jacobson. "Basic Use Case Modeling *(continued),*" *Report on Object Analysis and Design,* 1(3): 7–9, 1994. (See chapter entitled "Basic Use-Case Modeling *(continued).*")

5. I. Jacobson. "Use Cases and Objects," *Report on Object Analysis and Design* 1(4): 8–10, 1994. (See chapter entitled "Use Cases and Objects.")

6. L. Constantine and L.A.D. Lockwood. "Essential Use Cases: Essential Modeling for User Interface Design," OzCHI '94, November 1994, Melbourne, Australia.

7. I. Jacobson, M. Ericsson, and A. Jacobson. *The Object Advantage: Business Process Reengineering with Object Technology,* Addison–Wesley, Reading, MA, 1994.

8. I. Jacobson. "Use Cases in Large-Scale Systems," *Report on Object Analysis and Design,* 1(6):9–12, 1995. (See chapter entitled "Use Cases in Large-Scale Systems.")

9. I. Jacobson, K. Palmkvist, and S. Dyrhage. "Systems of Interconnected Systems," *Report on Object Analysis and Design,* 2(1), 1995. (See chapter entitled "Systems of Interconnected Systems.")

10. I. Jacobson and M. Christerson. "A Growing Consensus on Use Cases," *Journal of Object-Oriented Programming,* 8(1): 15–19,1995. (See chapter entitled "A Growing Consensus on Use Cases.")

11. I. Jacobson. *Concepts for Modeling Large Real-Time Systems,* Stockholm, Department of Computer Systems, The Royal Institute of Technology, September 1985.

12. J. M. Spivey. *The Z Notation: A Reference Manual,* Prentice–Hall, Englewood Cliffs, NJ, 1989.

13. F. J. van der Linden. *Object-Oriented Specification in COLD,* Technical report no. RWR-508-re-92007, Philips Research Laboratories, The Netherlands, 1992.

14. *The Unified Modeling Language for Object-Oriented Development,* Documentation set, ver. 1.1, Rational Software Corp., Sept. 1997.

15. I. Jacobson, S. Bylund, P. Jonsson, and S. Ehnebom. "Using Contracts and Use Cases to Build Pluggable Architectures," *Journal of Object-Oriented Programming*, 8(2): 18–24, 76, 1995. (See chapter entitled "Using Interfaces and Use Cases to Build Pluggable Architectures.")

16. J. Odell. "Approaches to Finite-State Machine Modeling," *Journal of Object-Oriented Programming*, 7(8): 14–20, 40, 1995.

17. *CCIT Specification and Description Language* (SDL), Recommendations Z.100, March 1993.

18. D. Harel. "Statecharts. A Visual Formalism for Complex Systems," *Science of Computer Programming*, 8: 231–274, 1987.

19. I. Jacobson. "Toward Mature Object Technology," *Report on Object Analysis and Design*, 1(1): 36–39, 1994. (See chapter entitled "Building with Components: Toward Mature Object Technology.")

20. I. Jacobson and S. Jacobson. "Beyond Methods and CASE: The Software Engineering Process with Its Integral Support Environment," *Object Magazine*, 4(8): 24–30, 1995. (See chapter entitled "Beyond Methods and CASE: The Software Engineering Process...")

22

A GROWING CONSENSUS ON USE CASES

Ivar Jacobson & Magnus Christerson, MARCH-APRIL 1995

PRACTITIONERS OF OBJECT-ORIENTED analysis and design have a plethora of ideas to choose from. There are several published methods and many other ideas in circulation. This is good, of course, but the practice of OO would be improved if we could build on each other's experience instead of defining overlapping and sometimes conflicting basic concepts. Now, leading methodologists are converging on some key concepts. One of these is the use case. This chapter gives our view of the growing consensus on the use case as a key OO concept.

BACKGROUND

There is a growing consensus that the use case concept is important: Rebecca Wirfs-Brock,[1] Grady Booch,[2] and Jim Rumbaugh[3] are incorporating it in their methods. (Jim Rumbaugh's column[3] presents the use-case concept in a manner very similar to our presentation of them.)

Nobody is happier than we are to see that our work is being recognized as key to object-oriented development. However, we want to clarify the relationship between use cases and objects. Because the use-case concept appears to be orthogonal to objects, it might seem sufficient to simply add this concept to an object-oriented method. However, because use cases have such a great effect on how you think and how you design a system, your understanding of them will fundamentally affect how you view and work with object models.

Use cases serve several important purposes. Among other things, use cases are the basis for:

- Defining functional requirements.
- Deriving objects.
- Allocating functionality to objects.
- Defining object interaction and object interfaces.
- Designing the user interface.
- Performing integration testing.
- Defining test cases.
- Determining development increments.
- Composing user documentation and manuals.

They also help define the system and control development by serving as the vehicle for:

- Capturing and tracing requirements.
- Envisioning an application.
- Communicating with end users and customers.
- Delimiting a system.
- Estimating project size and required resources.
- Defining database-access patterns.
- Dimensioning processor capacity.

In short, use cases are:

- The dynamic, black-box view of the system.
- The driver of development activities.

And there is more.[4-7] Of course, use cases certainly are not snake oil, or a silver bullet for software development. Much more hard work goes into successful software development. Object modeling, for example, is just as important.

USE CASES AND OBJECTS

The dualisms of use cases and objects are worth elaborating on. Use cases and objects provide complementary views of an application.

The use case is the *end user's* view. Through use cases, we understand the application's requirements. We interact with end users. And we focus on usability in application design. The object is the *developer's* view (although not every object-oriented evangelist would agree with that statement). Through objects, we understand the structure of the system and the interaction among pieces of functionality. Some object models do make sense to end users, e.g., an end user understands there are different types of accounts and that these have certain relationships to different types of customers. But it is often a waste of time to involve the end user in the practical details of object modeling.

Use cases and objects are related in that the use case is a tool to identify objects. Once you have the use cases in place, objects fall out in a straightforward manner. Objects are simply derived from the use cases. In our own work, this derivation is based on some simple, yet fundamental principles of what makes an application changeable and extensible.* Furthermore, you derive object interaction, class inheritance, and object aggregates from use cases. Because use cases define functionality that should be implemented by some object, you can use them to derive object responsibilities, which are thus traceable to use cases. The most interesting object interactions and class hierarchies are those involved in several use cases. A new concept for abstract use cases of this kind is the *pattern.* A pattern is the design of an abstract use case, or rather a generic abstract use case, because patterns typically do not belong to a specific application domain.

This use case–object dualism gives you a vehicle for moving back and forth between the user's view and the developer view (Fig. 22-1). The model provided by the use-case view shows how several objects participate in each use

---

* In the Unified Process, each use case has a corresponding use-case realization in the analysis and design models; such use-case realizations are actually stereotypes on collaborations in the Unified Modeling Language.[8]

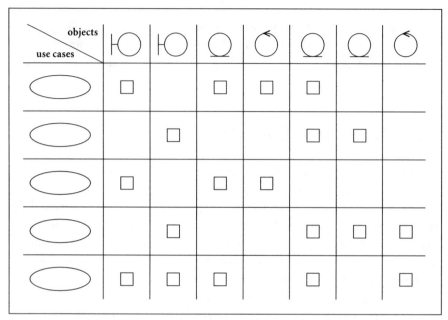

Figure 22-1. A use case–object matrix showing the dualism between the two.

case and also how each object may participate in several use cases and play a role in each of these use cases. This mapping is a key design transformation that forms the basis for traceability.

You derive objects one use case at a time, use case by use case. Each use case suggests certain object roles, which might lead to inconsistent and overlapping objects. Even if you tried to identify a common core set of objects before you begin, the various object views suggested from the use cases perspective are naturally inconsistent with each other. This is because each use case suggests object roles from the perspective of that single use case only. Other use cases may suggest conflicting responsibilities.

Obviously, the draft object model suggested by these different snapshots of the system must be harmonized and homogenized. The simplest cases involve synonyms (two objects that are the same but have different names) or homonyms (two objects that have the same name but are independent of each other). Most often, however, merging suggested objects to create a consistent model that still fulfills the use cases involves more creative activity than this. As you pursue this activity, it is very important to keep tractability to the use cases. Then when you modify an object's responsibility, you can easily see what use case might be affected and must be revisited. Changing one object might therefore change other objects. This is typical of object-oriented development.

THE OBJECT PERSPECTIVE

Taking an object perspective of this dualism, we see that an object participates in several use cases. The object designer must now define this object's responsibilities so that it is consistent and behaves as needed in every use case in which it participates. It is very easy to define behavior that is targeted to only one use case, but this is too specialized, and it undermines reusability when a new use case suggests a similar object responsibility. (In our OOSE method,[4] we handle this with control objects, which encapsulate behavior specific to a use case, and entity objects and interface objects, which encapsulate more general behavior and participate in several use cases.)

The mapping from a use case view to an object view also helps you verify requirements and design. You should not define an object that does not participate in a use case. Such objects do not originate from any requirements and thus cannot be tested properly, among other things. In the same way, you must not define a use case that has no objects allocated to it. Such designs do not meet all requirements. Use cases are common across all object models, and they tie object models together very efficiently.

USE CASES AS AN ENVISIONING TOOL

Use cases are just as helpful in the emerging field of user-oriented design as they are in object-oriented design. In user-oriented design, practitioners focus primarily on the user interface, and design the application based on how users act in their environment. Use-case modeling is preceded by an envisioning activity in which users participate to find the use cases and the associated user interfaces. It is very appropriate to do this envisioning work as a series of workshops in which user-interface designers observe users in the workplace, interview them, and ask them to describe in an episodic way different use scenarios, i.e., use-case instances. To better understand the user's needs, designers sketch the user interface as it evolves. When these designs are stable—and not before—prototypes are developed.

Booch[2] compares use cases to storyboarding in filmmaking. We go further and claim that the storyboard technique is a way to envision use cases.

We have seen several successful projects using storyboarding techniques together with use cases. Use cases can be used very well as a requirements capture and definition technique without even introducing object orientation! Work on user-oriented design, usability testing, etc., is very important in understanding the envisioning work.

USE CASE RELATIONSHIPS REVISITED

Having seen repeatedly how helpful use cases are, it is not surprising to us that others are embracing the concept and incorporating it into their methods. However, incorporating use cases into an existing method changes the foundation of the method because the use case concept affects all stages of development. It is therefore difficult to add it as just another technique on top of an existing method.

Most use-case concepts and extensions that have been incorporated into various methods are in line with our own thinking. We warmly welcome any suggestions on how to improve use case modeling. Let's not drive off in different directions due to misunderstandings. Instead, let's have an open discussion on new ideas. Two areas that appear to need some clarification are the generalization and extend relationship.

GENERALIZATION RELATIONSHIP

A use case can be thought of as a class that defines a virtually infinite set of instances, i.e., the executions of the use case that are actually possible. Use cases can be described formally, with some formal language, or informally, with plain text. Today we use plain text. Formalizing use cases, e.g., with state-transition diagrams and pre- and postconditions, could be a valuable extension but it could not replace plain text.

In describing use cases, you will sometimes note that two use cases share behavior. This common behavior can be defined with an *abstract* use case that is *used* by the *concrete* use cases. A concrete use case is the scenario a use case follows when it is executed.

You structure this commonality between use cases with the generalization relationship. Therefore, generalization is a relationship between use-case classifiers, and not between their instances. It is similar to inheritance between ordinary classes. The difference is that generalization implies a strict ordering of how the shared behavior is interleaved and extended by the concrete use case. The traditional concept of class inheritance in, e.g., C++, Smalltalk, or OMG, has no implied ordering of operations or attributes, and the order in which they are defined is of no significance.

In contrast, a concrete use case defines both when and how the abstract use case should be incorporated. When you change the abstract use case, you must also revisit the concrete use case to verify its correctness. The direction of the relationship (as always in our work) points out which use case that depends on the other. So, the concrete use case depends on the abstract use case.

EXTEND RELATIONSHIP

The extend relationship is similar to the generalization relationship. The main difference is one of changeability. In the case of extend, the *extension* use case depends on the concrete use case. In short, you use extend when you want to add functionality to a complete, meaningful concrete use case (one that, when instantiated, provides something of measurable value to some actor).

The semantics of the extend relationships now allows for extending the concrete use case without damaging it. Furthermore, the extension only takes place at a certain time, depending on the extension criteria. So, a use case instance can be executed with or without the extension. If you change the extension or add a new extension, you need not change the original use case. However, because the extended use case depends on the original, when you modify the original use case, you must revisit all its extensions. The extend relationship is also designed such that it should be possible to change the set of extensions at runtime, although not many commercial environments support this mechanism. In this way, you should be able to modify or enhance a system without shutting it down, which is often important in, for example, the telecom industry. The main difference between extend and generalization is thus not cardinality, but rather a matter of which use case knows what. Furthermore, both extend and generalization are relationships between definitions (classifiers), and not between execution entities (instances).†

---

† For more information refer to the chapter entitled "Basic Use-Case Modeling (*continued*)" for a more extensive treatment of use-case relationships.

INSTANCE RELATIONSHIPS

Why are there no relationships between instances of use cases? Indeed, several Objectory users have suggested the need for some kind of "consists-of" relationship between use cases. This is both syntactically and semantically feasible, but such a relationship would support functional decomposition, which would lead easily to a functional rather than object-oriented structure. Booch[2] reports a similar experience.

Instead, we prefer to move to object modeling as soon as possible after the functional requirements have been captured, defined, and validated with the end user. Doing refinement in terms of objects leads to a better decomposition than a purely functional decomposition. However, we do see a great need to do use-case modeling at various levels of abstraction. One example is detailed in a book on business process reengineering (BPR) with object technology.[9] Another example is decomposing a use-case model for each node in a network. Yet another is decomposing a use-case model for each subsystem in a large system. All of these are feasible, and because every use-case model is complete in itself, you should have traceability between various use-case abstraction levels. So the paradigm is, "This use case, defined in this way, corresponds to the use cases in these use-case models, each of which is separately defined," not "This use case is composed of these use cases."

OTHER APPROACHES

OMT/RUMBAUGH

In his *JOOP* column, Rumbaugh suggested how a use case concept could be introduced in OMT.[3] His actor and use case concept is very much in line with ours. Rumbaugh emphasizes domain classes as being equal to use case models when building the analysis model. In our work, use cases are more important than domain classes. Rumbaugh also introduces a new relationship, adds, between use cases, as a kind of instance aggregation. As we have just explained, we choose not to introduce any instance relationship between use cases because we do not want to encourage functional decomposition. Instead, we rely on generalization and extend.‡ Booch's *scenario* concept

---

‡ The UML has also added a third use-case relationship, called the "include" relationship.[8] See chapter entitled "Basic Use-Case Modeling (*continued*)" for a discussion of this new relationship.

corresponds to a use-case instance. A use case in the use-case model is a classifier from which we can imagine a virtually infinite set of use-case instances, just like we can create a virtually infinite set of instances from a class in C++ or Smalltalk. However, Booch introduces the scenario concept only informally, and then uses sequence diagrams to describe object interaction for a scenario.

RESPONSIBILITY-DRIVEN DESIGN/WIRFS-BROCK

Wirfs-Brock introduces use cases to support system requirements, object design, and user-interface design. She also suggests different levels of describing use cases. In this way, she provides an informal way of mapping different levels of use-case abstractions. She suggests a semiformal way to describe the interaction between actors and use cases. We have used similar techniques in some projects in which interfaces between subsystems had to be fixed early in projects. It works quite well.

Wirfs-Brock defines use cases at several levels. The highest level is the business scenario, which is refined into a more precise description of the actor's inputs to the system and the corresponding description of the system's responses. This captures the dialogue between an actor and the system; we have used sequence diagrams for the same purpose. In Wirfs-Brock's method, the system responses guide the developers to develop an object model and are further refined to include more details for the interaction, but still in user terms so that clients can be involved in reviews. System-response descriptions are the basis for further detailing the object model with object responsibilities. These more detailed system response descriptions are also the foundation for designing and tuning the user interface. She concludes, "Practical application of use cases can go a long way to improve our ability to deliver just what the customer ordered."[1]

OBJECT BEHAVIOR ANALYSIS

Another interesting contribution to use-case analysis and design is Object Behavior Analysis (OBA).[10] OBA is an extension of use cases; its contribution is primarily in the area of object-oriented analysis. OBA has no explicit support for use-case modeling. With OBA, you begin by identifying scenarios, which correspond to our use-case instances. A scenario is described with a script, and a script describes how different roles interact by sending messages to one another to perform the scenario.

Each message has an associated action that the receiver role takes. This is very similar to our robustness analysis. However, in OOSE we would do use-case modeling to explicitly identify use cases before doing robustness analysis. First we identify the different paths a use-case instance can follow; then, in robustness analysis, we identify the ideal objects needed to perform the instantiation of every use case. Our ideal analysis objects correspond to OBA's roles.

To define a robust object structure OOSE uses three object categories: boundary, control, and entity objects. After the ideal analysis, each use case is described in terms of interacting ideal objects. One technique for doing this is to use sequence diagrams. In OOSE, a use-case description then consists of several sequence diagrams. You give every sequence diagram an identity, in the same way that OBA suggests you identify a script. Just as you express the actions taken by an object instance when it receives a message, so can you associate actions to each activation in a sequence diagram.

Business rules can be expressed in a similar way. In a sequence diagram, you can express conditions such as alternative paths or exception handling in a manner similar to a script. From a modeling perspective, the underlying semantics of an OBA model and an OOSE robustness analysis model are very similar. The only difference is that we distinguish between three object categories, and the notation is slightly different. We use sequence diagrams, while OBA uses scripts.

WHAT'S NEXT?

The fact that most object-oriented methods seeming to merge and reach a consensus shows that object technology really is maturing. Notations still differ, but this is acceptable.

Of course, there are plenty of challenges left. One is how to synchronize the work of large projects, object-oriented or not. In our own work we are looking at introducing a formal interface concept between subsystems/packages.§ As long as interfaces do not change, teams can develop subsystems

---

§ For more information refer to the chapter entitled "Using Interfaces and Use Cases to Build Pluggable Architectures."

in parallel, with minimum synchronization. To reduce time to market, it is very important to reach stable interfaces as early as possible in a development project. It is easy to suggest interfaces early, but to suggest interfaces that are correct and will not change over time is much harder. Current methods are not very good at this. In our work, use cases are again proving to be a good tool for interface identification.

Other areas of interest, according to our priorities at Objectory Corporation[||], are:

- The process aspects of object-oriented development, i.e., how to really organize, manage, and perform predictable software development in large organizations.

- Large scale reuse: How to build architectures for reuse, layered systems, and mega-objects, and how to use frameworks to leverage the reuse of class libraries, etc.

- Integrating business modeling and systems development to create a seamless and clear path from business goals to implementation of support systems.[#]

To evolve the practice of use-case modeling, let use form a special use case–based design forum to exchange ideas and experiences, to evolve our ideas on how best to do use-case modeling. This could really be a field separate from object orientation; it is just as much related to user-centered design, for example.

[||] This took place in 1995.

[#] It is thus not a coincidence that these three issues recently have been treated in separate books.[9,11,12]

REFERENCES

1. R. Wirfs-Brock. "Designing Scenarios: Making the Case for a Use-Case Framework," *The Smalltalk Report*, (3)3, 1993.

2. G. Booch. "Scenarios," *Report on Object Analysis and Design*, 1(3): 3–6, 1994.

3. J. Rumbaugh. "Using Use Cases to Capture Requirements," *Journal of Object-Oriented Programming*, (7)5, 1994.

4. I. Jacobson et al. *Object-Oriented Software Engineering—A Use Case Driven Approach*, Addison–Wesley, Reading, MA, 1992.

5. I. Jacobson. "Basic Use-Case Modeling," *Report on Object Analysis and Design*, 1(2): 15–19, 1994. (See chapter entitled "Basic Use-Case Modeling.")

6. I. Jacobson. "Basic Use-Case Modeling (*continued*)," *Report on Object Analysis and Design*, 1(3): 7–9, 1994. (See chapter entitled "Basic Use Case Modeling (*continued*).")

7. I. Jacobson. "Use Cases and Objects," *Report on Object Analysis and Design*, 1(4): 7–9, 1994. (See chapter entitled "Use Cases and Objects.")

8. *The Unified Modeling Language for Object-Oriented Development*, Documentation set, ver. 1.1, Rational Software Corp., September, 1997.

9. I. Jacobson, M. Ericsson, and A. Jacobson. *The Object Advantage—Business Process Reengineering with Object Technology*, Addison–Wesley and ACM Press, New York, 1994.

10. K. Rubin and A. Goldberg. "Object Behavior Analysis," *Communications of the ACM*, (35)9: 48–62,1992.

11. I. Jacobson, G. Booch, and J. Rumbaugh. *The Unified Software Development Process*, Addison Wesley Longman, 1999.

12. Ivar Jacobson, Martin Griss, and Patrik Jonsson. *Software Reuse: Architecture Process and Organization for Business Success*, Addison Wesley Longman, Reading, MA, p. 497, 1997.

IN IVAR'S WORDS

Q: What made you invent the notion of a "use case"?

A: It evolved over many years. First of all, I worked in telecommunications in my early days, where the concept of "traffic case" existed. Such a traffic case was like a use case; it was, in fact, a telephone call. And there were many different kinds of telephone calls, and thus many different kinds of traffic cases. At that time we had no "cases" for other things than telephone calls. However, at that early time, I mean back in 1967, I had another term that was similar to use case and that meant the same thing: We called them "functions". A function crossed the whole system. A telephone call was a function, but functions were also more abstract things, and the term was not really well defined. We used this approach, "function-driven development," that is called now "use-case-driven development." We identified the functions, and then we designed the functions, like we do with use cases today. So the basic ideas are very old.

I identified the use-case concept in 1986, and when I had found that concept I knew I found something that solved many problems to me, because I could use this concept for everything that systems did, and for every kind of system. This helped me a lot to create a systematic software engineering methodology.

Q: It is interesting to see how quickly and broadly your use case concept was accepted by other methodologists. How could this happen so fast?

A: Most of the methodologists went into the objects world, and there was a lot of competition. However, the use case didn't compete with anything, and it solved a problem that everyone had. Even the concept of scenario was about something internal to the system, about internal interactions, but was not really specified.

One thing I did late was to publish. If you look at my 1987 paper, for the OOPSLA, it included all the basic definitions. But the problem I had was that I could sell my book, the Objectory book, in 1990–1991, for $ 25.00 a copy. So *why should I go and give it away to Addison–Wesley or any other publisher, to then get fewer dollars a copy, even if that was selling many more?*

Now I understand that I should have done it a little bit differently, but it's very hard to say, you have to be at the right time. Therefore, I think the other books helped us, because they had a big problem that was how to get from requirements to start an OO analysis and design. However, I refuse the idea that people publish their book, they were first with the idea: These were older ideas.

Q: Use case specifications are mainly textual. Previous methods, such as Structured Analysis, proposed the use of diagrams as a "common language" to reach an agreement between customers ("users") and developers. Why do you recommend textual specifications in the first hand?

A: In reality, today, customers and users of software don't want to read diagrams unless they are very simple. Examples of such diagrams are use-case diagrams that are so intuitive that everyone can read them. But pure text is something people don't need to learn a special language to understand.

We can of course use activity diagrams to describe use cases, and it's very nice, but there are some problems with that.

First, these diagrams quickly become very detailed, and it's not sure that they are more understandable because they are detailed, even if there is no doubt that at some point you need to specify them in more detail. But we think that the best way to specify those details is in terms of an analysis model, where you describe every use case as a collaboration among objects, instead of trying to detail the use case without talking about objects.

Secondly, activities can be very abstract, so it can be very hard to understand them, you really need to understand what has to be done, to understand the activities. So I'm very careful in introducing such a formalism in use cases. I think that when you go to analysis you get a much better formalism, a much better language to express details, because you talk about objects.

Q: Use cases have a double role in your method. First, they are used to elicit and to describe requirements coming from customers and users. Then, they drive the whole system development. Is one of these roles more important than the other?

A: No. But many methodologists, and many software developers, are very technology-introvert. If the use-case concept weren't so good in describing interactions, and helping to define system-internal object collaborations, they wouldn't have bought into it. So it does work as a very good sales argument to software developers: They would never have been accepted as widely as they are if they hadn't this impact on the design, if they didn't drive the development.

For me, anyway, both aspects are equally important. Use cases also manifest a very nice way to find the requirements and to capture requirements in some kind of diagram without going into the internals of the system.

(Extracts of the answers above reprinted with permission from Adriano Comai, an Italian IT consultant. They were first published at www.analisi-disegno.com and in the ZeroUno magazine (Italian translation).)

PART 6:
ARCHITECTURE AND LARGE-SCALE SYSTEMS

———

Whereas the previous part was about a software system's *function* (read: use cases), this part is more about *form* (that is, design and architecture). And as we will see, the universal fact that "function always has to compromise with form" also applies to software development.

We start by considering large-scale systems. These are systems of such complexity that they need to be decomposed into several smaller parts that in turn can be viewed as systems of their own. Creating models at two levels of a large-scale system—a superordinate level and a subordinate level—does this. Not surprisingly, having the notion of use cases in place helps significantly in this task.

This leads us to architecture in general. And luckily, it seems like the traditional art of creating software architecture is more and more becoming a science. Because in this part we find answers to important questions like "What is architecture?", What is a *good* architecture?", "How is an architecture described?", and "When do we develop the architecture in a software system's lifecycle?"

PART 6:
ARCHITECTURE AND
LARGE-SCALE SYSTEMS

———

23

USE CASES IN
LARGE-SCALE SYSTEMS

Ivar Jacobson, MARCH-APRIL 1995

U SE-CASE MODELING is an analysis technique for eliciting, understanding, and defining functional system requirements. I briefly
presented use-case modeling in the chapters entitled "Basic Use
Case Modeling"[1] and "Basic Use Case Modeling (*continued*),"[2] in which systems of moderate complexity were assumed.

This chapter shows how the use-case approach scales up to handle the construction of large systems. To build large systems, you must solve some
unique problems, including how to:

- Divide a large system into smaller autonomous systems.

- Define the interfaces among the smaller systems.

- Distribute the development work.

In this chapter, I will be presenting an extended use-case architecture and
system architecture; I show how employing use cases helps solve these problems. I also introduce the necessary method steps through an example.

USE-CASE MODEL INTRODUCTION

A use-case model consists of actors, use cases, and relationships among them.[3]

Actors represent everything that must exchange information with the system, including what are usually called users. When an actor uses the system, the system performs a use case. A good use case is a sequence of actions that yields a measurable result of values for an actor. The collection of use cases is the system's complete functionality.

Every system can be described with a use-case model. That is, any system can offer a number of use cases to a number of outside users, or actors.[4] Here, however, I consider only software and hardware systems.

SYSTEMS AT DIFFERENT LEVELS

In previous chapters, we have shown how to employ the use-case model to define the behavior of a complete system. This is fine for systems of moderate complexity, in which the number of use cases is small. But for very large systems, we must extend our architecture with features to manage the complexity of the system.

The use-case approach already supports a simple subsystem construct, which is a "transparent" package of objects. But this is not enough. We need a more powerful construct that can be developed separately and then connected with well-defined interfaces to form a large system. Therefore, we introduce a generalization of the system concept: Systems may contain systems recursively. For example, in Figure 23-1, the large system X contains three systems, X1, X2, and X3, which are developed by autonomous development teams.

When you must clarify what levels of system you are talking about, you can refer to the overall large system (e.g., system X in Fig. 23-1) as the superordinate system. Then, X1, X2, and X3 are referred to as subordinate systems. They are systems, not subsystems, and they should not be confused with the subsystem construct.

A large system can be divided into several levels of systems, but two levels are probably typical.

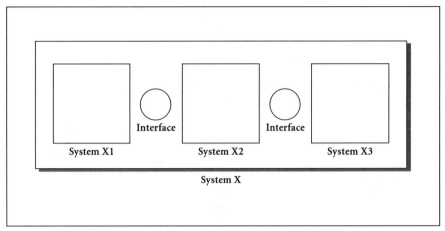

Figure 23-1. A superordinate system X containing three subordinate systems, X1, X2, and X3. The interfaces define the interfaces between the subordinate systems.

To distribute work among development teams so that each system can be developed separately, you must define the interfaces between each pair of communicating subordinate systems. An interface is here a definition of the services offered by a system.

Use-Case Models at Different Levels

Before you can divide a system, you must understand its overall requirements and structure. That is, you must define the behavior of the complete system, at least at a high level. The use case is our technique to model system requirements. However, the developers of each subordinate system should not have to worry about overall requirements; their requirements should be assigned to them.

The need for requirements on two levels leads to two levels of use-case models: a superordinate and a subordinate level. The superordinate use-case model (use cases a, b, and c in Fig. 23-2) defines the requirements of the entire system. The requirements of the subordinate systems are defined with a subordinate use-case model for each subordinate system. For example, the use cases a1 and b1 constitute the use-case model for system X1.

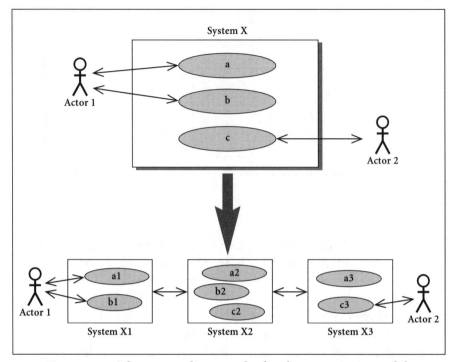

Figure 23-2. The superordinate and subordinate use-case models.

Use cases at the subordinate level that originate from the same use case in the superordinate use-case model are called subordinate use cases. For example, in Figure 23-2, b1 and b2 are both subordinate use cases of the superordinate use case b.

PHONE SWITCH SYSTEM EXAMPLE

A small telecommunications example, a phone-switch system, illustrates how to proceed from defining requirements for a large system to defining requirements for each subordinate system. In the use-case model in Figure 23-3, the superordinate use case Local Call routes a phone call from the location of a calling subscriber to the location of a called subscriber. The system looks up the called subscriber in the telecommunication network, sets up the incoming call between the called and the calling subscriber, supervises the call, and, when the call is finished, releases the network.

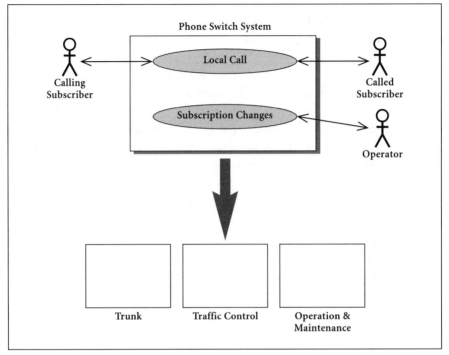

Figure 23-3. Model of a phone-switch system.

The other superordinate use case, Subscription Changes, describes how an operator changes the stored information about the local subscriber.

The phone-switch system is divided into three systems: Trunk, Traffic Control, and Operation & Maintenance (see Fig. 23-3). Just because these systems are part of an overall system does not mean they are small. Rather, they are of a size that is appropriate for a singular development team to handle.

The system divisions are found from the use-case descriptions or directly from the requirements specification. In OOSE[3] three different analysis object types—boundary objects, control objects, and entity objects—are used to model a system. These same types can be used to define a system's main responsibilities. So, the criteria for finding analysis objects can be used to identify systems. In this case, Trunk and Operation & Maintenance handle the communication with the subscriber and operator actors, respectively; they are (user) interface systems. Traffic Control controls the network and telephone lines; it is a control system.

SEQUENCE DIAGRAMS
AND SYSTEMS INTERFACES

Before you can divide the development work among the subordinate systems, you must distribute the requirements and define the interfaces among them. I use sequence diagrams[5] to do both. A sequence diagram describes how the behavior of a superordinate use case is distributed among the systems and how the systems communicate to implement the use case. In the phone-switch system, a sequence diagram for the first part of the use case Local Call would look like Figure 23-4.

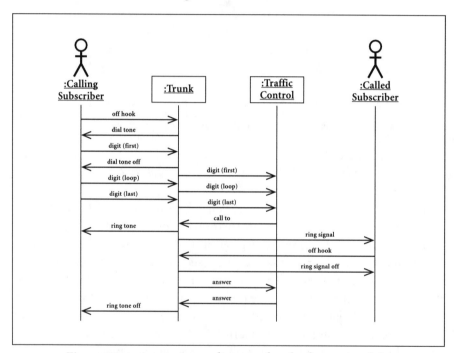

Figure 23-4. An sequence diagram for the first part of the Local Call use case.

You use the sequence diagrams to specify the interfaces among the systems. Interfaces are documented separately from the system that offers the interface. The interfaces of a system should be defined and approved long before the development of this system is finished. This means, for example, that a server system can be used by developers of related client systems before the inside of a server system is implemented.

256

SUBORDINATE SYSTEMS ARE SYSTEMS

Now that you have completed the modeling on the superordinate level, you can proceed to develop each individual subordinate system (in parallel of course).[6,7] We will concentrate on the Trunk. Three new actors to this subordinate system have been added, a Subscription Changer, a Coordinator, and a Digit Analyzer (see Fig. 23-5). They represent roles played by the systems interacting with the Trunk system; these actors behave in a way equivalent to the surrounding systems. However, a one-to-one correspondence between surrounding systems and actors does not necessarily occur. For example, the Coordinator and the Digit Analyzer together behave as Traffic Control. That is, two different actors represent Traffic Control, since it plays two different roles from the Trunk's perspective.

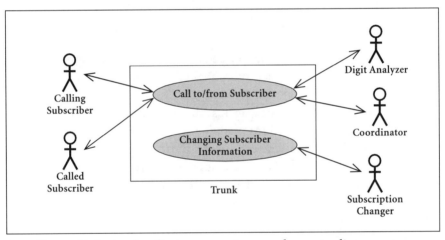

Figure 23-5. A subordinate system is treated as an ordinary system at the next level.

There are several reasons to view other systems as actors. First, the systems become less dependent on each other. This means that it will be easier to replace one system with another, as long as it conforms to the agreed-on interface. Second, by viewing a system as several actors that represent a separate role, respectively, you can easily let another system play one of these roles or even assign one of the roles to a system of its own. For example, the Coordinator role of the Trunk could be moved to another system's responsibilities.

To find the subordinate use cases of the Trunk, you use the sequence diagrams developed for the superordinate level. They give you enough information to divide the superordinate use cases into subordinate use cases. For example, the superordinate use case Local Call gives rise to the subordinate use case Call to/from Subscriber, and the superordinate use case Subscription Changes gives rise to the subordinate use case Changing Subscriber Information in the Trunk (see Fig. 23-5).

The requirements of the Trunk are completely defined by its subordinate use-case model and interfaces. Now Trunk can be developed in the same way as an ordinary system by a separate development team. We can identify the objects required to realize the use case, exactly as described in the chapter entitled "Use Cases and Objects."[5]

MAPPING DIFFERENT LEVELS OF USE-CASE MODELS

It is important that you be able to trace use-case models developed at different system levels. Clear traceability makes it easier to assign work when going from superordinate to subordinate use cases, and later, it helps verify the subordinate use-case models against the superordinate use-case model. A formal description method for mapping was introduced in 1985.[8]

Informally, the relation between superordinate and subordinate use-case models is interpreted as if all the use cases were equivalent, as seen from the actor's perspective. This means that the use case Local Call (see Fig. 23-3) and its subordinate use cases in Trunk and Traffic Control exhibit equivalent behavior to subscribers.

Thus, there is a type of equivalence relation between superordinate and subordinate use-case models. Each actor in the superordinate use-case model corresponds exactly to an actor in the subordinate model. Each use case in the superordinate use-case model corresponds to one or more use cases in the subordinate use-case model. Note that it is more important to identify good subordinate use cases than it is to maintain a one-to-one relationship between superordinate and subordinate use cases. In many cases, therefore, a superordinate use case will give rise to several subordinate use cases in the same subordinate system. Also, note that the name of a subordinate use case should explain the subordinate use case's behavior, which is probably not the same as the name of the superordinate use case.

Finally, each actor associated with a use case in the superordinate use-case model is usually associated with only one subordinate use case in the subordinate use-case model. (Theoretically, there is no reason why there cannot be more than one, but it is usually impractical.) This is true even in the special case in which a use case at the top level is allocated entirely, without being subdivided, to a single subordinate system.

SUMMARY

Informally, this is how you can employ use cases to define systems at different levels and relate use-case models at different levels to one another. This technique lets you continue to divide systems and use-case models in several steps. I believe, however, that even very large systems can be described with only one division, as described here.

ACKNOWLEDGMENTS

I am greatly indebted to Staffan Ehnebom at Ericsson HP Telecommunication AB and to the process-development team at Ellemtel AB for their valuable insights in how to develop large systems.

REFERENCES

1. I. Jacobson. "Basic Use-Case Modeling," *Report on Object Analysis and Design*, 1(2): 15–19, 1994. (See chapter entitled "Basic Use-Case Modeling.")

2. I. Jacobson. "Basic Use-Case Modeling (*continued*)," *Report on Object Analysis and Design*, 1(3): 7–9, 1994. (See chapter entitled "Basic Use-Case Modeling (*continued*).")

3. I. Jacobson, M. Christerson, P. Jonsson, and G. Övergaard. *Object-Oriented Software Engineering—A Use Case Driven Approach*, Addison–Wesley, 1992.

4. I. Jacobson, M. Erikson, and A. Jacobson. *The Object Advantage Business Process Reengineering with Object Technology*, Addison–Wesley, Reading, MA, 1994.

5. I. Jacobson. "Use Cases and Objects," *Report on Object Analysis and Design*, 1(4): 8–10, 1994. (See chapter entitled "Use Cases and Objects.")

6. R. Wirfs-Brock, B. Wilkerson, and L. Wiener. *Designing Object-Oriented Software*, Prentice–Hall, Englewood Cliffs, NJ, 1990.

7. B. Selic, G. Gullekson, and P. T. Ward. *Real-Time Object-Oriented Modeling.*

8. I. Jacobson. *Concepts for Modeling Large Real-Time Systems*, Department of Computer Systems, The Royal Institute of Technology, Stockholm, September 1985.

24

SYSTEMS OF
INTERCONNECTED SYSTEMS

Ivar Jacobson with Karin Palmkvist and Susanne Dyrhage, MAY-JUNE 1995

I N THE CHAPTER "Use Cases in Large-Scale Systems"[1] we presented an approach to modeling large-scale systems. A recursive system construct was introduced to model a system consisting of other systems, which is a way to manage the size and complexity of a large system. This recursiveness of the system construct is here further elaborated and presented as a general construct, which we refer to as a system of interconnected systems. We will also discuss some of the many situations where this construct is useful.

SYSTEMS OF INTERCONNECTED SYSTEMS

A system of interconnected systems is a set of communicating systems. There are several situations where this construct is useful, e.g., for a very large or complex system (S). Such a system is best implemented divided into several separate parts, each developed independently as a separate system. Thus, S is implemented by a set of interconnected systems, communicating with each other to fulfill the duties of S. The system S is then *superordinate* to the interconnected systems, and each of these is *subordinate* to S. This way, we get a separation of the superordinate system from its implementing subordinate systems, but with the relation between the different systems clear: Each subordinate system implements one subsystem of the superordinate system (see Fig. 24-1).

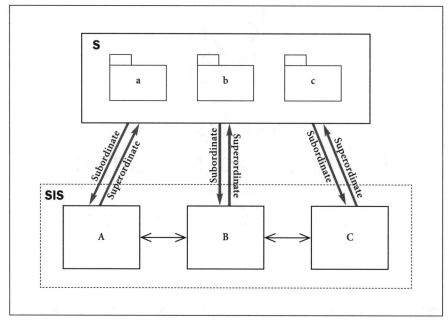

Figure 24-1. The specification of a system S is implemented by a system of interconnected systems (sis), where the systems A, B, and C are implementations of S's subsystems a, b, and c, respectively.

Separating the superordinate system from its subordinate systems has several advantages:

- The subordinate systems can be managed separately during all life cycle activities, including sales and delivery.

- It makes it easy to use a subordinate system for implementation of other superordinate systems by plugging it into other systems of interconnected systems.

- It means you can wait until late in the superordinate modeling process to decide if you need to develop entirely separate subordinate systems or if you can elaborate on the use-case and object models to implement the subsystems directly.

- It allows you to make internal changes to the subordinate systems without developing a new version of the superordinate system. New versions of superordinate systems are required only due to major functional changes.

Each subordinate system is associated with its own set of models, with strong traceability between these models and the corresponding models of the superordinate system. Thus, compared to the traditional recursion (system-subsystem-subsystem…) in most object modeling techniques today, recursion is enhanced by allowing recursion within more than one model. By doing so, each subordinate system can be managed as a separate system through all life cycle workflows: requirements capture, analysis, design, implementation, and testing. Naturally, the recursion may be extended to include more than one system division, even if this is seldom necessary in practice.

Workflows and Models for System Development

A natural assumption is that the superordinate system, as well as the subordinate systems, can be modeled with the same set of models and developed by performing the same workflows as for usual, noncomposite systems. Before we show how this can be done, these models and workflows—the development workflows that are performed to get the final result, and the implemented system (see Jacobson et al.[2])—have to be introduced. Examples of workflows are as follows:

- Requirements capture, with the purpose of capturing and evaluating the requirements, placing usability in focus. This results in a use-case model, with actors representing external units communicating with the system, and use cases representing sequences of actions yielding measurable results of value to the actors (see Fig. 24-2).

- Analysis, with the purpose of achieving a robust system structure, in the sense that it easily accepts modification and extension. This results in a model of objects grouped into subsystems of functionally related objects. The objects are of three different kinds to achieve a robust structure: boundary objects that handle all communication with the actors, control objects performing the use case-specific tasks, and entity objects corresponding to persistent objects (see Fig. 24-2).

- Design, with the purpose of investigating the intended implementation environment and the effect it will have on the construction of the system. This results in an object model, like the previous model, but this model is extended with specifications of how the objects communicate during the flow of the use cases. This might include definitions of interfaces (see Jacobson et al.[3]) for objects and subsystems, specifying their responsibilities in terms of provided operations. This object model is also adapted to the implementation environment in terms of implementation language, distribution, and so on (see Fig. 24-2).

- Implementation, with the purpose of implementing the system in the prescribed implementation environment. This results in components expressed in source code.

- Testing, with the purpose of ensuring that the system is the one intended and that there are no errors in the implementation. This results in a certified system that is ready for delivery.

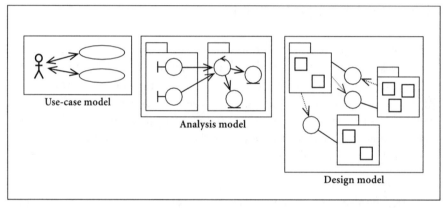

Figure 24-2. Three models of a system, each describing the system from a specific point of view, capturing specific characteristics of the system.

There is a natural order for these workflows, although they are not performed one after another but rather in cooperation with each other.

DEVELOPMENT OF A SYSTEM OF INTERCONNECTED SYSTEMS

In the previous chapter[1] it was shown how a use-case model could be used to model the responsibilities of the superordinate system. We will extend this to show how all the models above are used and interpreted for the superordinate system. Therefore each activity will be discussed in more detail with the focus set on a system of interconnected systems. We will also discuss the relationship between the superordinate system and the interconnected systems realizing it.

What we really have to do is define how the responsibilities of a system can be distributed over several systems, each one taking care of a well-defined subset of these responsibilities. This means that the main goal is to define the interfaces among these subordinate systems. When we have accomplished this, the rest of the work is performed separately for each subordinate system according to the "divide and conquer" principle. Therefore, this is all we have to do for the system as a whole, apart from testing it once implementation is done.

The first workflow is requirements capture. We have the same needs for requirements modeling for a system of interconnected systems as for any other system. A use-case model is a very natural way to express the results. The most straightforward way to look at this superordinate use-case model is to assume that it completely captures the behavioral requirements of the system. However, this is probably seldom the case. Since we need to implement the system with other systems, the system as a whole is probably quite complex. Therefore it is not a good idea to try to be exhaustive at this level. Thus, a superordinate use-case model usually gives a complete but simplified picture of the functional requirements of the system. There is actually no need to be too detailed at this level because the detailed modeling will be performed within each of the implementing subordinate systems.

The purpose of analysis is to achieve a robust structure of the system, which is of course of vital importance to a system of interconnected systems. The developers of the superordinate system must achieve a robust structure of subordinate systems, while they need not at all bother about the inner structure of these systems. We will therefore model a division of the system into smaller parts using subsystems. To get the right set of subsystems, and to get a first idea of how to distribute the responsibilities of the superordinate system over these subsystems, we develop an analysis model. The analysis objects should represent roles played by things in the system when the use cases are performed. Therefore the analysis model gives a simplified picture of the complete object structure, in analogy with the use-case model.

Functionally related analysis objects are grouped together into subsystems. Thus we get a subsystem structure that is ideal in the sense that it is based upon only functional criteria, e.g., we have not taken into account any distribution requirements.

Requirements regarding how the system should be divided into several sep-arate systems are taken into consideration when we design the superordinate system. The result of the design process may be a subsystem structure that is very different from the one we defined based upon functional criteria during robustness analysis. Thus we end up with a structure of real subsystems, which will each be implemented by a subordinate system (see Fig. 24-3). To be able to continue the development work for each such system separately, the interfaces are defined for the subsystems. In fact, the definition of inter-faces is the most important activity performed at the superordinate level, since interfaces provide rules for development of the subordinate systems.

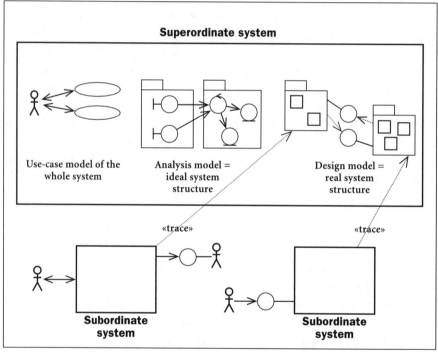

Figure 24-3. The superordinate system is described by a set of models, where the subsystems defined in the design-object model will be implemented by subordinate systems.

The next workflow is implementation. As already mentioned, implemen-tation of this kind of system is done by interconnecting other subordinate systems that together perform all the use cases defined for the superordinate system. Each subsystem in the design model of the superordinate system is implemented by a system of its own (see Fig. 24-3). In some cases there may already exist systems that can be used for this purpose, but in most cases we have to develop them. All models defined for the superordinate system serve as input to the subordinate systems development, and for each subordinate system the exact requirements are found by extracting all information that is tied to the corresponding subsystem in the superordinate system. The main requirement on a subordinate system is, naturally, that it conforms to the interfaces of its subsystem.

Each subordinate system is developed in the usual way, as a black box considering other systems with which it communicates as actors (see Fig. 24-3). We perform the usual set of workflows and develop the usual set of models, as described above, for each such system. If the models at the superordinate level are exhaustive we get complete recursiveness between the models at different levels, but as mentioned above, this is in practice seldom the case.

The final workflow is testing, which in this case means integration testing when the different subordinate systems are assembled and also testing that every superordinate use case is performed according to its specification by the interconnected systems in cooperation. Figure 24-4 shows the activities performed for development of the superordinate system and its subordinate systems. It is shown in terms of interacting business objects, cooperating in the development of a system of interconnected systems. This is a simplified

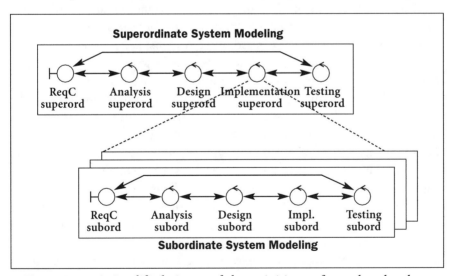

Figure 24-4. A simplified picture of the activities performed to develop a system of interconnected systems.

picture, which in reality would need several business objects.* The notation used is the one described in Jacobson et al.[5]

RELATIONS BETWEEN SYSTEMS

Now we have seen that the usual system development activities also can be applied to systems implemented by systems of interconnected systems. This is advantageous because it means that the one does not need to handle such systems in a way different from that used with other systems. We also get a nice separation of the superordinate system from its implementation in the form of other systems.

A final note on the independence between systems involved in a system of interconnected systems:

First we take a look at the subordinate systems. Each such system implements one subsystem in the superordinate system's design model. The subsystems depend on each other's interfaces and not explicitly on each other (see Fig. 24-5). Thus we may exchange one subsystem for another without affecting other subsystems, as long as the new subsystem conforms to the same interface. We get exactly the same relation between the corresponding systems. Each subordinate system views its surroundings as a set of actors. This means that we can exchange a system with another, as long as the new system plays the same roles toward other systems, i.e., as long as it can be modeled with the same set of actors. Systems refer to each other's interfaces as specified by the corresponding relations between subsystems and interfaces in the superordinate model. A subordinate system looks upon the interfaces of another system as offered by the corresponding actors, and therefore never has to refer directly to the other system (see Fig. 24-5). Note that Interface B occurs in several places in Figure 24-5, indicating that it is really the same interface referred to by subsystems in the superordinate system and by the corresponding subordinate system.

How about the superordinate system—what is its relation to its subordinate systems? It is independent of its implementing systems in the following sense: Each such system is only an *implementation* of what we have specified in the models of the superordinate system, it is not *part of* this specification.

---

* According to the Unified Process,[4] these "business objects" would be so-called workers operating on the superordinate and subordinate levels, respectively. See also chapter entitled "Designing a Software Engineering Process."

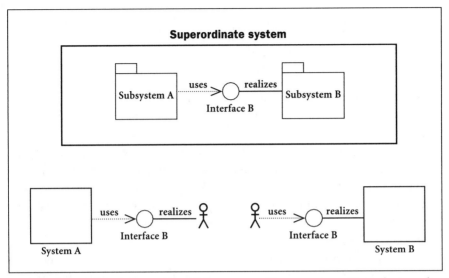

Figure 24-5. The subsystems of the superordinate system depend on each other only through their interfaces. The implementing subordinate systems therefore get the same kind of independence.

For practical reasons you have to define traceability links between systems at different levels, in order to trace requirements, but the most "tidy" way to do this is to define such links only between interfaces (see Fig. 24-5). In fact, one may even say that the subordinate systems are nothing more than implementations providing the interfaces defined in the superordinate models.

We can conclude that each system involved when a system is implemented by a system of interconnected systems is independent of the other *systems*, but they depend strongly upon each other's *interfaces*. Thus we have a very good platform for separate development of the systems!

APPLICATION AREAS

The architecture and modeling techniques for systems of interconnected systems can be used for different types of systems, such as:

- Distributed systems.

- Very large or complex systems.

- Systems combining several business areas.

- Systems reusing other systems.

- Distributed development of a system.

The situation may also be the opposite: From a set of already existing systems, we define a system of interconnected systems by assembling the systems.

In fact, for any system where it is possible to view different parts of the system as systems of their own, it is advisable to implement them as a system of interconnected systems. Even if it is a single system today, one may later have to split the system into several separate products, due to distributed development, reuse reasons, or customers' buying only parts of it, to mention some examples.

As a conclusion we will take a closer look at a couple of cases where the architecture for systems of interconnected systems can be used. For each of the examples we will show that the system in question has to be considered both as a single system and as a set of separate systems, indicating that it should be treated as a superordinate system implemented by a system of interconnected systems.

LARGE-SCALE SYSTEMS

The telephone network is probably the world's largest system of interconnected systems. This is an excellent example where more than two system levels are needed to manage complexity. It is also an example of a case where the top-level superordinate system is owned by a standardization body, and different competing companies develop one or several subordinate systems that must conform to this standard. Here we will discuss the mobile telephone network GSM to show the advantage of implementing a large-scale system as a system of interconnected systems.

The functionality of a very large system usually combines several business areas. For example, the GSM standard covers the entire system, from the calling subscriber to the called subscriber. In other words, it includes both the behavior of the mobile telephones and the network nodes. Because different parts of the system are products of their own that are bought separately, even by different kinds of customers, they should be treated as systems of their own. For example, a company that develops complete GSM systems will sell the mobile telephones to subscribers and network nodes to telephone operators. This is one reason for treating different parts of a GSM system as different subordinate systems. Another reason is that it would take too long to develop such a large and complex system as GSM as one single system; the different parts must be developed in parallel by several development teams.

On the other hand, because the GSM standard covers the entire system, there is reason to also consider the system as a whole, i.e., the superordinate system. This will help developers understand the problem domain and how different parts are related to each other.

DISTRIBUTED SYSTEMS

For systems distributed over several computer systems, the architecture for systems of interconnected systems is very suitable. By definition, a distributed system always consists of at least two parts. Because well-defined interfaces are necessary in distributed systems, these systems are very well suited also to be developed in a distributed fashion, i.e., by several autonomous development teams working in parallel. The subordinate systems of a distributed system can even be sold as products of their own. Thus it is natural to regard a distributed system as a set of separate systems.

The requirements for a distributed system usually cover the functionality of the entire system, and sometimes the interfaces between the different parts are not predefined. Moreover, if the problem domain is new for developers, they first have to consider the functionality of the entire system, regardless of how it will be distributed. These are two very important reasons to view it as a single system.

CONCLUSION

This chapter introduces architecture for systems of interconnected systems. This construct allows recursion not only within one model, but also between different models. The introduced architecture is used for systems that are implemented by several communicating systems. Their own models, separated from other systems' models describe all involved systems.

The examples given illustrate that the architecture for modeling systems of interconnected systems is useful in many different application areas. In fact, you may use the suggested architecture for any system where it is possible to view the different parts as systems of their own.[†]

[†] A recent book on reuse[6] is based on the SIS concepts as presented here, and is recommended for further reading.

REFERENCES

1. I. Jacobson. "Use Cases in Large-Scale Systems," *Report on Object Analysis and Design,* 1(6): 9–12, 1995. (See chapter entitled "Use Cases in Large-Scale Systems.")

2. I. Jacobson, M. Christerson, P. Jonsson, and G. Övergaard. *Object-Oriented Software Engineering—A Use Case Driven Approach,* Addison–Wesley, Reading, MA, 1992.

3. I. Jacobson, S. Bylund, and P. Jonsson. "Using Contracts and Use Cases to Build Pluggable Architectures," *Journal of Object-Oriented Programming,* 8(2), 1995. (See chapter entitled "Using Interfaces and Use Cases to Build Pluggable Architectures.")

4. G. Booch, J. Rumbaugh, and I. Jacobson. *The Unified Software Development Process,* Addison Wesley Longman, 1999.

5. I. Jacobson, M. Ericsson, and A. Jacobson. *The Object Advantage—Business Process Reengineering with Object Technology,* Addison–Wesley, Reading, MA, 1994.

6. Ivar Jacobson, Martin Griss, and Patrik Jonsson. *Software Reuse: Architecture, Process and Organization for Business Success,* Addison Wesley Longman, Reading, MA, 1997.

25

EXTENSIONS - A TECHNIQUE FOR EVOLVING LARGE SYSTEMS

Ivar Jacobson with Dave Thomas, JANUARY-FEBRUARY 1995

I N THIS CHAPTER, we describe a software engineering technique called Extensions—an approach for evolving large object-oriented software systems. It is well recognized that most of the effort in the life cycle is spent in the repair and enhancement of the system. No matter how well architected and designed the initial system is, over time, the system is transformed into one that traditionally has been increasingly more expensive to enhance and test. The fine-grained methods and differential programming provided by object-oriented computing greatly facilitate the process of software extension, thereby extending the useful life of a major system.

However, the use of object-oriented techniques introduces additional complexities in systems integration and testing.[1] In particular, both configuration management and testing are complicated by the granularity and inheritance of object-oriented programming. A second problem arises with regard to the description of the extensions, since as they get merged into the code base and distributed across the component library, an individual extension loses its identity. This makes it difficult to trace from a requirement, as described in a use case, to the code and vice versa. Extensions provide a disciplined approach for evolving a system wherein use cases are expressed as extensions to other (existing) use cases, as described in a previous chapter entitled "Basic Use-Case Modeling (*continued*)."[2] This eliminates unnecessary testing and preserves the traceability of new features/functions.

Evolving Object-Oriented Software

A well-designed system consists of a core set of classes for each system or subsystem.[1,3] To satisfy customer requirements the core system must be both changed and augmented. Experience has shown that much of the new functionality is easily added by extended existing classes and by added new classes that provide features that are substantially different from the existing system.[4]

In the ENVY/Developer[5,6] environment, for example, subsystems (collections of classes) are collected into applications that are each independently versioned and released. When a developer wants to add new functionality to a system, the developer defines new application classes that—if substantial—are themselves packaged into a new application.

In the process of adding new applications, it is often necessary to extend the behavior of an existing class in one or more other applications. We call such changes "extensions" and the classes that have been changed "extended classes." All the updates to the system can therefore be managed as the set of new, updated, and extended classes.

Testing

To fully test an object-oriented system, each class must be tested (module/unit test) and each component/subsystem must be tested (component test); finally, the entire system must be tested.[1] To test a class, the class and all its subclasses must be tested. In addition, any "super" methods that are used by or which use this class must be retested. Unfortunately, the time to test and retest a system can far exceed the time to perform defect repair and new feature development. Some have expressed concerns about the scalability of object-oriented programming systems for large embedded applications that contain many hundreds of classes.

Our experience with object-oriented technology in a wide variety of applications has been that object-oriented systems are much more evolvable than and need far less retesting than would be suggested by the above. The reason, of course, is that large proportions of the changes have effects that are localized to the class and/or method being changed. In the next section, we define Extensions, a particular type of change that facilitates software evolution while localizing testing to that portion of the software that has actually changed as a result of the extension.

EXTENSIONS

Extensions are a means for categorizing changes to a large system so that such changes can be applied and tested in a disciplined way. We define an Extension as the addition of a new feature/function that is a pure augmentation of the system. That is, a change is an extension if and only if it does not change the normal behavior of the underlying system that is being extended. When a change that is an extension is applied to the underlying system, only the extension needs to be tested, since there is no change to the behavior of the underlying system. In terms of an object-oriented system, this means that any additional behavior (methods) and state provided by the extension must be strictly an addition to the behavior and state of the existing system.

Unfortunately, it is generally undecidable if a change will preserve the underlying behavior of the system, so the responsibility for determining whether a set of changes is truly an extension is a human decision.

Clearly, it is possible to have a change/extension to an existing system that adds no new function but satisfies the property of being an extension. Examples include the use of an alternative representation of a component or the use of a new but equivalent algorithm. Although we agree that such changes may not require extensive retesting, we reserve the term "extension" for a major addition of new functionality that typically occurs over the life cycle of a large system.

The advantages of organizing large sets of changes into extensions is that it structures the testing and integration effort associated with implementing and releasing enhanced versions of the system. It means that the customer may only need to pay for (or wait for) the cost of developing and testing the requested extension. It also allows independent extensions to be implemented and tested concurrently, since there is no need to go through the full system test-and-release process.

We have observed that even in cases in which changes may not satisfy extension criteria, much of the change can be performed as an extension. That part of the change that is not an extension can then be subjected to more scrutiny.

Often in such cases, it may be easier to argue the correctness of the change through reasoning than by actually doing a full component test.

HISTORICAL NOTE

The principle of localized change is, of course, not new to good software engineers. For at least 20 years, large systems have been repaired in the field using machine-code "patches." Patch decks were usually distributed to the vendor and applied by a systems engineer from the vendor or the systems engineering organization of the customer. Unfortunately, in those days, it was common for large organizations to add their own patches to the system. It was also not uncommon for major applications vendors to provide patches for their products as well as portions of the underlying operating system. Just to make matters worse, it was not uncommon for some or all of the modules changed by the customer and/or the package vendor to be changed in the source, thereby defeating any straightforward application of absolute patches. This led to an extremely messy problem for the customer, since they were delegated the responsibility for merging and applying all of these absolute patches! The problem of merging and applying these patches forced numerous systems software managers to find techniques for managing the chaos.

Many systems programmers independently discovered a disciplined means for system extension based on applying patches to the underlying kernel system. The approach quite simply was to reduce the changes to the vendor code, making all patches simply *jump to* subroutines that preserved the absolute addresses used by vendor patches. Since the number of customer-applied absolute patches was now reduced to one per change and the vendors absolute addresses remained valid, this approach reduced the impact analysis of reinstalling the customer patches. This meant that all user changes had to be made in the form of patches, resulting in the development of tools that generated such patches from object code deltas, etc.

In this way, a system could be extended in a disciplined way by inserting a patch at a given address in the code and branching off to a subroutine that tested a flag and, if appropriate, supplied the additional behavior required by the customer or application. Provided the patch didn't change the existing behavior of the program, it could be applied and tested during the live operation of the system. Although we have never seen this systems programming technique documented, it was the survival secret for many mainframe systems and for large telecommunications systems.

IMPLEMENTING EXTENSIONS

Extensions are best described—you might say best *structured* (*structured* is used here in the normal sense)—in a way that does not change what already is understandable. The extension will describe both where the extension is inserted and the insertion. In the use-case model, this is expressed by letting one use case extend another already existing use case.

In the ATM example, we discussed the Cash withdrawal use case for customers who want to withdraw money from an ATM. Suppose we want to collect statistics on how often Cash withdrawal is used. To do this, we could extend the use case Cash withdrawal. Every time you execute Cash withdrawal, another use case counts and accumulates the number of times this transaction has been used (Fig. 25-1).

To be an extension, the set of changes represented by extended classes and/or near subclasses must preserve the behavior of the original system. Although in general it is impossible to guarantee this behavior, it is easier to argue if the code for the extensions is clearly separated from the code for the original system. It is still

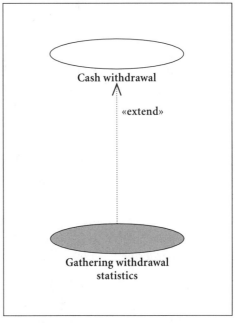

Figure 25-1. A common situation is having one use case collecting statistics regarding another use case, thus extending the other use case.

useful to have a tool that allows one to view the enhanced system as a single source code; otherwise, it is difficult to comprehend the system, since programming with extensions is really very much like programming with method combinations.

Extensions can be viewed as a set of additional classes that provide the state of the extension and a set of extended methods that provide the modifications to the existing methods that invoke the extension classes. These changes should be directly traceable to the extending use case that they implement.

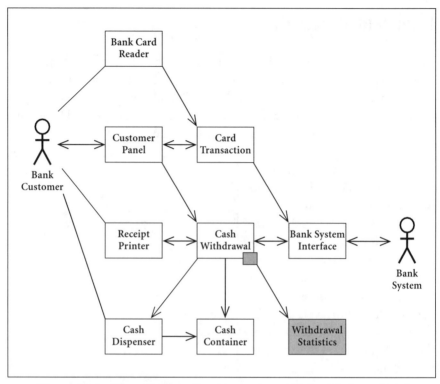

Figure 25-2. Class diagram for the use cases Cash withdrawal and Gathering withdrawal statistics. The extension is grayed.

Assume that the use case Cash withdrawal is designed as expressed in the class diagram depicted in Figure 25-2. The rectangles in the diagram are classes and the arcs are associations. The extension as expressed in the use case Gathering withdrawal statistics can now be implemented as one additional class (Withdrawal Statistics) and as a slight change to an existing class (Cash Withdrawal).*

In this example, we had to implement part of the extension as changes in existing classes. This is not always necessary, since some extensions can be implemented without affecting existing classes—which of course simplifies the implementation and maintenance of the extension.

Extensions should not modify the state of the kernel class, nor should they be visible to the preexisting clients of the kernel class. Even encapsulation

---

* The small rectangle overlapping the Cash Withdrawal class symbol in the diagram denotes the change of the class; this is not correct UML notation but included to simplify and clarify the discussion.

doesn't guarantee this, however, since extensions may change the time to execute a given method, therefore exposing their existence. If the system is implemented in a pure object-oriented programming style wherein every method is a single message, then extensions can be implemented using simple before or after method combinations.

Languages such as Beta (inner), CLOS (method combination), and Smalltalk (super) provide facilities for implementing such extensions. None of the existing object-oriented systems provides method combination at the statement level. We therefore feel that for large systems, the development environment should provide tools for managing extensions to avoid accidental implementation errors. It is important to be able to undo an entire extension. Configuration Maps[6] describe such a facility in an object-oriented configuration management system.

CONCLUSION

In this chapter, we have presented a software engineering technique called extensions. Extensions are a disciplined approach for evolving a system by adding a new set of features. They support the incremental evolution of a system without incurring the delays associated with a full systems integration, test, and release. Unfortunately, not all changes are extensions, nor is it even possible to formally verify that all extensions are in fact truly behavioral; however, the technique has proved so useful in practice that it merits inclusion in any software engineering process. There are at present no development tools that directly support extensions. We believe that life-cycle processes and tools should support the concept of extensions as distinct from a defect repair or update to the existing system.

REFERENCES

1. I. Jacobson, M. Christerson, P. Jonsson and G. Övergaard. *Object-Oriented Software Engineering—A Use Case Driven Approach*, Addison–Wesley, Reading, MA, 1992.

2. I. Jacobson. "Basic Use-Case Modeling (*continued*)," *Report on Object Analysis and Design*, 1(3): 7–9, 1994. (See chapter entitled "Basic Use-Case Modeling (*continued*).")

3. I. Jacobson. "Object-Oriented Development in an Industrial Environment," Proceedings of OOPSLA'87, Special Issue of *SIGPLAN Notices*, 22(12): 183–191, 1987.

4. I. Jacobson. "Language Support for Changeable Large Real-Time Systems," OOPSLA86, ACM, Special Issue of *SIGPLAN Notices*, 21(11), 1986.

5. D. Thomas and K. Johnson. "Orwell: A Configuration Management System for the Purpose of Team Programming," Proceedings of OOPSLA'88, Special Issue of *SIGPLAN Notices*, 23(11): 135–141, 1988.

6. M. Milinkovich and K. Johnson. *ENVY/Developer Reference Manual*, Object International, Inc.

26

USE CASES AND ARCHITECTURE

Ivar Jacobson, AUGUST 1998

I F A SOFTWARE PROJECT does not get started right, it is not likely to end right. To rush into construction too soon is to start wrong. To start right means: Get the requirements right and get them in shape to drive the development process. That means getting them into the form of use cases. Formulate an architecture and make it concrete as an executable baseline that guides construction. Get the process iterative and incremental, namely, use a series of phases (inception, elaboration, construction, and transition) and iterations within the phases that will enable you to attack first things first—but we leave this third step to the chapter entitled "The Unified Process Is Iterative."

These three steps lie at the heart of a good software process. Put this way, you probably agree. Unfortunately, there are still some people, undoubtedly benighted, who contend that the way to develop software is to hire good people, lock them in a room with a tight schedule posted on the wall, and let them do what they do best—write code. Please believe me—it doesn't work. Good people are always good to have, but they alone are not enough.

USE CASES DRIVE DEVELOPMENT

A requirement specification, often scores or hundreds of pages in length, has always been a difficult source from which to develop software. The major difficulties were structural. Specifications were structured as long lists of "shalls." Major and minor requirements were mixed. It was easy for these long lists to become wish lists. It was easy to add new stuff. But, there was no obvious traceability to usability.

The use case concept, as I reported in my 1992 book, *Object-Oriented Software Engineering,* was developed many years ago to avoid these difficulties. The concept is now widely used. It was developed out of experience and its value has been proven by experience.

Briefly, the use cases take the place of most of the textual requirements documents. Use cases capture almost all the requirements, functional as well as nonfunctional. While much of the use cases' content is drawn from direct contact with people who will be using the system, they are not the sole source. Use-case analysts put themselves—conceptually—in the position of users; they try to understand the roles they play; they try to understand the business setting in which they operate.

The use of the automatic teller machine, from which we all draw the monetary medium that sustains our daily existence, is an example of a "use case." We approach the machine with a confident step, insert our plastic card in the orientation that the machine insists upon, and read its response: "Enter your personal identification number." We obey. Then the digital logic within the machine conducts an exchange with a distant computer and establishes that we are indeed a valid customer with a positive account balance. It commands us to enter the sum we have in mind. If that does not exceed our credit limit, it counts the requisite number of bills into a dispensing device.

That is the essence of the ATM use case, though there are variations and additions, like what should it do when the plastic card has expired? The use case grows as the analyst, bank people, and representative customers think through all the possibilities. What are good use cases? A good use case is one that provides the user (a human being or another system) with "a result of value." This result of value is the criterion by which we judge the pertinence of the use case to the system. Applying this criterion gives the product team a means to avoid functions that sound interesting but, in fact, do not represent a result of much value.

Each use case captures a portion of the functional requirements. As use cases are put together, they become the use-case model. When the use-case model is complete—when it contains all the use cases—it completely describes the functionality of the entire system. In fact, it takes the place of the traditional functional specification. Furthermore, since most nonfunctional requirements are specific to a particular use case, we can attach nonfunctional requirements to the use cases to which they are relevant. Thus, the use case model with its related nonfunctional requirements captures all (or, at least most) requirements—functional as well as nonfunctional.

The old requirements specification described what the system was supposed to do. The use-case model goes one step further. It describes what the system is supposed to do for each user. In that respect, it is more concrete than the old specification. It pushes us to think in terms of value to specific users, not just in terms of functions that are "nice to have." There is a tendency under the old regime to add "bells and whistles," as the saying goes, because someone in the room is enamored of them, not because actual users are likely to have much use for them. Bells and whistles complicate the system, add to the difficulty of making everything work together, and extend schedule and costs.

At first, however, we are interested in putting together only a small percentage of the entire use case mass—perhaps 5 percent—enough to enable us to perceive the candidate architecture in the selected use cases (an inception phase activity). It is this candidate architecture, crystallized in a functioning proof-of-concept prototype that determines the feasibility of the proposed system. A little later, when we have worked out on the order of 10 percent of the use case mass, we can formulate the executable architectural baseline (an elaboration-phase activity). To find that 10 percent, however, we may have to explore, say, 40 percent of all the use cases to assure ourselves that we have not left anything in the shadow. By the end of the elaboration phase, we will have fleshed out, say, 80 percent of the use cases—enough to be able to make a bid.

Use cases and the use-case model are more than a means of specifying the system. They also drive system development. The use-case model leads to the analysis model, still in what we may call the "problem space." The analysis model serves two purposes: (1) to understand the use cases more precisely—the analysis model is the very best way to prepare a detailed specification of the requirements of the system; and (2) to identify a logical/ideal architecture of the system. In turn the analysis model becomes the design model, showing the system in the solution space. From analysis to design means taking care of the solution space—mapping the analysis model to the chosen platform (programming language, operating system, database system, etc.), middleware (GUI frameworks, standard protocols, etc.), and other reusable software, and then to implementation and components.

Starting from the use-case model, developers work through a series of models—analysis, design, implementation, deployment, and test. For every use case at the beginning, there is a corresponding realization of the use case in the design model. Once the model is available, testers can start planning the testing. Each use case maps directly to a set of test cases; each test case (maybe a group of them) corresponds to a path through the use case. Once the design is done, the testers use the sequence diagrams and the statechart diagrams to generate detailed test cases. The developers check each successive model for conformance to the use-case model. In fact, it is the testers' task to ensure that the components of the implementation represent the use cases correctly. Thus, the use cases, as a representation of the requirements, do more than initiate the development process; they bind it together. This binding together is the core of Objectory's use case-driven process.*

Progress from one model to the next is permitted through traceability, which is a great advantage when changes inevitably erupt. Change often appears at the use-case level, where it is comparatively simple to visualize. It is then pushed through the series of models to the code and the components—where it can be much more difficult to identify.

We call a development process operating in this way use case driven. But the use cases are not selected and fleshed out arbitrarily. Rather, they are keyed to the development of the architecture.

THE USE CASE DEFINITION

A use case specifies a sequence of actions, including alternatives to the sequence that the system can perform, interacting with actors of the system.

ARCHITECTURE ORGANIZES DEVELOPMENT

Trying to build a structure of any great degree of complexity without an architecture is foolhardy. It is architecture that provides the pattern within which we build structure. In the case of software, the most important goal is to get a good architecture. One thing we mean by good is that the architecture will be cost-efficient, not only in the current cycle, but also in future development cycles. And how do we achieve cost-effectiveness?

- Through a cost-effective balance between reuse of existing components or legacy systems and new construction.

- Through a cost-effective balance between "buy" of platform products, commercially available frameworks and components, and "build" of our own components (to satisfy the use cases).

---

* Consequently, this is the core of the Unified Process.

- Through achieving this balance in a way that will make the system resilient to future changes.

The role of architecture is:

- To conceptualize the design in a form that developers and stakeholders can understand.

- To guide construction during the first development cycle, and in the future evolution of the system.

- To enable management to structure the project and the organization itself around the architectural elements.

Why do we need an architecture? To begin to understand its place, let's take the example of products in general. Every product has both function and form. These are not big words, but their meaning in relation to a software product may not be immediately apparent. A much earlier product, for example, was the hammer. Its function was to drive something (a nail, perhaps) into something else (a wooden board, for instance). Its form was a hard-surfaced head on the end of a handle, the head to hit the nail and the handle to give the user something to hold on to and also a bit of added leverage.

Applying these concepts to software, its function is to implement requirements (or use cases). Its form is a collection of subsystems and the like, with the relations between them mediated by messages passed through interfaces. For a product to be successful, these two forces, function and form—and use cases and architecture—must be balanced (see Figure 26-1).

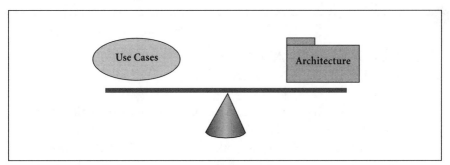

Figure 26-1. Use cases and architecture balance as function and form.

This balance does not just happen, especially in that locked room where the denizens are occupied with putting out lines of code. It happens best when the development process provides space and time in which it can happen, and rules on how to get balance. In software development, function and form evolve in parallel. On the one hand, the small percentage of use cases that were initially selected have to anticipate the architecture as it takes shape, must provide space in which the use cases that are developed later can be realized. We call a process putting this emphasis on architecture "architecture-centric."

THE ARCHITECTURE DEFINITION

Software architecture encompasses significant decisions about:

- The organization of a software system.

- The selection of the structural elements that comprise the system and their interfaces, together with their behavior as specified in the collaborations among the elements.

- The composition of the structural and behavioral elements into progressively larger subsystems.

- The architectural style that guides this organization: these elements and their interfaces, their collaborations, and their composition.

Software architecture is not only concerned with structure and behavior, but also with usage, functionality, performance, resilience, reuse, comprehensibility, economic and technological constraints and tradeoffs, and aesthetics.

KEEP USE CASES AND ARCHITECTURE IN BALANCE

Which comes first—use cases or architecture? If someone woke me up in the middle of the night and asked me this, I might say "...architecture." But after having coffee, I might say something like: "But how do I know what to build? Oh, that is through use cases." This is much like the question, "Which came first, the chicken or the egg?" that people probably began asking about 10,000 years ago, when settled agriculture first appeared. We will not try to solve that problem here—Charles Darwin probably already

OBJECTORY IS NOW THE UNIFIED PROCESS

The Objectory process was first released in 1987. It has evolved over all the years based on user and customer feedback. During the past two years we have made many important improvements to the process. The three most important improvements are: (1) focus on architecture, (2) controlled iterative and incremental development, and (3) the application of UML for modeling. It now supports in depth the whole life cycle including business modeling, requirements capture, implementation, and test. It also includes project management and configuration management, yet it still maintains all the old core values of Objectory: use case driven analysis and design. Objectory is also designed using engineering techniques. We used a version of Objectory for process engineering to design Objectory for software engineering. This allows Objectory, in principle, to be specialized for every product.

Because Objectory is the recommended software development process for using UML, it was natural to call it the Unified Process. It made life simpler for everyone. Thus, from now on I will use the name the "Unified Process" to talk about our process: the use case driven, architecture-centric, and iterative and incremental process.

The Unified Process is published in a book.[1] Grady Booch and Jim Rumbaugh are coauthors. The Unified Process also exists in the form of a product from Rational Software Corporation, called the Rational Unified Process. The book is a textbook to present workflows, the artifacts, the activities, and how UML is used for different purposes. However, the book is not enough to help a whole team of developers work as a concerted effort to develop commercial software together. For this you should use the Rational Unified Process. (Refer to the interviews with Dr. Jacobson in Part 4 that discuss this issue in depth.)

has, anyway. They evolved together over millions of iterations. We are sure, however, that in software development use cases and architecture must evolve together—must be kept in balance during this evolution.

The reasoning (somewhat simplified) goes like this: The first step is to create an approximate architecture based on our general understanding of the application domain and a limited understanding of the specific system. In other words, with little detailed knowledge of the use cases. We get the lower layers (platform, frameworks) of the system this way. The second step is to expand our knowledge to reflect those use cases that are architecturally significant and adapt the approximate architecture to support that set of use cases. Then we expand our knowledge again and modify the architecture. With each step we increase our knowledge of the use cases and embody that knowledge in the growing architecture. In time, we achieve a baseline architecture that guides development.

These steps, of course, we call iterations, a subject we intend to explore further in the chapter entitled "The Unified Process Is Iterative." For now we stress that Objectory,† which is driven by use cases and centered on architecture, and keeps the two in balance with iterations—is what industry needs.

---

† And now the Unified Process.

REFERENCE

1. I. Jacobson, G. Booch, and J. Rumbaugh. *The Unified Software Development Process*, Addison Wesley Longman, 1999.

27

ARCHITECTURE IS ABOUT EVERYTHING—BUT NOT EVERYTHING IS ARCHITECTURE

Ivar Jacobson, MARCH 1999

WHAT IS THE MOST IMPORTANT THING to get right when developing a new software system? You may think this is a stupid question. However, if I had to answer it—and I had to pick only one answer—I would say "architecture." Then I would try to amplify that one-word answer.

"You cannot get the right architecture if you don't look at what use cases to provide," I would say. "You cannot get the right architecture if you don't consider the technology that is available." There is quite a list of considerations.

Getting the right architecture assumes all those things. Because it does, the architecture is the most important thing to get right.

WHAT IS ARCHITECTURE?

What do we really mean by "architecture of software systems"? Searching the literature on software architecture yields many answers that seem to be whatever is on the author's mind at the time. It's reminiscent of the old parable in which a group of blind men give a variety of descriptions of an elephant—a big snake (the trunk), a piece of cord (the tail), and so on.

We might next look at the historical discipline that gave rise to the word "architecture" itself—building, which embodies many layers of technology: the excavation, foundation, structure, walls and floors, elevator shafts, electrical, air conditioning, water, sanitation, and features for specialized occupants. The role of architects is to fit all these layers together. They make the total product intelligible to clients. At the same time, they provide guidance to all the other participants in the building process.

That is what we want architecture to do for the software development process.

ARCHITECTURE IS ABOUT EVERYTHING

The architecture of a software system covers the whole system, even though parts of the architecture may be only "one inch deep." For important parts that are not initially understood clearly by the participants, the architecture goes as deep as it must to make the part clear. In areas in this category, it may go down to executable code so the stakeholders and developers can see it run, and can feed back their insights.

In covering the whole system, the architecture provides clients, developers, and the stakeholders with a common vision. Having a common vision, they can work together more effectively and attain a product that meets users' needs, yet doesn't overshoot the resources available.

For an architecture to be "good," we mean:

- It is resilient to future changes.
- It is simple to understand.
- It is designed to evolve.
- It separates responsibilities between subsystems.
- It balances what to make and what to buy (or accommodates reuse).
- It is designed to harvest reusable building blocks.

ARCHITECTURE IS NOT EVERYTHING

Architecture in the construction industry is about the significant things, and the same is true in the software industry. Software architecture sorts out the significant things about the system. This little bit, this significant bit—the architecture—eventually grows into the whole system. The architecture is like the skinny system; it contains the skeleton and the most interesting muscles (code). It grows through the development work to become the full-fledged system; all the muscles are added. The system is the end result of this development process; it is the "everything," but the architecture comes first. It is less than everything, but it is enough to serve as a guide for the development project.

First, however, note that the meaning of architecture varies with the type of building or product. The architectural drawings for a villa are different from those for an office building. The drawings for buildings are different from those for bridges, cars, or television sets. Thus, architecture has meaning (unless you are a philosopher) only in the context of what kind of product you are building.

For example, if you are building a software system, architecture means extracts from the artifacts of the system. Thus, if you build the system based on functional decomposition, you get very different sets of artifacts as compared to building based on components. Consequently, you get a very different meaning to architecture depending upon which approach you use.

Now, because it is our experience that component-based development gives us the best system-life-cycle behavior, the issue becomes: What is architecture in this context? To answer that question, we need to know what kind of artifacts this approach requires.

MODELS ARE EVERYTHING

Before we explain this provocative heading, let us consider the ultimate result we seek:

- What kinds of drawings do you need to get a good system?
- What do you need when you plan the whole project?
- What do you need to mitigate risks?
- What do you need to make a bid?
- What do you need to proclaim that "this is the architecture"?
- What do you need when you build the system?
- What do you need after you have developed the architecture into the initial release to maintain and further develop the system?

You need a lot of experience to answer these questions. You need to have been through a number of development cycles. You need to understand what it means to develop many different types of software for different applications. You need to have been in both the maintenance part of the life cycle and in developing new generations of existing products. Even all that is not enough. You also need to know what a good system looks like, what kinds of building blocks you should use, what kind of infrastructure (operating system, etc.) you should base your product on. You should know, in general, what reusable building blocks are available in the application area of your system.

Beyond these needs as separate considerations, you have to balance them. Once you have this balance in place, you have found the kinds of drawings you need for the system. In addition, what should be contained in each of these sets of drawings is obviously dependent on who is going to use them. For instance in house construction, the drawings for the electricians are different (that is, they use a different notation) from those for the plumber. Moreover, the electrician and the plumber don't want to have their notations on the same drawing. They prefer to work from different drawings.

In software development, similarly, we say that we provide workers with models uniquely suited to their work. A model is a complete description of the system from a particular perspective. In the 30 years of experience that has resulted in the Unified Process, we have identified the need for a number of models. Some of the most important are:

- *The use-case model,* which captures the functional requirements of the system and many nonfunctional requirements specific for a use case. The analysts develop this model for users and the customers.

- *The analysis model,* which refines the use cases as collaborations among conceptual objects. It identifies reusable building blocks; it identifies a structure resilient to future changes; and it specifies structure and behavior that should be preserved in the design and implementation. The analysts, with the participation of customers, develop the analysis model for the developers.

- *The design model,* which is a blueprint of the implementation. It identifies all classes, subsystems, interfaces, and components. It is built by the developers.

- *The deployment model,* which describes the physical computer structure and the allocation of components to the different nodes in the network. It is designed by the developers.

- *The implementation model,* which includes all the components—files as well as executable components. It is the result of the developers' work.

- *The test model,* which identifies all the test cases and test procedures, needed to perform the tests. It is prepared by the testers.

The number of models may vary for different applications and organizations. The model concept is very powerful and has been adopted by UML. Personally, I expect the number of models to grow once we have a stable foundation model set and as we get more and more tool support for the process.

Building models is what software development with the Unified Process is all about. (This is why we used such a provocative heading.) This is why models are everything we do. (Not quite true, but almost.)

ARCHITECTURE AND MODELS

Now you may well ask, "Why don't we have an architecture model made by the architect for the developers?" That is a good question. There could very well be one. Suppose we had one. What would it look like? It would identify all that is significant about the system, but not everything. In particular, there are lots of drawings that are not architectural.

Thus, an architectural model would contain all the significant subsystems, classes (active classes and some realizations of conceptual classes), components, nodes (in the computer architecture), and the most significant parts of the interfaces. (In many cases the most significant subsystems means all the subsystems.) The architectural model would also describe how these structural elements collaborate to realize the most important use cases. In brief, it would describe a system, small in relation to the whole system, with the focus only on what is significant.

An architectural model would contain an extract from the use-case model (including only those use cases that were critical to the architecture), and extracts from all the other models: analysis, design, deployment, implementation, and test.

In effect, this new hypothetical architecture model would consist of extracts from all the other models. In the Unified Process, instead of employing a special architecture model, we create an architecture description composed of

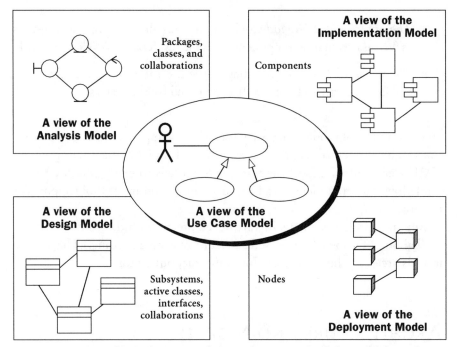

Figure 27-1. The architecture description is views of the models in the Unified Process.

extracts from the other models, or as we say, views of the models, that is sufficient to present the architecture.

Thus, an architecture description includes views of the models (see Fig. 27-1). There is a view of the use-case, analysis, design, deployment, and implementation models. Since the test is performed just to verify the architecture, we don't include it in the architecture description.

Since a view of a model is an extract, a view of the use-case model looks like a use-case model itself. It has actors and use cases but only those that are architecturally significant. In a similar way, the architectural view of the design model looks like a design model but it contains only those design elements that realize the architecturally significant use cases. It contains collaborations for all significant use case realizations, and so on.

There is nothing magical about an architecture description. It looks like a complete system description with all its models (there are some differences that we will come back to in a later chapter), but it is smaller. How small is it? There is no absolute size for an architecture description, but in our experience, for many systems, it should be about 50–100 pages. That range applies to single application systems; architecture descriptions for suites of applications will be larger.

For a discussion on architecture, refer to the chapter entitled "The Steps to an Architecture."

28

The Steps to an Architecture

Ivar Jacobson, July 1999

RCHITECTURE IS *about* everything but it is not everything, as I explained in my previous chapter. The "everything" is the completed models of the system we are building and the architecture is a well-selected extract or view of these models. The architecture includes the most significant constructs of the system. But, how do you get an architecture? That is what this chapter will talk about.

When Do You Develop the Architecture?

The architecture is developed in early iterations of the very first life cycle of a new system. In the Unified Process, it is primarily done during the elaboration phase. Actually, we can define the elaboration phase as the one in which you need to get a stable architecture. If you do not have a stable architecture you are not yet done with the elaboration phase. Having a stable architecture is a prerequisite to making a good plan—a plan with high credibility—to guide the construction phase. In the elaboration phase you carry out each iteration in the usual way, that is, you start with requirements capture and follow with analysis, design, implementation, and test. In this phase, however, you focus particularly on the architecturally significant use cases and their related requirements. As always, the use cases drive your work in every iteration. The result is an implementation of a small portion of the ultimate system, what we might call a skeleton of the system with a few software "muscles." More formally, we call it the architectural baseline. This baseline is more than a set of extracts from the models; it actually runs—to a degree.

WHICH USE CASES ARE ARCHITECTURALLY SIGNIFICANT?

The architecturally significant use cases come from two sources:

- Those that help us mitigate the most serious risks.

- Those that are the most important to users of the system.

However, to sort out those significant use cases, you have to find most of "all of them." You do this to make sure that you cover all the important functionality of the system. You want to leave nothing in the shadows. Let us explore this a bit further.

USE CASES THAT MITIGATE THE MOST SERIOUS RISKS

In principle, we can map all technical risks to a use case or a scenario of a use case. To accomplish this goal, we have to select the use cases in such a way that we mitigate the risk if we can realize the use case's functional and non-functional requirements. This principle is valid, not just for risks pertaining to requirements and architecture, but also for verifying the underlying hardware and software. This principle means that judicious selection of pertinent use cases enables us to exercise the key functions of the underlying architecture. We establish that we have a workable architecture baseline.

USE CASES MOST IMPORTANT TO USERS OF THE SYSTEM

The second category of use cases that we explore in the elaboration phase are those that cover the main tasks or functions of the system. To find them, you ask yourself the question, "Why are we building this system?"

You find the answer in the word "critical." That is, you look for the use cases critical to the operation of the system. In addition, you look for the use cases to which important nonfunctional requirements are attached—requirements such as performance, response time, and so on.

These two categories of use cases, those related to important risks and those pertinent to essential operations, enable us to find the architectural skeleton of the system. To this skeleton, in the construction phase, we will add the rest of the functions required.

DON'T LEAVE ANY
USE CASES IN THE SHADOW

In the elaboration phase, we are trying to sort out only a small percentage of the use cases on which to base the architectural skeleton. After all, in this phase our time and staff are limited. At the same time, we want to at least look at all the use cases that could possibly impact the architecture. We do not want to leave any functionality in the shadow. We don't want to discover too late that our architecture is not stable. To be sure of our architectural baseline, we need high coverage of the use cases that might affect the architecture. Moreover, we need high coverage, not just for the architecture, but also for predicting accurately the costs of developing the product in the first cycle. Finding out in a later phase—or even in a later generation of the life cycle—that our architecture cannot accommodate a newly discovered functionality is a risk that we want to avoid.

To avoid leaving any functionality in the shadow, we find in practice that we need to "cover" about 80 percent of the use cases in the elaboration phase. By "cover," we don't mean to elaborate every last detail; it is enough to understand the use case and its impact on the system. It is enough to locate it in the use-case model. We are not trying to design at this point; we are trying to formulate the architecture. It is not necessary in the typical project to detail all of the use cases. Parts of them are usually sufficient. In fact, some of the descriptions may come to only a few lines.

In simple projects where the risks are low, we may detail only a minor fraction of the use cases. In more complicated projects with higher risks, we may detail 80 percent or more of the use cases.

So now we understand which use cases we need to start from to drive the work on the architecture.

THE ARCHITECTURE BASELINE IS A SYSTEM—
BUT IT IS A "SMALL, SKINNY" ONE

What exactly do we mean by "architecture baseline"? It is a set of models that depict the most important use cases and their realizations. The models

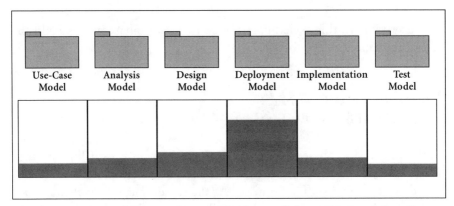

Figure 28-1. At the time of internal release of the architecture baseline, the models are worked out only to the extent of defining the architectural skeleton.

include the use-case model, the analysis model, the design model, and so on, as shown in Figure 28-1. Each model is only partly completed, as shown in the figure, just enough to represent the architecture baseline. Note that we have an implementation model, though it is only a small part of the eventual system. At this point, the baseline is "small and skinny."

By the end of the elaboration phase, we have also reached a number of decisions:

- The standards to rely on.

- The systemware and middleware to use.

- The legacy systems to reuse.

- The distribution needs we have.

As we see in Figure 28-1, the architecture baseline contains partial versions of the same models that will eventually represent the full-fledged system. It is a skeleton of subsystems, components, and nodes of the system with little of the musculature in place. However, this skeleton does possess "behavior." The implementation model is executable code. This skinny system is capable of evolving in the next phase into a system capable of initial operation. Some changes to the structure and behavior may prove to be necessary during this evolution, but they are intended to be minor. By definition, the architecture at the end of the elaboration phase is to be stable. If, at this point, it seems not to have reached stability, you must continue the elaboration phase until you achieve this goal. The later success of the project and product rests on a stable architecture.

At the time of internal release of the architecture baseline, the models are worked out only to the extent of defining the architectural skeleton.

The shaded slice of each model corresponds to the degree of completion of that model at the time of internal release of the architecture baseline at the end of the elaboration phase. The shaded and unshaded parts together (the whole rectangle) represent the completely developed model, as it will appear at the end of the life cycle, at the time of customer release.

After the internal release of the architecture baseline, we could define several other baselines, representing further internal releases of new versions of the models. Each of these additional versions would build on top of one another, starting with the first additional increment on top of the architecture baseline. Each new version would evolve from the earlier versions.

We note, however, that a project does not evolve one sequence of model buildup independently of the other model sequences. For example, a use case in the use-case model corresponds to a use-case realization in the analysis and design models and to test cases in the test model. Also, the performance requirements of the use cases must be met by the process and node structure of the deployment model. Accordingly, to assist developers in working from one model to the next or back again, model elements from one model to the next are connected through «trace» dependencies.

THE ARCHITECTURE BASELINE AND THE ARCHITECTURE DESCRIPTION

The internal release at the end of the elaboration phase consists of more than the model artifacts. That "more" is the architectural description. It is developed concurrently with the models. In fact, it is often developed ahead of the activities that lead to the architectural version of the models. The architecture description guides not only the development team for the first life cycle, but also subsequent teams in the life cycles to come. It is the standard guidepost, now and into the future. Since the architecture baseline should be stable by this point, the ongoing standard will continue to be stable.

The architect can adapt the architecture description to the needs of the project and the stakeholders. On the one hand, he could extract pertinent views from the versions of the models that make up the architecture baseline. On the other hand, he could revise these extracts to make them easier to understand. In any case, the architecture description includes extracts or views from the models at this time.

As the system evolves, the models become larger in later phases. The architect may make changes or even add views from the new versions of the models. However, if architectural stability had been achieved at the time of the elaboration phase, subsequent modifications of the architectural description should not upset that stability. These changes or additions should be in the nature of refinements or clarifications.

The Architecture Baseline Is Operational

The fact that we implement, integrate, and test the architecture baseline assures the architect, other developers, and stakeholders that this skeleton is operational. Executable code actually runs. That reality cannot be matched by any amount of "paper" analysis and design. Moreover, this operating baseline provides a working demonstration in which customers, users, and the developers themselves can discover problems that might elude them in a pile of papers (or electronic equivalents). Now is the time to correct misunderstandings; now is the time to stabilize the architecture.

Architecture: The Most Important Determinant

In chapters entitled "Use Cases and Architecture" and "Architecture Is About Everything—But Not Everything Is Architecture" we have presented what an architecture is, how it is represented, when and how it is developed. It is worth paying a lot of attention to architecture, since in our experience over many years, the single most important determinant of an application's quality is the quality of its architecture.

29

USING INTERFACES AND USE CASES TO BUILD PLUGGABLE ARCHITECTURES

Ivar Jacobson, Stefan Bylund, Patrik Jonsson, & Staffan Ehnebom, MAY 1995

T HE USE OF OBJECT TECHNOLOGY in mature software development organizations has lead to system models being built in terms of large-grained building blocks, often called subsystems.[1-6] In most cases it is important to model subsystem dependencies, i.e., how instances of classes within different subsystems depend on each other during a system's execution. This can be accomplished by using *subsystem interface specifications*, or simply *interfaces* as we call them here.

The subsystems and their interdependencies define a system's large-grained architecture. We achieve a *pluggable architecture,* in the sense that subsystems can easily be substituted in a model if they have the same interfaces, as a consequence of having clearly defined interfaces on subsystems.

Thus, subsystems and interfaces, or similar constructs, are well known to the object-oriented (OO) community. However, these constructs are not enough; they need to be extended by other constructs to describe the dynamic behavior of subsystems with interfaces. This is unique to our approach: being able to describe the behavior of systems in terms of interfaces realized by subsystems. To accomplish this, we exploit use cases.[1, 7-9]

SUBSYSTEMS AND INTERFACES

Subsystems might be used to model *layered architectures*[10] by letting subsystems represent different layers, or *distributed applications*,[11,12] where a subsystem represents a node in a distributed system. In these contexts it is important to model the client/server dependencies between subsystems. We have here concentrated on the modeling of such dependencies by using interfaces (see Fig. 29-1).

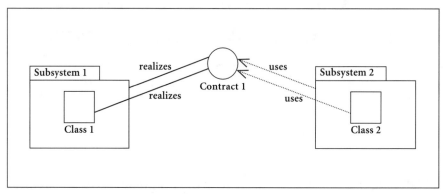

Figure 29-1. Interfaces in relation to classes and subsystems.

Assume that we have two subsystems, subsystem 1 and subsystem 2, that contain classes whose instances will interact. In this case, an instance of class 2 will send stimuli to an instance of class 1. Instead of modeling this with a relationship between the classes, we use an interface (interface 1) between them that specifies the public operations available from class 1. We then use a *realizes* relationship from class 1 to interface 1 to specify explicitly the connection between an interface and its implementation (i.e., a class). To model that an instance of class 2 will communicate with an instance of class 1, we have a uses relationship from class 2 to interface 1. We also model these dependencies on a subsystem level with uses and realizes relationships from the subsystems to the interface. Note that these subsystem relationships correspond to the relationships from their contained classes to the interface. Moreover, an interface does not itself contain any realization (or implementation) definitions for the defined behavior; it just serves as a definition to be used by the client of a specific behavior. The idea of using interfaces is to achieve the following:

- **Implementation independence.** A subsystem and its contained classes depend only on interfaces realized by other subsystems, and not on the internal design of other subsystems; thus, a subsystem's internal design can easily be changed without affecting other subsystems depending on it.

- **Pluggability.** Different subsystems realizing and using the same set of interfaces can be exchanged with each other if they have the same externally observable behavior. Note that such exchanges require that the static as well as the dynamic aspects of an exchanged subsystem are preserved by the new subsystem.

- **Abstraction.** One interface can represent behavior that is implemented by many arbitrary classes and subsystems interacting with one another. Such an abstraction can be useful to a client of a complex subsystem.

- **Division of work.** An important use of subsystems is to specify *a part of the total system;* such a part of the system can be designed and implemented by a specific group of people. In this context, it will be the interfaces realized by a subsystem that define what has to be designed and implemented inside the subsystem. It will also be the subsystem interfaces that serve as the basic *synchronization points* for different work groups.

- **Separate interface management.** Interfaces can be managed separately, in a systematic way, if they are separated from implementations.

We have found that it is very important to model both the static and *dynamic* aspects of subsystems and their interfaces in order to meet these requirements. It is also important to understand interfaces from a process perspective[1] to be able to discuss responsibilities, change requests, division of work, top-down development, and so on.

A Telecom Example

Here we introduce an example to illustrate our ideas, a simplified telecom switching system.[1] We will concentrate on the use case Local call and its actors A-subscriber and B-subscriber (see Fig. 29-2).

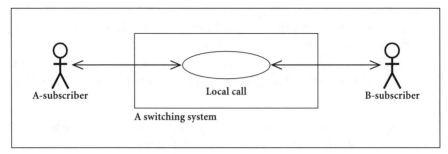

Figure 29-2. A telecom switching system, with the use case Local call and its actors.

An A-subscriber is a person issuing a local call (i.e., a caller), and a B-subscriber is a person answering such a call (i.e., a recipient). A local call goes from an A-subscriber to a B-subscriber connected to the same switch. The diagram of Figure 29-3 is a view of the classes that participate in the flow of the use case.

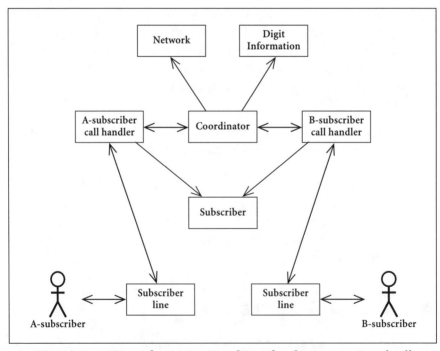

Figure 29-3. View of participating classes for the use case Local call Arrows denote interactions between objects.

Note that the names of the symbols are class names but that the diagram describes how instances of these classes are associated. Of course, the classes themselves can also be associated with instances of classes, but for simplicity we do not consider that case in this chapter.

There are classes whose instances represent the network (Network), phone numbers (Digit information), and subscribers (Subscriber). There is also a class (Subscriber line) whose instances handle interaction with the subscribers. Finally, there are three controlling classes, one for each subscriber (A-subscriber call handler and B-subscriber call handler) and one for the whole system (Coordinator), whose instances coordinate the subscribers' behavior. The part of the use case that we are interested in can be illustrated more precisely with a sequence diagram (Fig. 29-4), where the responsibilities of the use case have been allocated to classes appearing in the diagram in Figure 29-3.

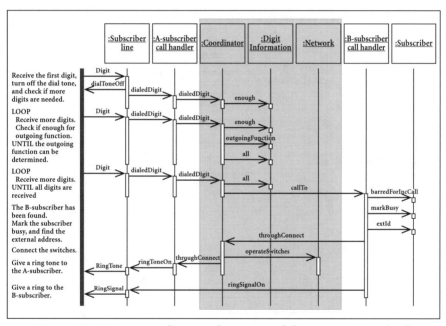

Figure 29-4. Sequence diagram for a part of the use case Local call. The grey part covers objects whose classes are defined by the same subsystem (see Fig. 29-5).

On top of each object lifeline in the sequence diagram there is a symbol with a class name. Each lifeline has a set of *activations* (rectangles), where each activation denotes a *way* through an operation that is performed by an instance of the class at the top of the lifeline. Each activation has one incoming arrow, denoting a stimulus transmission; the name on a stimulus transmission can be the name of a message corresponding to the name of the operation that will be performed.

In this manner, we may continue designing our system, use case by use case, finding all the classes needed. For each use case we then create a view of participating classes, together with one or several sequence diagrams describing its behavior in terms of interacting objects.

THE SUBSYSTEMS OF THE EXAMPLE

We assume the subsystem partitioning of Figure 29-5.

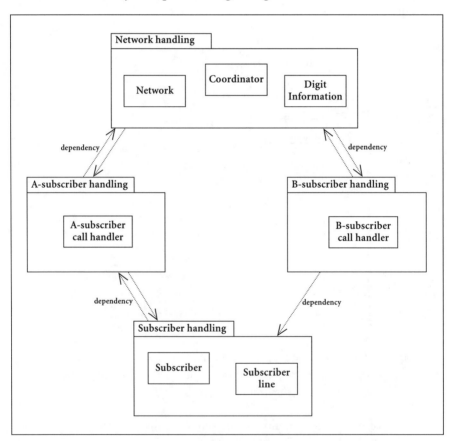

Figure 29-5. Subsystem partitioning of the telecom example.

The dependency relationships between subsystems are used to specify that instances of classes contained within different subsystems interact. Note that in reality, a subsystem is not needed when it contains just one class such as the A-subscriber handling subsystem; we use this partitioning in our example just to illustrate our ideas.

Now, assume that we want to build for pluggablility regarding the subsystem Network handling. The internal design of the subsystem might change, and instances of other classes might realize its behavior. A model such as the one above (Figs. 29-3 and 29-4) would require that we change all diagrams where the classes contained in Network handling appear, e.g., the diagrams of Figs. 29-3 and 29-4. Moreover, all descriptions in the model (such as use case descriptions) where classes within Network handling appear must also be modified.

We solve this problem by defining interfaces on the Network handling subsystem that remain the same regardless of its internal design. We can split our model into two (or more) levels, where one high level perceives the Network handling subsystem as a black box realizing and using interfaces and another, lower level presents the internal behavior (and the specific design) of the subsystem. Then, when we want to change the internal design of the Network handling subsystem (e.g., add or remove classes within it), we only need to substitute the lower level design. The higher level design will be the same as long as the interfaces are the same.

Building for Pluggability—a High-Level View

Now, for each subsystem we define the interfaces that are relevant for performing the use cases. In this example, we use interfaces of Figure 29-6.

Here, the interfaces realized by each subsystem are for simplicity shown by "gluing together" the interface symbol with the subsystem symbol (although a correct notation would call for realize relationships[11]); for example, the interface C is realized by the Network handling subsystem. We also have the following relationships from the contained classes to the interfaces (compare with Figs. 29-3–29-5): The class Coordinator realizes the interface C, A-subscriber call handler realizes A, B-subscriber call handler realizes B, Subscriber line realizes L, and Subscriber realizes S. The subsystems that contain a class realizing an interface thus also realize the interface; the subsystems that contain a class using an interface also use the interface. The arrows in the diagram are uses relationships, from subsystems to interfaces, meaning that instances of classes within a subsystem use (interact with) instances of classes contained in another subsystem.

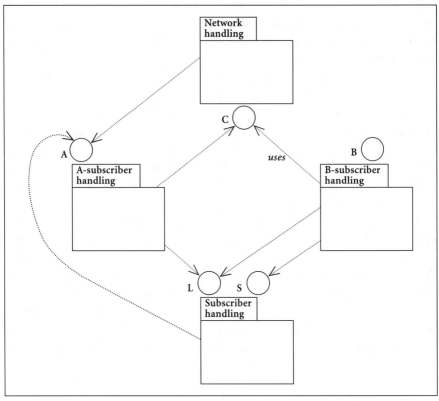

Figure 29-6. View of participating subsystems and interfaces for the use case Local call.

Usually, a subsystem contains a large number of classes. In that case, we only have to create interfaces for the classes that should be visible from the outside of the subsystem.

Note that the diagram in Figure 29-6 is just a higher level view of the diagram in Figure 29-3. In the same manner, we can translate the sequence diagram in Figure 29-4 to the sequence diagram over subsystems (Fig. 29-7).

On the top of each lifeline there is a symbol with a subsystem name instead of a class name as in Figure 29-4. Here it is specified how the subsystems interact to perform a part of the use case. All arrows (stimuli transmissions) in the diagram are associated with an interface, followed by the name of a stimulus corresponding to an operation defined in the interface. Note that these stimuli have the same names as the stimuli defined on the objects as shown previously (Fig. 29-4). To simplify, it could be said that the subsystems interact "through" the interfaces.

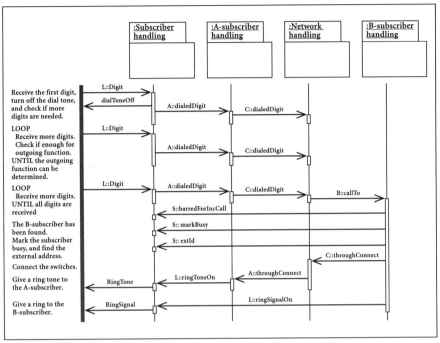

Figure 29-7. Sequence diagram where the behavior of Local call is distributed among subsystems.

In a stimulus transmission in Figure 29-7 there will be one instance whose class is contained within the subsystem—namely, the one that realizes the interface, that receives the stimulus; when this instance performs the corresponding operation, it will *lead to* the sending of the outgoing stimuli. It may not necessarily be the receiving instance that performs the sending; it can also be another instance of a class contained within the subsystem. Thus, the activation can in this context denote a *way* (or sequential thread) through several operations on different instances of classes within the subsystem. As an example, consider the stimulus transmission C::dialedDigit to the subsystem Network handling. Since C is realized by the Coordinator class within Network handling, it will be an instance of Coordinator that receives the stimulus dialedDigit. In the sequence diagram of Figure 29-7 we can see that the third time such a stimulus is received, it will lead to the sending of the stimulus B::callTo to the subsystem B-subscriber call handler; however, the diagram does not tell us which instance sends this stimulus. In this case, we happen to know from Figure 29-4 that it will be an instance of Coordinator that sends the stimulus.

Note that in this high-level view of the design it would be easy to substitute the Network handling subsystem with another subsystem realizing and using the same interfaces, as long as they have an equivalent behavior.

BUILDING FOR PLUGGABILITY—A LOW-LEVEL VIEW

Given the high-level design above, we want to complement it with low-level views describing the internal design of the subsystems. The diagram in Figure 29-8 is a view of participating classes (and interfaces) for the part of the use case Local call that is local to the subsystem Network handling.

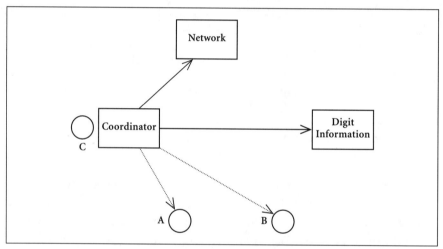

Figure 29-8. View of participating classes and use cases for the use case Local call, local for the Network handling subsystem.

Here the interfaces realized by a class are shown by gluing together the interface symbol with the class symbol; for example, the interface C is realized by the Coordinator class. The arrows between the classes are the same relationships as before (Fig. 29-3). An arrow *to* an interface means that it will be an instance of a class realizing the interface that receives a stimulus. For example, an arrow to the interface C denotes that one or several stimuli are received by an instance of the Coordinator class. But from this low-level perspective, we do not know *what* specific classes will realize the interfaces A and B.

Following these ideas, we can also create a local sequence diagram (Fig. 29-9) for the Network handling subsystem. That diagram is almost the same as the

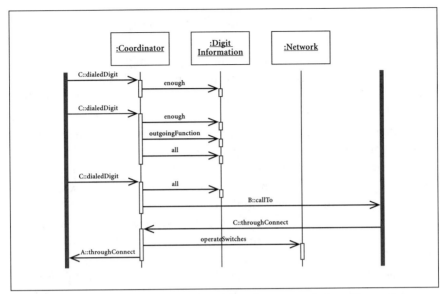

Figure 29-9. Sequence diagram, local for the Network handling subsystem regarding the use case Local call.

shaded part of Figure 29-4. The only difference is that interfaces are used on the stimulus transmissions when interactions cross subsystem borders.

Note that the two diagrams in Figures 29-8 and 29-9 illustrate part of the internal design of the Network handling subsystem. If the subsystem is to be removed from the system, all its local diagrams and description documents will also be removed. However, since the other subsystems use its functionality through interfaces, they can remain unchanged if another equivalent subsystem is put in the same place. With *equivalent subsystems* in this context, we mean two subsystems that *realize* and *use* the same interfaces, and when they are in the same externally observable state, they respond in the same way when receiving the same stimuli.

TRACEABILITIES BETWEEN VIEWS AT DIFFERENT LEVELS

As we have shown above, the model will contain class diagrams and sequence diagrams describing how both objects and subsystems interact. Some of the diagrams are refinements of others. It should therefore be possible to trace abstract diagrams (e.g., views of participating subsystems) to their refinements (e.g., views of participating classes) and vice versa. This could be supported by hypertext links between the diagrams themselves.

A DESIGN METHOD FOR PLUGGABLE SUBSYSTEMS

We have so far introduced interfaces in a way that might lead the reader to believe that one should be working bottom-up during design activities. This is, of course, a possible way of working, and it is suitable for instances when an already existing design is abstracted by means of interfaces and included in a higher order system. We will now show top-down design as another possible approach to a system design. A top-down approach allows for an early decomposition of a system into subsystems with strict interfaces, which simplifies a process for working in parallel for system designers. Our proposed design working-order is similar to the approach taken in Jacobson et al.[1] in that it takes a number of specified use cases and actors as input.

First, a system is designed in terms of directly contained subsystems SS1...n. The design working-order is recursive in the sense that the different subsystems SS1...n can be designed in terms of their contained subsystems, and so on, all the way "down" to the classes.

STEP 1: IDENTIFY THE HIGHEST-LEVEL SUBSYSTEMS

There are several ways to identify the highest-level subsystems, ranging from simple approaches where subsystems are elicited from a written system specification to approaches where an OO system analysis is carried out to identify the subsystems.[1,12,13] We will here assume that we have some rational approach to identify these subsystems. The result of this step could be some thing similar to Figure 29-10.

STEP 2: DISTRIBUTE THE USE CASES OVER THE SUBSYSTEMS

Create a sequence diagram for each use case and distribute the flow of each use case across the subsystems. Define an intersubsystem stimulus transmission whenever behavior defined in one subsystem emits a stimulus that activates behavior defined in another subsystem.

Since the behavior defined in a subsystem is only accessible through the interfaces realized by that subsystem, it is now necessary to define through which subsystem interface a transmitted stimulus is to be received. Identifying the interfaces realized can be done in different ways. One approach we propose is that interfaces are identified by making an OO analysis. Such an analysis, the purpose of which should be to identify the main object roles of the system, determines which analysis objects perform

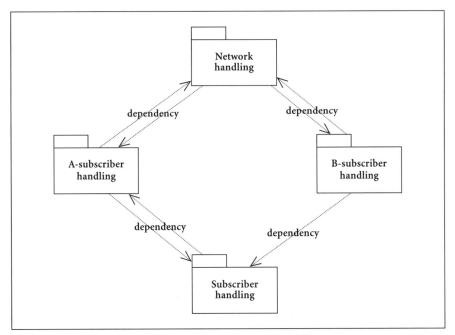

Figure 29-10. Subsystem partition of the example.

intersubsystem communication and serves as a sound OO input to identifying the interfaces of the design subsystems.

The result of this work-step could be something similar to Figure 29-7. Also define which interfaces are *used* by a specific subsystem.

STEP 3: SPECIFY THE OPERATIONS REALIZED THROUGH THE INTERFACES

Now it is possible to collect all use cases' requirements on each subsystem. This can be done by collecting and analyzing the operations paths from each sequence diagram that involves the subsystem. All of these activations serve as candidate operations in the interfaces of the subsystem, but they have to be coordinated so that different use cases utilize the same behavior through the same operation name. The result of this step could be something similar to Figure 29-11.

STEP 4: DESIGN EACH SUBSYSTEM INTERNALLY

With the interfaces used and realized by a subsystem and the sequence diagrams that involve the subsystem, it is possible to design the subsystem

---

Interface: C
Description: Analyzes phone numbers and connects different subscribers.

Operations:
    dialedDigit: aDigit
    Description: Receive a dialed digit, store it, and analyze the sequence of
        the received digits.

    throughConnect: bSubscriberID
    Description: If the call is through-connected to the b-subscriber line,
        the network switches are connected and the a-subscriber
        line is notified.

Figure 29-11. An interface example.

internally. This is carried out *within each subsystem,* quite similar to the work steps 1–3 above (i.e., recursively) with the difference that sequence diagrams are created *within* each subsystem for the local part of each use case that involves the subsystem.

The recursion ends when a subsystem contains only classes, which means that no further recursion is necessary within the subsystem.

The internal design of a subsystem will sometimes show that the design on a higher level does not make optimal use of the subsystem. This means that the higher level designs sometimes need to be adapted when the internals of the subsystems are understood better, something that is particularly true early in the design phase.

EXPERIENCES

The basic idea behind interfaces—to design for pluggability—is a well-known one that has been used for several decades. A predecessor of OO software engineering[1] (and Objectory) (and thus also a predecessor of the Unified Process) was developed in 1967 to support the design of the Ericsson AKE and AXE systems family.[14] The backbone of the architecture of these systems was made up of the interfaces between different subsystems. Another could replace a subsystem as long as it offered the same interface. The interfaces of the whole system were documented in a library managed separately from the subsystems. A designer of a subsystem had to realize and use subsystem interfaces as defined in the library. We managed a construct called a *hole* that was a kind of virtual or abstract subsystem, and every incarnation of that subsystem had to comply with its interfaces to fit into the hole. Thus, the basic ideas are not new, they have been certified for 25 years. What is new, however, is to structure the subsystem interfaces in terms of interfaces describing types instead of just a list of all the signatures of the subsystem.

Related Work

We do not know of any work regarding the modeling of *dynamic behavior* in terms of interfaces and subsystems. But there is some work regarding interfaces and interfaces that are similar to "our" interfaces.

Rebecca Wirfs-Brock et al.[2] introduced contracts. "[A] contract between two classes represents a list of services an object (a client) can request from another object (a server)."

The CORBA[15] specification uses *interfaces*, "description[s] of a set of possible operations that a client may request of an object." Interfaces, as defined here, are similar to our interfaces.

COM[16] defines an interface as "an interface that an object supports (implements)."

Koistinen has in his thesis[17] introduced something similar to our interface: a *primitive interface*, "an interface corresponding to one class." Component (subsystems) can then use and realize these primitive interfaces in a way similar that of our approach. However, no constructs for describing behavior discussed in the thesis.

Conclusion

We have provided an outline of how pluggable architectures can be built using interfaces; as a consequence, we have shown how to build both high-level and lower-level views of the same model, and also how these different views relate to each other.

What we believe is unique in our proposal is the integration of the idea of an interface with a dynamic use case construct. This allows design to be carried out top-down while maintaining functional characteristics of the design, as expressed in use cases.

ACKNOWLEDGMENTS

The authors are greatly indebted to several individuals working at Ellemtel Development AB and Ericsson Hewlett-Packard Telecommunications AB, who have provided substantial input to the work that led to this chapter. It is of course impossible to do justice to all that have been involved, but we thank Jari Koistinen and Christer Johansson.

EDITOR'S NOTE

The notion of "interfaces" in this chapter was originally called "contracts," but was renamed due to the UML.[11] And although the UML currently adds more details and expressive power regarding both subsystems and interfaces, the basic reasoning in this chapter about their overall use in the development process still applies, and was also an important input to the creation of the UML.

REFERENCES

1. I. Jacobson, M. Christerson, P. Jonsson, and G. G. Övergaard. *Object-Oriented Software Engineering—A Use Case Driven Approach*, Addison–Wesley, Reading, MA, 1992.

2. R. Wirfs-Brock, B. Wilkerson, and L. Wiener. *Designing Object-Oriented Software*, Prentice–Hall, Englewood Cliffs, NJ, 1990.

3. G. Booch. *Object-Oriented Design with Applications*, Benjamin/Cummings, Redwood City, CA, 1991.

4. S. Shlaer and S. J. Mellor. *Object Lifecycles—Modeling the World in States*, Prentice–Hall, Englewood Cliffs, NJ, 1992.

5. K. Walden and J. M. Nerson. *Seamless Object-Oriented Software Architecture*, Prentice–Hall, Englewood Cliffs, NJ, 1995.

6. B. Henderson-Sellers and J. Edwards. *The Working Object*, Prentice–Hall, Englewood Cliffs, NJ, 1994.

7. I. Jacobson. "Basic Use-Case Modeling," *Report on Object Analysis and Design*, 1(2): 15–19, 1994. (See chapter entitled "Basic Use-Case Modeling.")

8. I. Jacobson. "Basic Use-Case Modeling (*continued*)," *Report on Object Analysis and Design,* 1(3): 7-9, 1994. (See chapter entitled "Basic Use-Case Modeling (*continued*).")

9. I. Jacobson. "Use Cases and Objects," *Report on Object Analysis and Design,* 1(4): 8–10, 1994. (See chapter entitled "Use Cases and Objects.")

10. D. Garlan, R. Allen, and J. Ockerbloom. "Exploiting Styles in Architectural Design Environments," Proceedings of the *ACM SIGSOFT '94 Symposium on Foundations of Software Engineering,* December 1994.

11. The Unified Modeling Language for Object-Oriented Development, Documentation set, ver. 1.1, Rational Software Corp., September 1997.

12. I. Jacobson. "Use Cases in Large-Scale Systems," *Report on Object Analysis and Design,* 1(6): 9–12, 1995. (See chapter entitled "Use Cases in Large-Scale Systems.")

13. I. Jacobson, S. Dyrhage, and K. Palmkvist. "Systems of Interconnected Systems," *Report on Object Analysis and Design,* 2(1), 1995. (See chapter entitled "Systems of Interconnected Systems.")

14. I. Jacobson. "Object Orientation as a Competitive Advantage," *American Programmer,* 5(8), 1992. (See chapter entitled "A Large Commercial Success Story..." for a refined variant of this essay.)

15. OMG and X/Open. The Common Object Request Broker: Architecture and Specification, rev. 1.1, 1991.

16. Microsoft Corporation and Digital Equipment Corporation. Common Object Model Specification, Draft version 0.2, October 1994.

17. J. Koistinen. *Large-Grained Modularization of Object-Oriented Software,* Lic. thesis, Report no. 94-015, Dept. of Computer and System Sciences, Royal Institute of Technology and Stockholm University, May 1994.

In Ivar's Words

Q: Architectural Patterns are a hot topic today. Jim Rumbaugh described patterns at a level above the usual object diagrams or process, but where do you think patterns really fit in and do you think there are any constructs that can take advantage of them?

A: Absolutely, but first let me say that we have always had patterns in software. Everyone that is using software has used patterns in design; however, something new about patterns is that we have given names to them; we have identified and placed our finger on it and said this is a pattern and this is a pattern and everyone doing similar work will recognize these patterns and that means reuse. To me a pattern or most of the patterns we have heard about today, say utility patterns, are relatively simple patterns belonging to the utility layer in the software architecture of systems and I don't believe they give us the expected value.

A pattern is a problem definition with a solution that can be reused over and over again—this is the definition of a pattern. I think one of the missing points in the work on patterns today is that they have only formalized the solution part of a pattern leaving the problem definition part as just textual. So for me today's pattern is just the solution part where the problem definition is what I would capture as a use case.

The pattern people have identified basic utility patterns to be reused. To really get a lot of value, however, we need to find the business patterns that are reused in a business. Our approach is to identify the abstract use cases for the business tool you design. We use the term business tool instead of information system because it is more telling. Abstract use cases are the part of the concrete use cases that you can most reuse. These shared abstract use cases correspond to the solution part of patterns. The solution part of a pattern is a number of interacting objects described through interaction diagrams. Patterns with both a problem part and a solution part will be reusable when you design tool support for a business.

And to go one step further, a framework is then an integrated set of patterns in a business. So at least in my higher layers, a framework consists of a set of interconnected objects that provide a number of solutions to abstract use cases that are reused.

Q: In one of your books you mention the "building block approach" that has evolved over the years, and I know you have an article where you discuss megaobjects, in ROAD, with frameworks and patterns, and application objects and component objects. Is this still an evolving model, this kind of object differentiation, or stereotyping, is that going anywhere?

A: Now we are talking about objects of a higher level. We are talking about megaobjects, and we now have a new concept which we call a system of interconnected systems, which is actually a technique for designing really large systems, like networks of systems, for instance in telecommunications. The whole telecommunications network is a huge system of interconnected systems and you do use cases on the top level, the whole system, and then you identify subsystems. These subsystems make up the next level and become systems in their own right, and that means that you do use cases for these subsidiary systems, and you do designing and implementation for all of them. So systems of interconnected systems, I wrote about that in two papers, with a number of colleagues, one in ROAD, and one in JOOP, and we already have tool support for that. So you can design a family of systems that are interconnected.

Another thing, if you look at my first book, at the difference between application systems and component systems, and application objects and component objects, that was just the very beginning of designing a family of systems. And since then, I've been working together with two other people, Martin Griss, who is the reuse Rabbi inside HP, and Patrik Jonsson, who is one of my colleagues at old Objectory. We have been working on how to design to obtain reusable assets.

And there are two components here. Architecture on the one hand—there should be a number of architecture styles so that designing a family of systems is supported. And on the other hand you need to have a number of development processes—not one single process—but you need a number of processes to design a family of systems. For instance there is a process to design every component system, and you have a process to design every application system, and you have a process to design a whole family of systems. And you need a process to integrate other systems, such as relational databases, operating systems, laptop systems, and integrate them into something that can be used by the application systems. This work to design a Reuse Driven Software Engineering Business is something that is described in my reuse book.

Q: What do you think about the state of software reuse today ?

A: You know this is primarily an understanding about what reuse really is and how you can achieve reuse. I think my book was the first one that really talks about the difference between application systems and component systems. However, I felt that I had to be very brief, otherwise I would never get out the book.

To get reuse you have to design an architecture that gives you reuse for a family of systems. Then you need a number of processes to be able to develop and maintain this architecture. Finally you need an organization that incorporates these processes and produces the selected architecture to be able to succeed. To be able to present this rather advanced idea I first needed to present basics in object-oriented software engineering, I did that in my first book. Then I needed to describe how you engineer an organization so that it has the development processes to produce the architecture. I did that in my second book. Now we can bind it all together and describe how you really get reuse in a systematic way. This was presented in the reuse book. I view this book as the most advanced work I have participated within since it stands on top of everything else I have been doing: on top of my work in software engineering, business engineering. Architecture becomes more large scale and there is a need for different specializations of the process for different layers in the architecture.

Anyway, I think that one of the fundamental issues of reuse is: How do you define the reusable components for an industry or for businesses such as banking or insurance? I believe that instead of only designing objects and then retrieving them, a design and architecture for reuse must be in place and an organization must have the processes in place to design this architecture. This is the real key to reuse.

For example, the Unified Process is designed to be reusable because it can be adapted to any organization through the use of reusable process elements designed when we engineered it. There are in this case two types of elements. We talk about workers and artifacts. Workers represent the different types of people you need when developing software, such as use-case designer, class designer, tester. Artifacts model the different work products that are the result of the process such as a use-case model, a class, a test specification. These *elements are reused through mechanisms such as inheritance and can then be specialized to become any required process. Our customers engineer their own processes and then reuse them in their next generation when they change them again. And Rational has a process framework with tool support which we can specialize for every customer, for every application of the framework. This is what we do.*

In the same way, families of processes, or process frameworks, can be developed for particular businesses or industries such as insurance which can then be sold or reused by that industry. Many such frameworks were developed while working with our customers and with our own people and their ideas and this learning went into our approach. And now this same process will support the use of UML with the evolution of Rational's approach and the improvement and union of the Booch and OMT methods. And now Rational can offer all of this together in a single product, the Rational Unified Process.

PART 7:
EPILOGUE

IN THIS PART WE CONCLUDE with yet more interesting aspects of the Unified Process. For example, we can read about its relation to some of its forerunners, namely to the Objectory process and to the OOSE textbook method. We can also read more about the Unified Process being component-based and iterative; these are some absolutely essential characteristics of a successful software development process.

As a final touch I recommend the interview section at the end of this part, where amongst other things we can read about Dr. Jacobson's plans, visions, and dreams for the 21st century.

Part 7:
Epilogue

30

OBJECTORY IS
THE UNIFIED PROCESS

Ivar Jacobson, APRIL 1998

T HE METHODS WAR IS OVER. We have a standard. The Object Management Group adopted the Unified Modeling Language (UML) as a
standard in November 1997. It is a widely supported standard,
driven by Rational, but supported by the whole software industry: HP, IBM,
Microsoft, Oracle, and many others.

What it means, fundamentally, is that all the different methods found in
the software industry are now moving to one modeling language: UML. This
represents an incredible success to the user community. Its members now have
a single modeling language for making blueprints of their developed software.
Moreover, this new standard is far better described than any modeling language in the past. It covers more of the life cycle than anyone did before, and
tools will support it. Tool competition will move from the necessity, and the
investment cost, of having to support many different modeling languages to
supporting just one: UML. And they will be able to do that well.

However, having a standard modeling language like UML is not all you
need. You also need to know how to use it. You need a software development process by which you develop your software and model it using UML.
You need to know what artifacts to develop—artifacts such as use cases, subsystems, classes, collaborations, nodes, architecture, and models. You need
to know what workflows to perform. Moreover, not all development
processes result in good systems that are understandable, easy to evolve new
requirements for, resilient to future changes, and capable of high-level reuse.

Using the wrong process gives you a bad product—a product that is hard to use and manage during its life cycle. Although the artifacts that you develop with a poor process may, thanks to UML, be understandable, and you may be able to move them from one tool to another, they may not represent a well-designed product. Thus, even if the methods war is partially won, it is not over. The user community still needs a well-proven process that is automated. It needs a process that helps developers' organizations attain good products.

The Unified Process is one such process. The Unified Process relies on more than 30 years of experience derived from component-based design. It represents the coming together of the process developed by Grady Booch, Jim Rumbaugh, and me, with heavy impact from other people within Rational: primarily Philippe Kruchten's work on architecture and Walker Royce's work on project management.

On the one hand, we tried to make UML process-independent (you can use it with any process). On the other hand, we designed UML to be optimal for use in a generic and unified process. For instance, the UML specification contains an entire section titled, "UML Extension for the Objectory Process for Software Engineering."

It is not possible, of course, in the brief space of a chapter, to explore all the ramifications of both UML and Objectory. Grady, Jim, and I are currently writing two books on UML and one book on the process. I am the principal writer for the one on process.[1] In this chapter, however, I am going to focus on just one point: the Objectory process facilitates component-based development. It has long been evident that putting together existing components is much more effective than building software from scratch. That is what Objectory has always done. It is also evident that component-based development is on the path to the future. And that is where Objectory leads.

WHAT IS COMPONENT-BASED DEVELOPMENT?

A *component* is a significant piece of software that has a distinct function and well-defined interfaces (see the sidebar, "Definitions in Component-Based Development"). By component-based development (CBD) we mean *composing* a system from components and interconnecting them via *interfaces.* An interface specifies the use of a component, actually a set of components, that is, a set suited to the same interface. The concept of *component* assumes that a component exists in an architectural context and that this context, in turn, is characterized by its interfaces.

CBD also encompasses the act of *decomposing* a system into components. This decomposition, in turn, is an aspect of architecture development. In decomposing a proposed system, the architects and developers are working to develop an architecture, the lowest level of which is made up of components. Some of the components they identify, they may have to build anew for the system under consideration. They may also intend that the new components will be general enough to have further use in other applications—that is, harvesting components. Other components they identify, they may seek in already existing component banks.

Further, CBD enables developers to replace one component with another, provided that the new component provides and uses the same interfaces. The new component may better carry out the functions to which the original component was devoted, or it may implement additional functions that were not originally contemplated. Later, in a new generation of the product, developers may readily substitute components that adapt the product to the new generation.

Thus, we have, so far, a system and its components. In between these two endpoints we have subsystems. Architects and developers compose subsystems to form systems. Subsystems, in turn, may form a hierarchy from lower-level subsystems to higher0level subsystems. The lowest-level subsystems consist of components.

Systems created by means of CBD have the very great advantage of being *understandable*, even though the functionality and technology concealed in the individual components are very complex. This property, understandability, may sound rather unimportant—something about which technicians don't really care—but it is, in fact, of the utmost importance. The ability to understand a system has to do with its structure. A structure that is going to be understandable doesn't just happen. It has to be managed into existence.

Therefore, *managing* in this sense is what system development is all about. It means managing the system during its entire life cycle—dealing with new requirements, new technology, new developers, and new customers. If the current group of developers, not to mention later generations, has trouble understanding the system, they have trouble developing it or, later, producing a new generation. In contrast, building systems on the basis of interchangeable components results in software that is robust and resilient

HISTORY OF THE OBJECTORY PROCESS

Objectory has been in development for more than 30 years.

1967-69: The original approach I presented in 1967 was used to develop a new generation of switching systems at Ericsson in Sweden. The approach relied on a number of original ideas that, to my knowledge, were unique at that time:

- Components were containers of code as well as data, and they conformed to a set of interfaces, the code was in assembler, and the interfaces were macros defined outside the component.

- Using the term "software architecture" was a key selling point for customers.

- The interfaces were the core of the architecture.

- Use cases were used to drive the development work.

- Collaboration diagrams and sequence diagrams were used to describe collaborations.

- State diagrams were use to model behavior of objects.

- Components interacted by sending signals to one another.

to the inescapable changes. These attributes, in turn, lengthen the lifetime of the software.

HOW DO YOU FIND COMPONENTS?

CBD certainly sounds promising. It must be wonderful to be able to develop software products just by putting fairly large-scale components together. It sounds so simple! But is it? No!

Let us count off some of the difficulties. The first is: How do you find components? Aren't there millions of components out there in the billions

Ericsson used this approach to develop a product that has become the largest commercial success story in the history of Sweden.[2] Much of the success is attributed to this approach.

1976–82: The original approach was the major source of inspiration for the standard modeling language SDL, which was the first object modeling standard ever adopted.

1987: Objectory was founded. It represented a major simplification, generalization, and formalization of Ericsson's experience. It also incorporated techniques from ER modeling to support building data-intensive systems. Unifying these worlds gave us a process that, during the next several years, would be used heavily in nearly every segment of software development.

1995: Objectory went through a major improvement and more unification. Objectory was influenced by work from Grady Booch, Jim Rumbaugh, Philippe Kruchten, and Walker Royce, primarily on architecture and iterative development. Rational's 14 years of experience from component-based design was incorporated in the process.

1997: Objectory incorporated the Unified Modeling Language and it became the Unified Process. The Rational Unified Process is the product manifestation of the Unified Process, and is currently provided by Rational Software.

of lines of existing code just waiting to be picked? Well, not quite. Much current software is just lines of code. There is no architectural description of it, no series of models of it (such as the UML now proposes to provide), no consistent interfaces to place components between. If you did, in some fashion, manage to find a component, it probably would not fit with anything else you already had.

The second difficulty is that components work only in an architectural setting, as I have already pointed out. Lego and Tinkertoy function well between them. Similarly, most of today's software functions where it is, but would not function somewhere else. This is because those lines of code were not designed to work with anything beyond the system in which they were originally embedded.

The third difficulty is that components, to be reusable, must satisfy technical constraints. For example, they must be designed to work on top of a platform specified by programming language, operating system, database management system, and other system software.

The fourth difficulty is that components must, perforce, be available within business constraints, such as who is going to finance their availability: Will that entity be able to modify them as technology progresses?

There is hope, however. In the *Software Reuse* book,[3] we described a technique to build a family of systems based on an architecture with systems of systems, subsystems, frameworks, patterns, facades—constructs now in the UML. Moreover, UML will help, too, by providing standard representations of reusable components at each workflow level.

A few vendors are making stabs at these difficulties, but overall you still have to rely very much on yourself. That, of course, takes commitment and financing. Before management commits, however, they want to see a process capable of utilizing components. Now they can: Objectory.

DEFINITIONS IN COMPONENT-BASED DEVELOPMENT

The following sets of definitions have been agreed upon within the team of methodologists at Rational and reveal where we are heading:

- A *component* is a physical and replaceable part of a system that conforms to and provides the realization of a set of interfaces.

- A *interface* is a collection of operations that are used to specify a service of a class or a component.

- *Component-based development* (CBD) is the creation and deployment of software-intensive systems assembled from components, as well as the development and harvesting of such components.

- *Automating component-based development* (ACBD) is the use of process and tools to improve productivity, quality and time-to-market using component-based development.

What Is the Difference Between Component-Based Development and Object-Oriented Development?

To me, they have always meant the same thing. That is, the semantics were the same. Calling it component-based development is a change for the better in the terminology. Component-based development still means that we do object-oriented design, but in implementation we get less dogmatic. Component-based is a more practical term telling what it is all about.

Object-oriented means something more puristic to many others. In Objectory we have always had the more practical approach. We allowed a subsystem of classes modeled in design to be implemented as a piece of code in any language, that is, as a component. In many other OO approaches, developers had to follow the OO paradigm all the way down to executable code, that is, they had to implement the design in languages such as Smalltalk, C++, and Java. With component-based development, we are not so dogmatic about this practice. We still think it is advantageous to use an OO programming language to implement the models developed using UML, but we also realized that a lot software is already in existence, and that it will remain in existence for many years to come. As long as the legacy software can be described as a set of components having well-defined interfaces, it can be used in our design. Some modern languages, such as Ada and Visual Basic, are adequate for many purposes, but are not pure OO. In fact, what is inside may be Cobol, Basic, C, C++, or Java. What matters more is that what is inside is important, and that its interfaces to other components are consistent and enduring.

Another difference is in how people have applied object-oriented modeling. One of the mechanisms in object-oriented modeling is inheritance. It is a powerful mechanism, certainly, but it has been applied as if it were the most important mechanism for getting reuse. Misuse of inheritance can result in what has been called "ravioli" code or "jo-jo" programming. In Objectory, to avoid this outcome, we recommend a very limited use of inheritance.

For instance, developers should employ inheritance between classes in one subsystem and classes in another only with the utmost care. Inheritance between classes within a lower-level subsystem, called a service package in Objectory, presents only a minor problem, because the classes in question end up in the same component when they are implemented. In contrast, inheritance between classes within two different service packages presents a potentially serious problem, unless the developer takes special care. By care, I mean allowing inheritance between different service packages or frameworks only if the service packages have been designed and documented for reuse, and only if they have passed a precise verification process.

Inheritance is a powerful mechanism, but it is not the only way to achieve reuse. Another, often more powerful, mechanism is the composition of parts into a whole. This technique can be applied to the small: A class can be an aggregate of other classes. It can also be applied in the large: A subsystem can consist of a set of classes all providing some set of use cases to the surrounding subsystems.

Real reuse depends on reusing something larger than a class. It means reusing big chunks of code: whole subsystems or service packages, sets of interfaces, and frameworks.

What Is Objectory?

It is a software development process. It takes new requirements as input and produces artifacts in the UML as output. The work to produce a new release is divided into four phases:

1. *Inception:* establishes core architecture; identifies and reduces critical risks, assures feasibility.

2. *Elaboration:* establishes mainline architecture, identifies and reduces significant risks, plans and estimates the construction phase.

3. *Construction:* builds product in a series of iterations, resulting in increments or builds.

4. *Transition:* moves product into the hands of users.

Within each phase, architects and developers carry iterations through a set of workflows:

- Requirements capture, based on use cases.

- Analysis and design, including an architecture.

- Implementation.

- Test.

Showing how all this comes together to achieve component-based development has proved to be a book-length effort. However, we emphasize three key ideas:

1. Use case driven.

2. Architecture-centric.

3. Iterative and incremental.

See related chapters entitled "Use Cases and Architecture," "Architecture Is About Everything—But Not Everything Is Architecture," "The Steps to an Architecture," and "The Unified Process Is Iterative."

EDITOR'S NOTE

The name "Objectory" as it appears here is actually the name of a full-fledged process product that is configured and implemented in real software development organizations. Objectory has recently been renamed to the "Rational Unified Process," which is a newer and refined version of the Objectory product that is continuously under development and provided by Rational Software Corporation.

However, this subject is a bit more delicate, since the Objectory product was based on and inspired by a textbook version describing its fundamental methodology, called OOSE.[4] The OOSE book is a textbook to be used for education. It is intended to introduce people to the fundamental ideas, and it presents a number of modeling techniques and a number of method components. But to use it for real software development, it needs to be "processified" into a real software engineering process. This is what Objectory did.

Similar to this, the Rational Unified Process also has a textbook counterpart;[1] this is the Unified Software Development Process, or the Unified Process for short. So, when we refer to the Unified Process, we actually refer to the fundamental and conceptual ideas of its methodology; and when we refer to the Rational Unified Process, we refer to the productified software engineering process, and all that comes with that.

Refer to Part 4, "Process and Tools," for more discussion about this subject.

REFERENCES

1. I. Jacobson, G. Booch, and J. Rumbaugh. *The Unified Software Development Process,* Addison Wesley Longman, 1999.

2. I. Jacobson. "A Large Commercial Success Story Based on Objects," *Object Magazine,* May 1996. (See chapter entitled "A Large Commerical Success Story…")

3. I. Jacobson, M. Griss, and P. Jonsson. *Software Reuse: Architecture, Process and Organization for Business Success,* Addison–Wesley, Reading, MA, 1997.

4. Ivar Jacobson, Magnus Christerson, Patrik Jonsson, and Gunnar Övergaard. *Object-Oriented Software Engineering—A Use Case Driven Approach,* Addison–Wesley, Revised Fourth Printing, 1993.

31

THE UNIFIED PROCESS IS
ITERATIVE

───

Ivar Jacobson, DECEMBER 1998

A S I DISCUSSED IN THE CHAPTER "Use Cases and Architecture,"[1] use case driven and architecture-centric are two of the three essential characteristics of the Unified Process. They have a clear technical impact on the product of the process. Being use case driven means that every phase in the drive toward the eventual product corresponds to what users actually do. It drives developers to ensure that the system meets the users' real needs. Being architecture-centric means that, in the early phases, development work focuses on achieving the architectural pattern that will guide system construction, ensuring a smooth progression not only in the development of the current product release, but throughout the product's entire life.

Achieving the right balance between these two keys—use cases and architecture—is similar in nature to balancing function and form in the development of any product. The balance between them grows with time. Asking which one comes first, however, is similar to asking, "Which came first, the chicken or the egg?" Actually, the chicken and the egg came about through almost endless iterations during the long process of evolution. Similarly, in the shorter process of software development, developers work out this balance between use cases and architecture consciously through a series of iterations. Thus, the iterative and incremental development approach constitutes the third key area of the Unified Process.

DEVELOP IN SMALL STEPS

The third key—the iterative and incremental development approach—provides the strategy for developing a software product in small, manageable steps, or iterations. Each iteration consists of the following activities:

1. You plan a little.

2. You specify, design, and implement a little.

3. You integrate, test, and run each component a little.

Once you are happy with a step, you take the next step. In between each step you get feedback that allows you to adjust your focus for the next step. Then you take a few more steps, and when you have taken all the steps you planned to take, you have developed a product that you can release to your customers and users.

The iterations in the early phases are mostly concerned with scoping the project, removing critical risks, and baselining the architecture. Then, as we proceed through the project and gradually reduce the remaining risks and implement the components, the shape of the iterations changes and they become increments.

A software development project transforms a delta (or change) of users' requirements into a delta (or change) of the software product. With an iterative and incremental approach, this accommodation of change is done little by little. In other words, we split the project into a number of *miniprojects*, and each one is an iteration. Each iteration has everything a software development project has: planning, working through a series of workflows (requirements capture, analysis and design, implementation, and testing), assessment, and preparation for release.

An iteration is not an entirely independent entity; it is a stage within a project. It draws heavily from being part of a project. We say it is a miniproject because it is not, in and of itself, the result that the stakeholders have asked us to achieve. Also, each of these miniprojects is like the old waterfall activities. We might label each iteration a *miniwaterfall*.

The iterative life cycle repeatedly delivers tangible results in terms of several internal (though preliminary) releases that demonstrate the added increments and demonstrate the reduction of the risks that were concerns. These releases may be shown to customers and users, who can provide valuable feedback to validate the work.

The project manager tries to order the iterations to create a straight path that allows the early iterations to provide the knowledge basis for the later iterations. Early iterations in the project result in increased knowledge of the requirements, the problems, the risks, and the solution space; whereas later iterations result in additive increments that eventually make up the external release—the customer product. The ultimate success for the planners is a sequence of iterations that always proceeds in a forward direction, and never has to go back two iterations to patch up the model because of a requirement learned one iteration too late. We do not want to climb a mound of melting snow, taking two steps forward and sliding one step back.

WHAT ITERATION IS NOT

Some managers have the perception that "iterative" or "incremental" is a fancy name for "hacking." They fear that the words merely conceal the reality that the developers don't know what they are doing. In the inception phase, even early in the elaboration phase, there may be some truth behind this feeling. For example, if they have not yet resolved critical or significant risks, then the assertion is true. If they have not yet proven the underlying concept, or established an executable architectural baseline, then the assertion is true. If they have not yet figured out how to implement the requirements that are central to the phase they are in, the assertion is true. They do not yet, "know what they are doing."

Does it do any good for them to pretend that they do know? Does it do any good to base a "plan" on insufficient information? Does it do any good to track to this unreliable plan? Of course not.

Just for the record, let us emphasize what the iterative life cycle is not:

- It is not random hacking.

- It is not a playpen for developers.

- It is not something that affects only developers.

- It is not redesigning the same thing over and over until they finally chance on something that works.

- It is not unpredictable.

- It is not an excuse for failing to plan and manage effectively.

In fact, controlled iteration is far from random. It is planned. It is a tool with which managers can better control the project. It reduces, early in the life cycle, risks that may be hazardous to the progress of development. Internal releases after iterations enable stakeholders feedback, leading, in turn, to earlier correction of the project course.

ITERATIONS DURING THE LIFE CYCLE

The life cycle of a software project is divided into four phases (see Figure 31-1). Each of the phases concludes with a major milestone:

- The inception phase concludes with the life cycle objectives milestone.

- The elaboration phase concludes with the life cycle architecture milestone.

- The construction phase concludes with the initial operational capability milestone.

- The transition phase concludes with the product release milestone.

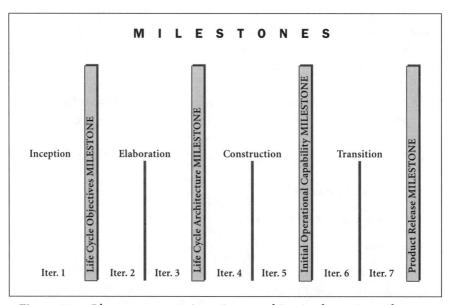

Figure 31-1. Phases aggregate iterations resulting in the major milestones where management makes important business decisions. (The number of iterations is not fixed, but varies for different projects.)

The goal of each major milestone is to make sure that the different models evolve in a balanced way during the life cycle of the product. I mean "balanced" in the sense that the most important decisions impacting those models are made early in the life cycle; these are the decisions about risks, use cases, and architecture. Later in the life cycle, work should be able to proceed at increasing levels of detail with higher quality.

The primary goals of the *inception phase* are to set the scope of what the product should do, reduce the worst risks, and prepare the initial business case, indicating that, from a business standpoint, the project is worth pursuing.

The primary goals of the *elaboration phase* are to design the architecture, capture most of the requirements, and reduce the second worst risks. By the end of this phase, we have an executable architectural baseline, and we are able to estimate the costs and schedule and plan the construction phase with high fidelity. At this point, we should be able to bid.

The primary goals of the *construction phase* are to develop the complete system and to ensure that the product can begin transition to customers.

The primary goal of the *transition phase* is to ensure that the product is ready to be released to the user community. Also, during this phase of development the users are trained to use the software.

Within each phase, there are lesser milestones, such as meeting the criteria for each iteration. Each iteration produces results, called *model artifacts.* Thus, at the end of each iteration, there will be a new increment to the use-case model, the analysis model, the design model, the deployment model, the implementation model, and the test model. This new increment will be integrated with the result of the previous iteration into a new version of the set of models.

At the minor milestones, managers and developers decide on how to proceed to the subsequent iterations. At the major milestones at the end of each phase, managers make crucial decisions and decide on schedule, budget, and requirements.

This division in phases helps management and other involved stakeholders evaluate what has been done during the low-cost inception and elaboration phases, before they decide to commit to the high-cost construction phase. Economy of scale is the goal of the construction phase. The number of people on the project increases during this phase. They develop the bulk of the system functionality, build on the architecture that was baselined during the elaboration phase, and reuse existing software as much as possible.

While each iteration is a sweep through the requirements capture, analysis, design, implementation, and testing workflows, the iterations have different emphases in different phases (see Fig. 31-2). During the inception and

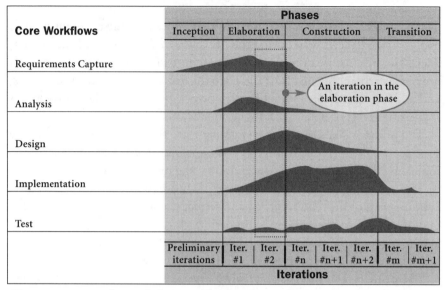

Figure 31-2. Emphasis shifts over the iterations, from requirements capture and analysis, toward design, implementation, and testing.

elaboration phases, most effort is spent on capturing requirements and architecture work (early analysis and design). During construction, the emphasis shifts to detailed design, implementation, and testing. Although it is not shown in the figure, the early phases are heavy on project management and developing an environment—process and tools—for the project.

In summary, a life cycle resulting in a customer release is made up of a sequence of iterations that are grouped into four phases. Some of the iterations, particularly the early ones, help us understand the risks, establish feasibility, build the initial core of the software, and make the business case. Others, particularly the later ones, add increments to it until we have created a product that is ready for external release.

REFERENCE

1. I. Jacobson. "Use Cases and Architecture in Objectory," *Component Strategies,* 1(2): 70–71, Aug. 1998. (See chapter entitled "Use Cases and Architecture.")

In Ivar's Words

Q: Do you expect for the Unified Process a success and an impact on the IT industry analogous to that of the UML?

A: Yes, absolutely yes, and we have very good reasons to believe that. We are making inroads into many corporations today, and it's our goal to get there. We don't think it would be an easy thing to make the Unified Process a formal standard, it would be so much hard work and so much opposition, so we'd rather do it in small steps. Instead of going and forcing people through a standard, let people convince themselves. And I think that everyone that looks at the Rational Unified Process will become convinced this is the way they've got to do it, as soon as they have started to look at it. There is nothing even close to it. Many people tried to say that there is, but what is it that they have? They have something that can be compared with my book, but they don't have anything that can be compared with a full-fledged process. If you just look upon it in terms of substance, and depth, and experience, and so on, and if you compare … How old is Approach A, or Approach B? Do we know that it works, for large projects? We know that ours works. It's really very different.

Q: How much of Objectory is left in the Unified Process?

A: If you look just upon the basic ideas, we basically only covered requirements, analysis, and design in Objectory. If you look upon these things, what was in Objectory in the old days is still there. But there's a lot of new stuff that has been added. We had very little about implementation, very little about testing, nothing about configuration management and version control, and nothing about project management. Iterative development was primarily something we recommended, but it was not enforced by the process, we didn't really tell about the differences among the various iterations, so I think the core ideas are still there, but there are lots of other things that have been added. The Rational Unified Process is really teamwork; we have a lot of people that have been involved, whereas the Objectory Process was primarily my ideas, my work that we implemented. But, given the smaller resources we had, it was still quite a lot!

Q: The Unified Modeling Language was a collective creation. And so the Unified Process. But in the latter, your own contribution is more clear, more apparent. UP roots are more in the Objectory / OOSE ground than in the Booch method or in OMT. Does this reflect a sort of "division of labor" among the Amigos?

A: I don't think that we have divided on purpose. Some people are experts on everything, and it's hard to see that anyone of us three would agree that there is an area in which we don't have any expertise. Honestly, I think there is no division of work. It's a fact that we started from Objectory, when developing the Unified Process, and from there we have evolved. And of course, you cannot move from object modeling, just object modeling. There is not a simple way to go from approaches like OMT, or Booch, to do what we did in Objectory. So it is easier to go the other way round, thinking about use cases and then you have objects and classes and subsystems to design.

Q: What do you consider as the the major contributions of Objectory to the Unified Process?

A: Spontaneously, I could have mentioned the actual process: use cases, use case driven; each use case corresponds to a use-case design (collaborations in UML) and a use-case test set. Multimodeling (use cases, analysis, design, implementation, and testing) with traceability between models. Focus on architecture. Services and other subsystems, system of systems to build family of systems (all now in the UML). I could also have mentioned business modeling and user-interface modeling and design based on use cases.

Having said this let me also say that the new version of Objectory, that, is the Unified Process, is much more complete; it has identified separate workflow activities to deal with requirements, a much more explicit architecture and iterative development. Implementation and testing are full-fledged workflows. Project management, environment management, configuration management are now part of the process. The Unified Process is a great improvement. A step that from a product point of view can be compared with moving from one generation to the next.

However, what I am most excited about in Objectory is its approach to engineering of process and the consequences that will give us. Since 1987 we designed Objectory as a system of itself, we used the Objectory business modeling approach to design the Objectory software development product. We have done so for 12 years today. Thus we use terms like workflows (which are realizations of abstract business use cases in UML), workers (in UML), artifacts (business entities in UML). Earlier we used interaction diagrams to describe workflow; now we use activity diagrams with swim-lanes.

Now, why is this so important?

First, it allows us to deal with process development in an engineering-like way. It is not book writing but engineering of software business elements. It is extendable, it allows us to have many people working concurrently and nearly independently. It allows us to make specializations of Objectory, so Objectory is a true process framework. We have only implemented this partially, but we have a concrete vision. In the future, I think Rational will not only market one kind of process but many kinds of processes: several requirement management processes, several different business engineering processes, reengineering legacy systems to component-based systems, several processes for framework development, support processes, processes for software production. We will design not only processes but actually complete software engineering businesses.

Secondly, once we have a designed process specialized for a customer, we can install this process in our envisioned process management tool. When an instance of that process is created, that is when a project is started, then instances of workflows, workers, artifacts are created and our tools are properly attached to the right workers. We enact the process description and the tools. The new work on Unified Process with mentors is a step in this direction. This is a way that leads into the future, where we will be able to become the true market leaders as well.

Q: Now the greatest part of the "unifying" effort is done. Are you going to rest, and capitalize on it, or are you moving forward to other areas of interest? What next?

A: There is one part of me that says: I want to go ahead, and look for what needs to be done, to create a much better world, and we have a lot of things to do. In a way, UML is a standard, and that's wonderful. But it doesn't mean that these are new ideas—we just got them consolidated. In the last years, I don't think I've done anything really new, I pushed the adoption process more than the creation process. Now a part of me wants to take a next step. What is beyond the Unified Process? What is beyond UML? I think it is still an evolution, not a revolution, but there are some important steps that need to happen in software, to get up to the level of extremely high quality which we need to develop the systems we will want to develop in the 2020s, or something like that. These are much larger systems than we can think of today, and more complex, and we need to be able to develop these systems. We need a much better infrastructure than we have today, in terms of operating systems, programming languages, UML integrated with programming languages, maybe part of the UML will be a programming language, with action language semantics and so on. That's one thing I'm constantly thinking of.

The other thing is to capitalize on business engineering. There is something really interesting to get done, there. The Rational Unified Process is very well prepared for the Web. Many of the companies who develop Websites are using the Rational Unified Process today, specializing it a little bit, so it fits for their special purposes, but it's the same process. I would like to see that we extend and make the right decisions to make the required model improvements, in the Rational Unified Process, changes that make it clearly, without any doubt, "the" process for Website applications design.

I'm also going to write a revision of my book The Object Advantage for the end of this year. The Internet and ideas like one-to-one marketing will have a lot of impact on this revision. We need to make the book more approachable for business people, and not only for software people. We will show how to use it in the context of business, not only in the context of software. The basic ideas are already there, it works very well, customers are happy, but today we need to take that through the barrier of IT, solving the problem existing with the acceptance of technical notation. For example, activity diagrams are very useful for business modeling.

(Extracts of the answers above reprinted with permission from Adriano Comai, an Italian IT consultant. It was first published at www.analisi-disegno.com and in the ZeroUno magazine (Italian translation).)

Q: Will there be any other specific areas that people will turn attention to or that are in real need of attention?

A: Yes, there will be no end. We will always find new interesting things but I certainly believe that objects are the platform from which we can develop and extend our experience in getting more and more technology. Objects are *important but they are just the easy part. So we have to extend the method-ology, we have to extend the design with new architectural styles and it is not enough with objects and use cases. We need systems of interacting systems to be able to design networks including large systems and legacy systems. We need to go on with use-case engineering, which has just started, and there is much progress to be made in moving the development work to the front end so that we can spend less time in the back end of the software engineering process and more time in the front end so we make the right decisions early on. That means that we need to have languages to talk about the most impor-tant issues in the early phases. Here use cases will be developed as a large exten-sion, we will be able to find formal means for use cases so we can certify that the design and implementation really support the use cases.*

Another important point of view on what we have been doing so far is designing the software engineering process, but we have only been starting to provide the means of implementing the process. That is where I think we can do a lot of development in the future, how to get the process really online and supporting people in their everyday work. So not only do you design the process but also you instantiate the process when you design a project and you will instantiate the workers and artifacts that you define.

Another direction of research is to define higher level architectural styles, where constructs like layers, systems, subsystems, interfaces, patterns, and frameworks are just components of different architecture styles. And we need languages like the UML to do that. The best way is by identifying some con-cepts and getting them accepted and agreed upon as a standard, then the whole community will move in the same direction and we will stand on each other's shoulders instead of on each other's toes.

And that is a very large community to talk about, and if we all had some kind of standard to work with we would be very powerful. So I see an accel-eration of the maturity in the software community in the near years to come. Even if you have to teach people through education to change and to move in the same direction, young students moving in more similar directions than they have done in the past will move faster; there is no doubt about that.

Q: Finally, what are your visions or dreams for the 21st century ?

A: We all have dreams. Just a little over 25 years ago, I had a dream. I dreamed that the technology known today as "object-oriented" could be used to design telecommunications systems. I dreamed that this technology would be generalized and given a wealth of wholly different applications. I dreamed that the computer scientists who—in those days—ridiculed this technology and saw it as a dead-end street would one day accept it. I dreamed that this technology would in time become an indispensable element in the mainstream of computer science.

25 very exciting years have passed, and I have seen my dreams become reality. I have also experienced that using object technology as a means of competing in the market has resulted in singular commercial success for those who have been foresighted enough to have chosen it. Commercial success is, after all, the real proof of a technology's viability.

However, 25 years ago I had yet another dream. I dreamed that the object concept could be used to model phenomena in many different disciplines— not only man-made ones (computers, businesses, constructions in general), but also natural ones (living systems, physical systems) as well. What I hoped for was that we would be able to develop an object notation with simple, intuitive semantics to use for teaching in the schools. Already at the elementary level, students could be taught this kind of notation parallel to learning basic arithmetic. Later on, physics, biology, chemistry, psychology, sociology, economy, and astronomy could all use this type of notation instead of having to use the individual systems each subject has developed for the purpose. With a shared technique of this kind, we would be better able to understand complex connections and find it easier to see similarities in ostensibly divergent subjects. It might even be possible to find a framework that could be used in several different subject contexts.

(Extracts of the answer above reprinted with permission from IEEE. It was first published in the article "Object Orientation—The Model of the 21st Century?" by Ivar Jacobson, in IEEE Software. © 1992 IEEE.*)*

INDEX
